International Financial Management

AMIT GAUTAM
Professor
Institute of Management Studies
Banaras Hindu University (BHU)
Varanasi, Uttar Pradesh

TWINKLE JAISWAL
Former Wealth Manager, ICICI Bank
Doctoral Fellow (UGC)
Institute of Management Studies
Banaras Hindu University (BHU)

ADITYA KESHARI
Former Assistant Manager, HDFC Bank
Doctoral Fellow (ICSSR)
Institute of Management Studies
Banaras Hindu University (BHU)

PHI Learning Private Limited
Delhi-110092
2025

In fond memory of ***Shri Asoke K. Ghosh*** *(October 1942 – February 2024), Founder Chairman and Managing Director of PHI Learning, whose vision endlessly inspires.*

The Legacy Continues....

Published by Pushpita Ghosh, PHI Learning Private Limited, Rimjhim House, 111, Patparganj Industrial Estate, Delhi-110092 and Printed by Syndicate Binders, A-20, Hosiery Complex, Noida, Phase-II Extension, Noida-201305 (N.C.R. Delhi).

₹595.00

INTERNATIONAL FINANCIAL MANAGEMENT
Amit Gautam, Twinkle Jaiswal and Aditya Keshari

ISBN-978-93-91818-97-5 (Print Book)
ISBN-978-93-91818-98-2 (e-Book)

The export rights of the book are vested solely with the publisher.

Contents

List of Figures

List of Tables

Preface

With the advancement of information and communication technologies, the international business has widened its horizon, national boundaries have become hazy and globalisation is the buzzword of the moment. But a growing trend of deglobalisation has also been observed worldwide especially after the expanding popularity of conservative governments in various parts of the world together with COVID pandemic. The growing economic rivalry between United States and China for substantial footprints in business across the countries as well as the ongoing Russia-Ukraine War and its impact on whole Europe, besides the slump in economies of developed countries has also accentuated the deglobalisation trend. The turbulence arising out of such contradicting megatrends is making the global financial scenario more complex and volatile, and thus, it has become pertinent for scholars and practitioners in the field of business and finance to understand and manage the intricacies involved in Financial Markets.

The book starts with the opening chapter that discusses Globalisation, expanding trade across the globe and International Business. Then, it goes on to discuss in detail the reverberations of megatrends in geopolitics and its implications on businesses worldwide. In the subsequent chapters, the discussion on FDI, international monetary system and exchange rate regimes observed worldwide with the focus on foreign exchange market is provided.

Furthermore, the financial risks arise to firm due to its international nature and the volatility in foreign exchange rates (i.e., Foreign Exchange Exposure) and its management is explained with practical examples wherever necessary. Then, the focus shifts to Financial Markets and accordingly international money market, bond market and equity market and its various phenomena is included in order to provide an understanding of how to raise funds as well as the cost of capital in international markets.

The book is designed for the undergraduate and postgraduate students, professionals and researchers in the field of management, commerce and economics. The book will equip the readers with the conceptual and practical understanding of global business scenario, major theories that explain why businesses go international, global monetary system, global financial markets and their complex amalgamation. The inclusion of on-going megatrends in macroeconomics, the resultant geopolitics and its implication for the businesses worldwide makes the content more relevant. The book has used a balanced blend of theory and empirical features in order to elucidate the complicated nature of international business competing in the global market.

The prime distinguishing feature of this book from the other resources is that it covers all the major topics of international finance in a succinct way as per the demand of the readers exploring the subject area. However, the book does not claim to cover every dimension of broad study area of international financial management.

The book is designed keeping in mind the Indian context. Hence, the data, illustrations and cases used have a reference to India.

In this continuation, we would like to acknowledge the support extended by various persons in the completion of this book specially our colleagues and fellow researchers who have given valuable inputs as and when required for making the book more enriching and thought provoking. We also thank our parents and family members for their constant support throughout the journey of writing.

At last, we would like to pay our rich tribute to the almighty for providing us that needful insight which is being required for the creation of the intellectual output in the form of this book.

Amit Gautam
Twinkle Jaiswal
Aditya Keshari

List of Abbreviations

ADR	American Deposit Receipt
APT	Arbitrage Pricing Theory
BCA	Balance on Current Account
BIS	Bank of International Settlements
BKA	Balance on Capital Account
BOP	Balance of Payment
BRA	Balance on Reserve Account
BSE	Bombay Stock Exchange
CAD	Canadian Dollar
CAPM	Capital Asset Pricing Model
CCAPM	Conditional Capital Asset Pricing Model
CIA	Covered Interest Arbitrage
CNY	Chinese Yuan
ECB	European Central Bank
ECU	European Currency Unit
EME	Emerging Market Economy
EMH	Efficient Market Hypothesis
EMS	European Monetary System
EMU	Economic and Monetary Union
ERM	Exchange Rate Mechanism
ESCB	European System of Central Banks
EU	European Union
EURIBOR	European Interbank Interest Rates
FDI	Foreign Direct Investment
FEDAI	Foreign Exchange Dealers Association of India
FOMC	Federal Open Market Committee
Forex	Foreign Exchange
FRN	Floating Rate Note

GATT	General Agreement on Tariffs and Trade
GBP	Great Britain Pound
GDP	Gross Domestic Product
GDR	Global Deposit Receipt
IAPM	International Asset Pricing Model
IBRD	International Bank for Reconstruction and Development
ICSID	International Centre for Settlement of Investment Disputes
IDA	International Development Association
IFC	International Finance Corporation
IFE	International Fisher Effect
ILO	International Labour Organisation
IMF	International Monetary Fund
IMM	International Monetary Market
INR	Indian Rupee
IRP	Interest Rate Parity
JPY	Japanese Yen
LIBOR	London Interbank Offered Rate
LPG	Liberalisation, Privatisation, Globalisation
LSE	London Stock Exchange
MIGA	Multilateral Investment Guarantee Agency
MNC	Multinational Corporation
NASDAQ	National Association of Securities Dealers Automated Quotation
NSE	National Stock Exchange
NYSE	New York Stock Exchange
OECD	Organisation for Economic Co-operation and Development
OPEC	Organization of the Petroleum Exporting Countries
OTC	Over The Counter
PPP	Purchasing Power Parity
QSD	Quality Spread Differential
RBI	Reserve Bank of India
SDR	Special Drawing Right
SONIA	Sterling Overnight Interest Rates
UNCTAD	United Nations Conference on Trade and Development
US	United States
USD	United States Dollar
VAR	Value at Risk
WTO	World Trade Organization

CHAPTER 1

Introduction

LEARNING OUTCOMES

After reading this chapter, the reader will be able to:

- Define International Financial Management
- Differentiate between Domestic and International Finance
- Discuss the Scope of International Finance
- Explain Globalisation: Its Evolution, Benefits and Challenges
- Relate Macro-Economic Megatrends and Globalisation
- Explain Implications and Effects of Globalisation on Indian Industry

1.1 MEANING OF INTERNATIONAL FINANCIAL MANAGEMENT

As the world has become highly integrated economically, it has changed the business environment of firms irrevocably. Firms have expanded their area of operation and forayed into international markets to take advantage of the enlarged opportunity set. Thus, it has become impossible to manage the finances of a corporation with only a narrow understanding of financial management in domestic context.

International financial management is concerned with the investment and financing choices that multinational corporations must make given the global environment of their operations. It looks at the dynamics of foreign direct investment, currency exchange rates, balance of payments, global financial markets, and other financial management issues.

Decisions about investments and finance often include valuing uncertain future cash flows. The impact of exchange rate risk on these decisions is a crucial aspect of the global context. In order to facilitate rational decision making in an international setting, the technique must take into account the extra complexity that exchange rate risk and currency rate forecasts present.

Political risk is another concern that businesses may experience while operating internationally. Political risk includes everything from sudden alterations to tax laws to outright takeover of foreigners' assets. Political risk results from the ability of a sovereign state to alter the "game's rules" without providing adequate remedy for those who are harmed.

Then, the international markets are highly imperfect. The barriers to trade and finances like exorbitant transaction and transit costs, knowledge asymmetry, legal restrictions and discriminatory taxation exists there.

All these factors together make it pertinent to study management of finances in global context.

1.2 INTERNATIONAL FINANCIAL MANAGEMENT AND DOMESTIC FINANCIAL MANAGEMENT

In the backdrop of globalised world, International Financial Management seems natural extension of Domestic Financial Management but yet there is a substantial difference between them. International Financial Management focus on cross country coverage of sources and instruments of financing, such as, American Depository Receipts, Euro Currency Issues, International Bond Markets, etc. that may be more cost competitive in comparison to Domestic Financial Markets but the process of raising and managing funds are complex.

The investment options are also diversified for a multinational enterprise than that of an enterprise operating in a domestic setting. The rules and laws make International Financial Management more complex than Domestic Financial Management, although the basic concepts of corporate finance govern both. Decisions relating to management of earnings in global scenario require deep understanding of the country-wise policies for repatriation of profit or reinvestment in the host country. Nonetheless the prevalence of more than two hundred odd currencies make the decision variables in international arena more challenging but also full of opportunities.

The homogeneity of Domestic Financial Environment makes it easy to take decision for firms operating in it but the International Financial Management not only encompasses majorly the perspective related to Domestic Financial Management, such as, money and capital market involving Central Bank of the country, regulatory institutions of equity and bond but also includes the aspects which are unique in global setting such as geo politics, trade, foreign direct investments, portfolio investments, cross listing of stocks, etc.

The capital budgeting decisions are also viewed differently in international setting by considering and defining risk and discount factors incorporating many other variables which may seem marginal or not present in case of Domestic Financial Management. Multinational Enterprises are also exposed to the cross country financial issues related to sales cannibalisation while dealing with product launching in international markets.

International Financial Management also differs from Domestic Financial Management in terms of working capital management also. The decision related to cash management essentially involve a choice between centralised or decentralised cash management, managing global supply chains involve inventory decisions like single vendor or multiple vendor system. Also, the receivables management pose substantial differences through the medium and mechanism of funds transfer across the countries.

In short, the above major differences between the International Financial Management and Domestic Financial Management are explained in detail in the coming chapters for the avid readers to develop an understanding of the subject under hand.

1.3 SCOPE OF INTERNATIONAL FINANCIAL MANAGEMENT

A multinational corporation's international financial management has its own method for dealing with business situations and is also a complex process. The procedure became more complicated as a result of the globalisation of foreign markets, be the money markets, bond markets, or stock markets. In a global context, investing in or raising capital from these markets is tedious due to the interdependence of domestic and foreign markets. The process connected not only the market but also the organisations, who have a tendency to embrace an international business strategy. International finance has evolved in a fragmented manner, therefore defining its scope will be helpful.

Several commercial businesses are entering global markets outside of their historical and customary borders due to the need for profit as well as the ease of communication, travel, and technical advancements. A global corporation is increasingly acceptable in the business world compared to businesses operating within a nation's borders. Financial organisations can expand their scope and scale of business by international diversification through the foreign direct investments and portfolio investments.

In order to protect their own nation from economic and financial instability and to improve people's quality of life, policy makers must simultaneously increase employment, productivity, and sustainable growth. Since countries are more susceptible to the economic and financial instability of other nations in a globalised world, the economic and financial stability of a nation is a problem on both a national and international level. So, it covers the role of the IMF, the World Bank, and other global economic institutions in assisting foreign trade and bringing stability among the nations.

Balance of payment is another yet a crucial part of international financial management which includes a systematic accounting record of all economic transactions during a given period of time between the residents of the country and the rest of the world. A sound balance of payment can help the economies to avoid the currency crisis.

Organizations are confronted with a wide range of risks while international trade, with foreign exchange exposure being the greatest including transaction, translation and economic exposure. By the use of instruments like futures, options, and swaps, international financial management offers ways to mitigate exchange rate risk.

The growth of global banking, along with the transnational expansion of banks through branches and subsidiaries, aids in the expansion of MNCs' financial and economic globalisation. International banking also makes it easier for individuals to make financial transactions internationally.

The money market is essential to the growth of economies because it offers borrowing power and lends money for short periods, often with maturities of one year or less. The trans-border financial transfer policies of different countries' currencies control the international money market. The past currency crises and steps that can be taken to prevent them from happening in future must be addressed while discussing the international money market.

The majority of countries use the international bond market to help pay for their fiscal deficits. Progressive globalisation of financial markets and capital flows, the adoption of anti-inflationary policies, and the use of flexible exchange rates have paved the road for effective money raising. The development of debt markets is motivated by a number of broad factors. The most important rationale is to create market interest rates that represent the opportunity cost of money at each maturity, which will improve financial markets more comprehensive.

In continuance, the international equity market expands and draws businesses looking to raise money on the global market through the issuance of ADRs and GDRs. Due to the lower cost of capital in developed countries than in developing countries, it is crucial for businesses to create an optimum capital structure while balancing the risk and cost involved.

1.4 GLOBALISATION

Take a look at things around you, the mobile phone that you are using might be manufactured by a Korean or Chinese company, the applications in the phone might be developed in various different countries, the smart watch from an American company, the battery in those watch might be manufactured in China, the car that you use might be of a German brand but manufactured in India. This is the level of interconnectedness of trade and commerce around the world. With the development of modes of transportation, communication and information technology people and businesses around the world have become more interconnected and interdependent.

The value of goods and services traded globally has reached a whooping level of $28.5 trillion and the flow of Global Foreign Direct Investment has increased to $1.65 trillion in the year 2021 which is approximately 4 times the level of trade in the year 2000 ($ 6.82 trillion) and a 78% increase of flow of FDI from the year 2000 ($1.3 trillion) respectively (UNCTAD's Global trade update).

Globalisation means being global. It refers to the growing interconnectedness and interdependence of the world's economies, populations and cultures through the cross-border movement of goods, capital, people, technology and information.

In general, we use the term Globalisation in economic and financial context but it is a much broader phenomena and includes other fields. The term Globalisation encompasses following facets:

Political

The development of international organizations like United Nations, International Monetary Fund, etc. in the last decade as well as their growing influence and interference in the local political and economic policies is a result of political Globalisation. The political aspects of a country are highly influenced by the world politics in general and regional politics in particular.

Earlier, there were two major political blocks in the world, western (which represented liberal democracy) and communist, but with the growing acceptance of democratic ideas worldwide, the communist block is shrinking and the world is moving towards the political pervasiveness of liberal democratic ideas.

Economic

The interconnectedness of local economies has given rise to the global economy, where every single economy is a part of larger global system. With growing liberalisation, i.e., removal of trade barriers and reduction of restrictions in the flow of capital, the international trade has developed and the production of goods and services has dispersed globally. Economic Globalisation is connected with the capitalist system which is based on the belief of free market (works on the laws of demand and supply).

A great example of Economic Globalisation is Stock markets around the world. The volatility of one market has a direct or indirect spillover effect on all the other domestic markets around the world.

Social

Globalisation has accelerated the interaction and amalgamation of cultures that has resulted in the loss of unique cultures and creation of a supra-culture. The taste, preference and life style of people are continuously evolving. Increasing number of people are migrating to developed countries in hope of better employment and quality of life, leaving behind their unique culture and identity.

Look at the major urban centre in any country and you will find people wearing similar clothes, coming out of a fast-food chain or mall, clicking pictures for their social media feed using similar mobile phones. This is the impact of globalisation on society.

Technological

The dissemination of technology around the world, generally to less developed nations from developed nations is termed as technological Globalisation. In today's world, technology developed in any part of the world is being used by everybody around. Take example of blockchain technology, it was first developed and used in cryptocurrency by a Japanese named Satoshi Nakamoto in 2008, but now it is being used by people around the world in multiple domains like healthcare, logistics, Internet of Things, NFTs and so on.

Environmental

Environmental globalisation accounts for the idea of considering planet Earth as a single global entity as we all share the same atmosphere. Effects of environmental degradation in one part of the world effects everyone. The less developed countries contribute the least to the environmental pollution but they will suffer the most due to the lack of resources compared to developed nations (who are the highest contributors to global pollution).

1.4.1 History of Globalisation

Humans have been involved in trading goods since the beginning of their origin. But at the start of 1st century BC, a new phenomenon occurred; people in Rome started using luxury silk products manufactured thousands of miles away in China. The route through which Silk was transported earned its name as Silk Route and various other luxury goods like spices and gems were also added to the trade. This was the beginning of Global Trade.

The next major development was the trade of Spices mainly through Mediterranean and Indian Ocean routes from East (as far as Indonesia) to West (to the other corner Spain) (7th–15th centuries). Spices were traded through sea since the ancient time but by the medieval era, they become the major product of the International Trade. Globalisation was still a farfetched phenomenon, but now there existed the land and sea trade routes between East and West.

During the period of Renaissance in Europe, major scientific developments took place and the Europeans started the exploration of world for the purpose of trade and commerce. They discovered America and reached to Africa and India, initially for the expansion of trade but then started colonization. They set up the Global supply chains but it was mostly to exploit the colonies and hence cannot be termed as Globalisation in true sense. (15th to 18th centuries)

First wave of Globalisation (19th century to 1914) started with the domination of Great Britain on world both in terms of geography and technology. The invention of steam engine, the industrial weaving machine, telephone, etc., revolutionized the trade and commerce. The trade grew at an average rate of 3% for a century and the contribution of exports to global GDP became 14% at the end of year 1914. The People sitting in London could order various products manufactured around the globe through telephone and expect the delivery at their doorsteps. While Britain and other European nations benefitted the most from this development, there was a dark side too. Large nations like India and China which earlier used to be a major power and trading economies, were either not allowed to or were incapable of adapting the global trends.

In 1914, the outbreak of First World War then the great depression in the America in 1930s and the Second World War disrupted the world economy. By 1945, the global trade as a percentage of GDP had fallen to a low level of 5%.

TABLE 1.1 Evolution of Globalisation

Globalisation Era	*Age of Discovery*	*Globalisation 1.0*	*Globalisation 2.0*	*Globalisation 3.0*	*Globalisation 4.0*
Leading Exports	Raw Material	Industrial Goods	Factories	Global Supply Chain	Digital Goods
Leading Nations		Great Britain	USA and Soviet Union	USA	USA and China
Exports as Percentage World GDP	Less than 5%	6–14%	5–15%	15–20%	
Enabling Era	Scientific Revolution	1st Industrial Revolution	2nd Industrial Revolution	3rd Industrial Revolution	4th Industrial Revolution
Enabling Innovations	Ship, navigation	Steam Engine	Means of Transport	Internet	Artificial Intelligence and Cloud Computing
Characterizing GDP trend	Europe	Britain	World	United States	China

Once the World War was over, Global trade started picking up but this time it was fuelled by the US and the Soviet Union [Second wave of Globalisation (1945–1989)]. By 1989, the trade once again rose to pre-world war level. This was accompanied by the sudden rise of middle class in west.

With the fall of Soviet Union, Globalisation became the central force. The institutions like World Trade Organization (formed in 1995), encouraged countries to enter into free-trade agreements and reduce barriers to trade. At the same time, the adoption of Internet worldwide worked as a facilitator of trade and commerce. It allowed the further integration of global supply chains. As a result, the global exports rose to a remarkable level of 25% to the GDP (Third wave of Globalisation).

Fuelled by the development of Digital technologies like Artificial Intelligence, Blockchain, Internet of Things, Robotics and Virtual reality, a new wave of Globalisation with digital world at its front, is at our doorstep (Globalisation 4.0). The world economy is undergoing transformation; many traditional industries have closed and new have formed. Although this new wave is exciting, it has few challenges as well. The rising inequality, social instability and climate related constraints have made people question the Globalisation and the economic system it underpins. Many countries are again gravitating towards protectionism and trade wars are once again prevalent.

In the words of Klaus Schwab (executive chairman, World Economic Forum)—"Globalisation 4.0 has only just begun, but we are already vastly underprepared for it."

1.4.2 Benefits of Globalisation

Globalisation accelerated the trade of goods and services as well as the movement of capital and human resources across the world. This has benefitted both the developed and less developed worlds in utilising the available resources. The amalgamation of capital and technology from developed world with the natural as well as human resources of developing and less developed regions has helped in efficient production and dissemination of goods and services.

The development of free-trade policies across the world has significantly contributed to global economic growth which also resulted in the growth of industries worldwide. The technological advancement that we witness today is the outcome of this only.

It has been observed that the countries that opened their economies for international trade has benefitted in multiple ways. China, after opening up its economy in 1970s has witnessed a striking growth. From a developing country with more than 50 percent of its population below poverty line, it has managed to retain average growth of 8% for multiple decades and pull its population out of poverty. It has become the manufacturing hub of the world and is now competing with US to become a global leader.

India, on the other hand, was close to default on international obligations in 1990s, when under the pressure of International Monetary Fund, it embraced LPG (Liberalization, Privatization & Globalisation) policy. After this, India has also managed to accelerate the economic growth and has reduced the poverty and unemployment in the country. It has become a major IT hub with companies like Infosys and Wipro competing with global players.

The interconnectedness of the countries also made it easier for humans to migrate to other developed countries for better education and employment opportunities. The migration is advantageous for both host and source countries. Host countries are able to attract brains from the world that contribute in the development of their country. The best example of this is USA.

The migrants send valuable foreign exchanges to their country, a lot of them also return to their source country after learning valuable skills and become a valuable resource for their country.

1.4.3 Challenges of Globalisation

No doubt Globalisation has benefitted the global population but it has been criticized on multiple grounds as well. It has resulted into growth of income and wealth disparities between people and nations. As per a Credit Suisse Global Wealth Report, it is recorded that top 1% of the individuals own about 48.5% of world resources. Difference of per capita income on PPP basis between richest and poorest country enlarged to 165 times in 2022 from 70 times in the year 2000.

Also, it is said that some countries benefit more from free trade than others. Globalisation has also resulted in increasing interference of international organizations (which are dominated by developed western nations) in domestic policies of developing world.

The growing wealth and influence of large multi-national corporations has been a major concern. It has negative consequences for social justice, democracy and environment especially in less developed part of the globe. They interfere in the policies of a country through continuous lobbying and push their agenda of neoliberal policies that promote privatization and deregulation in practically all the areas.

As the world has become more interconnected and interdependent, the crises in one part of the world have spillover effect on others. The global financial crises that started because of the structural issues in the United States spread to whole world and caused slump in growth rate of even developing countries like India and China.

The economic growth and increasing productivity of industries that are the main outcomes of globalisation are contributing to the loss of natural resources and environmental degradation. The economic growth results in rise in living standards of the people which in turn affects the demand for goods and services. The fulfilment of such demand requires more production that eventually leads to unnecessary use of natural resources, and also contribute to greenhouse gas emissions and global warming. The growing consumption of goods worldwide is also creating a big garbage problem, especially plastic pollution.

1.5 MACRO-ECONOMIC MEGATRENDS AND GLOBALISATION

According to recent estimations of World Trade Organisation (WTO), world trade is expected to slump in the year 2023 due to the multiple shocks to the economy.

Growing import bills for food, fuels and fertilizers could increase the food insecurity and debt distress in the developing world. Import demand is expected to soften due to the slump in developed world economies.

High energy prices in Europe due to Russia-Ukraine war, will squeeze the household spending and raise manufacturing costs. Monetary policy tightening in US will result into a slump in interest sensitive industries like housing and automobiles.

Policy makers have to choose between controlling inflation, providing employment as well as promoting clean sources of energy.

1.5.1 Covid Pandemic and World Trade

The Covid pandemic has had destructive effect on the health and economy of the world. As per the UN report on Covid-19, 3 million plus cases were reported with more than 0.2 million deaths in the first four months of 2020. There has been a slump of 6 percent year on year in world production in the first quarter of 2020. It was followed by a drop of 11.2 percent year on year in the next quarter of 2020 (United Nations Industrial Development Organisation). Since World War II, it was the largest reduction in output volume. The decline in production as well as trade were of similar depth to those at the trough of the global financial crises of 2008 (as can be seen in Figure 1.1). Apart from the human suffering, the pandemic interrupted almost every sphere of life. Offices, factories, schools and other public places got shut, travels were limited, there was shortage of many essential goods and social life became a farfetched dream. The interruptions resulted in job losses and the people were deprived of their means of livelihoods especially those who were employed in unorganized sectors.

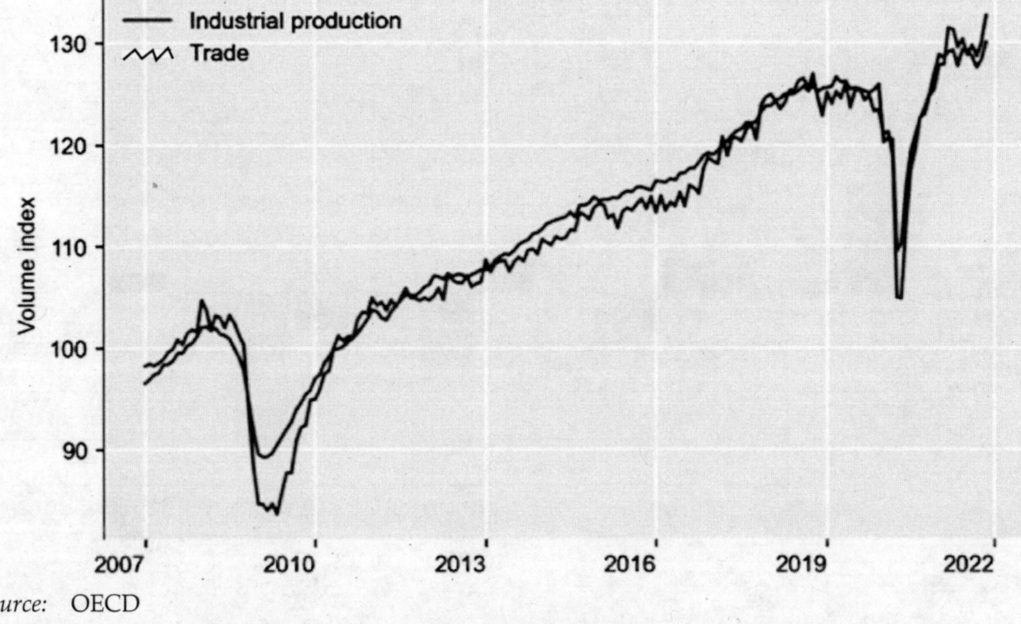

Source: OECD

FIGURE 1.1 Volume of World Trade and Industrial Production.

While the condition has improved, the recovery has been volatile. As per an ILO report of 2022, global working hours were below pre-pandemic levels by 3.8 percent in the first quarter of 2022.

In today's interconnected world, the pandemic spread like a wild fire across the globe. The massive slump in trade and investment was the outcome of this. Though both trade and investment recovered after a while, the revival was unequal across industries and nations. The IT industry boomed during the period on the back of digitalization whereas industries like automobiles and apparels went through the toughest phase. Some countries like Finland and South Korea were least harmed by the Covid pandemic, on the other hand, nations that were heavily dependent on tourism like Sri Lanka went into economic crises.

The global economy recovered from the Covid-19 crisis. Economic growth bounced back with trade and investment reaching higher levels in 2021 than prior to the pandemic. The world economy grew 5.6 per cent in 2021, the fastest in nearly 50 years (UNCTAD, 2022a).

But the world economy entered into a "two speed" recovery path with the beginning of the year 2022. The developing world, on one side, became much more vulnerable to the external shocks, on the other side it became harder for them to recover from the pandemic setback. The developed countries, for example, US economy grew at a rate of 5% whereas the average growth of Sub-Saharan countries was about 3.5% only. Figure 1.2 shows the per capita income growth of emerging nations as well as low-income nations relative to the advanced economies. It can be seen that the pre-pandemic growth in per capita income was higher in emerging and low-income nations but the Covid pandemic has changed the scenario. If we exclude China from the emerging nations, both emerging and low-income nations are performing worse than the advance economies.

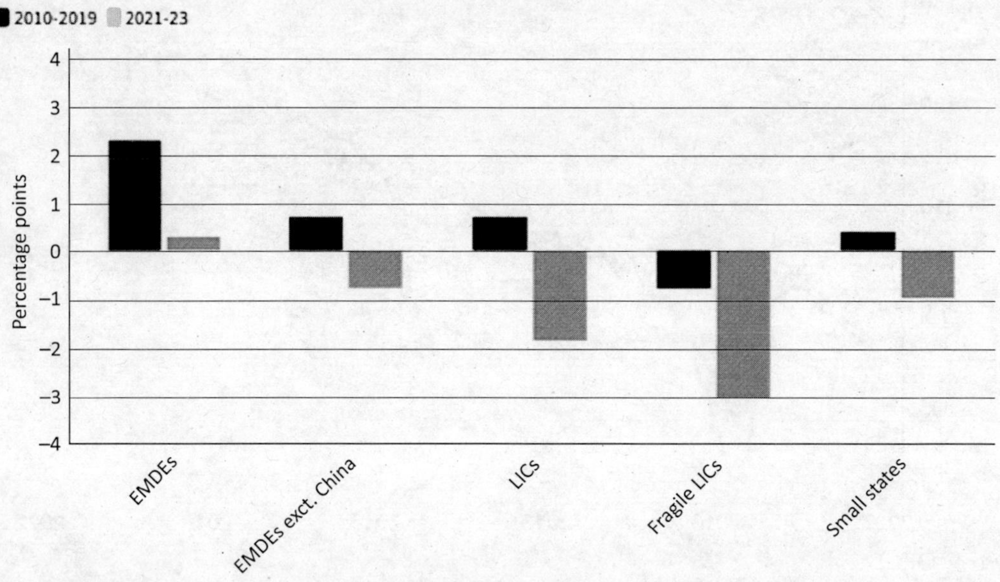

Source: World Bank

Note: EMDEs = emerging market and developing economies; LICs = low-income countries; Fragile LICs = fragile and conflict-affected LICs. Relative per capita income growth is computed as a difference in per capita GDP growth between respective EMDE groups and advanced economies.

FIGURE 1.2 Per capita income growth relative to advance economies.

UNCTAD forecasts that uneven growth trends will continue in 2022 and beyond. Several advanced economies already surpassed their pre-pandemic levels of output, while many developing countries may need several years. On current trends, many developing countries are facing a lost decade (UNCTAD, 2020a; United Nations, Inter-Agency Task Force on Financing for Development, 2022).

While the pandemic was major concern for the world for two years, it has largely vanished from the headlines. The world's attention has been shifted to Europe because of the ongoing war between Russia and Ukraine.

1.5.2 Russia Ukraine Crisis

The conflict between Russia and Ukraine has increased the uncertainty about the recovery of world economy in general and economy of Europe in particular, and triggered tumult in global financial markets.

Even before the conflict the inflation was rising in developed countries like United States, United Kingdom, Germany and other European nations because of the aid provided to people and industries during Covid as can be seen in Figure 1.3. As the conflict began between the two countries, the prices of commodities like oil, natural gas, metals and food escalated as Russia is a significant exporter of vital commodities like natural gas (2nd largest), oil (3rd largest), wheat, neon, titanium, palladium and ammonium nitrate. On the other hand, Ukraine is the significant producer of sunflower (largest), corn (6th largest), wheat (7th largest), barley, beet, rapeseed, soya and sugar. The high commodity prices are not only disruptive for the recovery from the Covid pandemic but the higher prices for much longer period increases the risk of long-lasting inflation, and thereby increases the risk of economic slump.

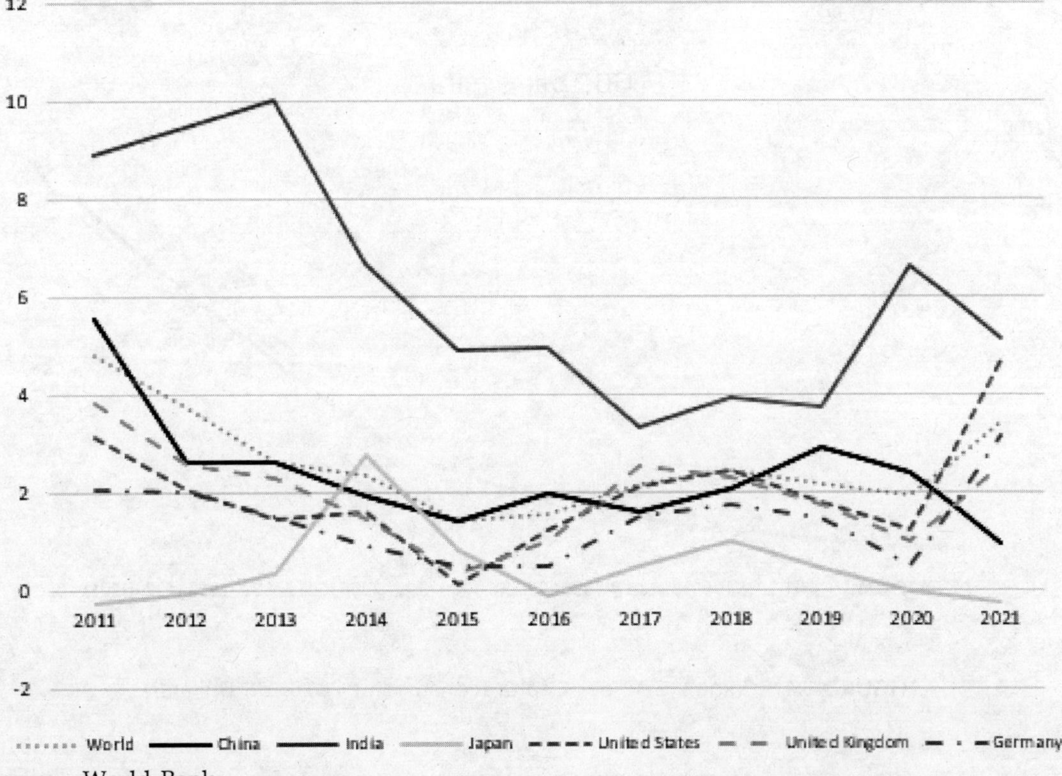

Source: World Bank

FIGURE 1.3 Annual inflation in percentage (consumer prices) from 2011–2021.

While the economies of Russia and Ukraine will suffer inevitably. There is huge effect of war in Europe. European countries especially Germany, Italy and some other eastern countries are heavily dependent on Russian oil and natural gas for its energy requirements. It is not possible for them to replace Russian imports in the short to medium terms.

The shot up in fuel and food prices has increased the inflation, which will have a negative impact on household consumption. The increased fuel prices have a negative effect on industries as well. There will be increased uncertainty in the commodity as well as financial markets. Due to the war, the supply chain has also been disrupted.

If the crises in eastern Europe escalates, it can trigger the wave of deglobalisation, as was observed during the inter-war period, when world trade contracted to 5% of the GDP from about 14%.

1.5.3 China's Role in World Trade

Since the opening of its economy in 1970s, China's economy has grown tremendously. It has recorded an average annual growth of over 9 percent and lifted 800 million plus people out of poverty. The Gross Domestic Product per Capita of China has grown from \$381 in 1978 to about \$ 11,200 in 2021 (see Figure 1.4). Once considered as a low-income country, China has now become a middle-income country. It has a huge influence on other developing economies like India through trade and investments.

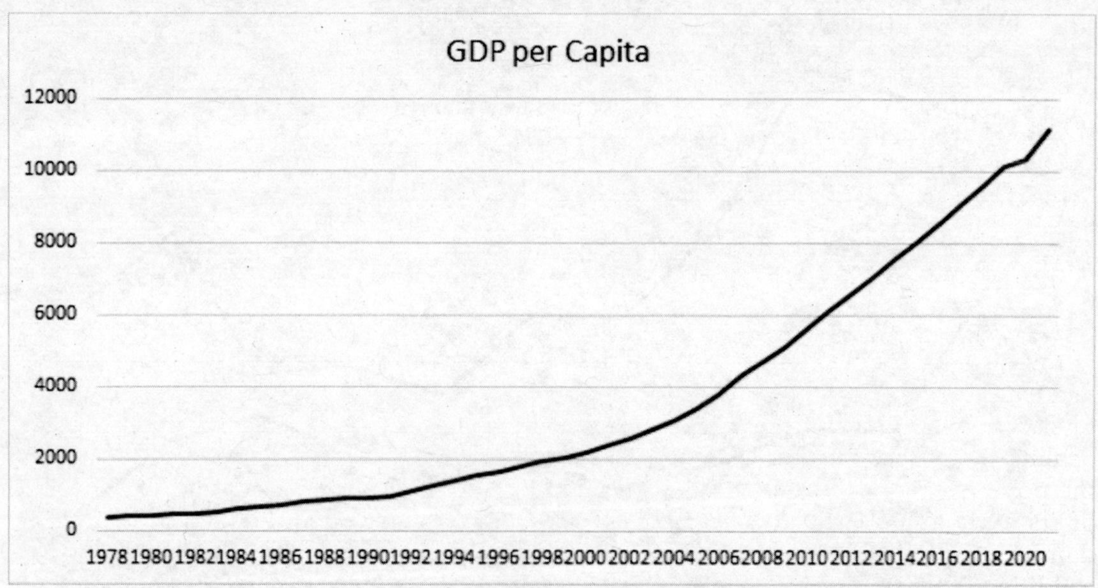

Source: World Bank

FIGURE 1.4 China's GDP per Capita (constant at 2015, US Dollars).

China has shown a tremendous growth in low-cost manufacturing, exports and investments and has become an engine of global growth. Exports have been the focal point of Chinese economy. In 1978 (the year when China opened its economy), it was exporting goods and services worth of $6.8 billion only. Exports grew vastly between 2002 to 2008 from $333 billion to $ 1.5 trillion. There was a setback that year then because of the global financial crises. After that it again started ascending till 2014 to $2.46 trillion. It again slumped on account of geopolitical conflicts in the year 2015. Since then, the China's growth is volatile (Figure 1.5) on account of multiple factors, of which the most prominent one is growing protectionism around the world, especially in United States.

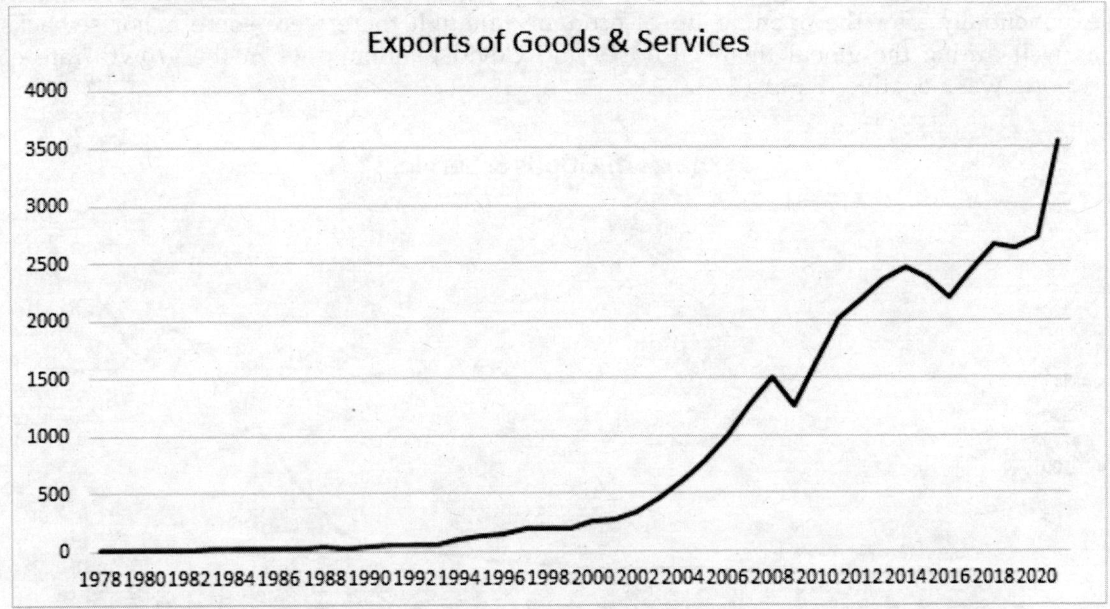

Source: World Bank

FIGURE 1.5 Total Exports of Goods and Services from China (in Billion US Dollar).

Over the past few years, the growth of China is moderated amidst multiple domestic and external shocks. As per World Bank projections, China's GDP growth rate is expected to slow drastically to 2.8 percent in 2022 from 8.1 percent in the year 2021. China is still dealing with the Covid pandemic. The real state sector is going through a major distress, the population is also aging and it's witnessing major protests across the country because of its zero Covid policy. Apart from internal issues, the Russia-Ukraine conflict has dampened the external economic environment with rising inflation, tightening financial conditions and slowing global growth.

1.6 IMPACT OF GLOBALISATION ON INDIAN INDUSTRIES

During mid eighteenth century, India was the largest economy in the world with a contribution of 25% in the global trade, but the contribution fell to 2% by the beginning of twentieth century. After gaining independence from colonial rule in 1947, India chose to follow protectionist policy, in order to develop domestic capabilities. The focus during the initial phase was on investing in heavy industries and the dominance of state in economic development. But soon the problems in economy became unavoidable with a high inflation and dwindling foreign exchange reserves. Thus, in 1990s the government introduced many reforms in the economy in order to move towards liberal trade policies and embrace the phenomena called globalisation.

Globalisation of the Indian Industry took place in its various sectors such as steel, pharmaceutical, petroleum, chemical, textile, cement, retail, and BPO.

As can be seen in Figure 1.6, the exports of goods and services from India has risen exponentially after the opening up of economy, though there were some major setbacks as well during the global financial crises and Covid pandemic when the growth rate of exports was negative (Figure 1.7).

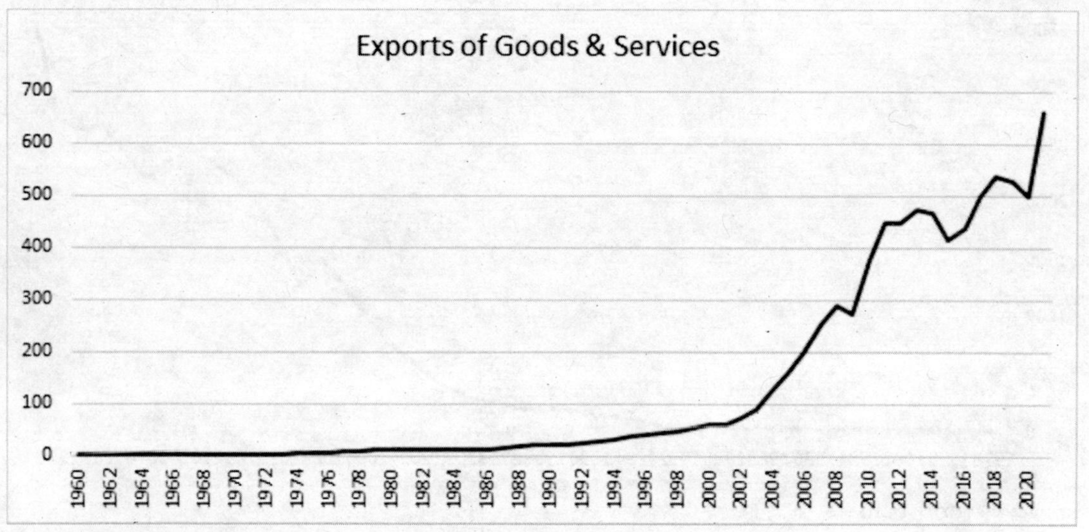

Source: World Bank

FIGURE 1.6 Exports of Goods and Services from India (Figures in billion US Dollars).

Globalisation allowed foreign firms to enter into Indian markets, with them they brought advanced production and distribution technologies. This improved the industrialization of country and increased competitiveness. The domestic players also had to improve their processes in order to survive. This overall proved to be beneficial for both consumers and industry.

The various negative Effects of Globalisation on Indian Industry are that due to the opening up of economy to foreign players, the competition has increased. Multinational companies from developed world being technology savvy and having huge financial resources were efficient and cost effective in production and thus were being preferred by local consumers. This reduced the market share and profit available to domestic industries. This happened mainly in the pharmaceutical, manufacturing, chemical, and steel industries. Also, with the import of technology, the requirement of labour in industry has been reduced which has caused the job losses especially to blue collar workers.

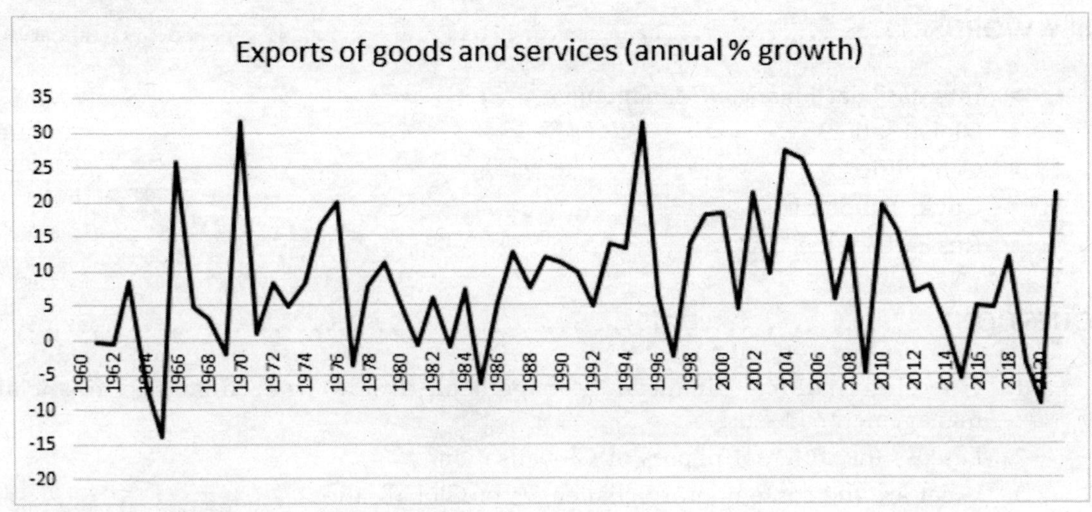

Source: World Bank

FIGURE 1.7 Percentage Growth in Exports of Goods and Services from India.

SUMMARY

1. Globalisation means being global. It refers to the growing interconnectedness and interdependence of the world's economies, populations and cultures through the cross-border movement of goods, capital, people, technology and information.
2. It has evolved from the trade of selected commodities to its current vibrant form where all the nations are a part of global ecosystem.
3. Globalisation has accelerated the global economic growth, helped many countries alleviating the poverty as well as improved efficiency of utilization of resources.
4. It has been criticized by many on the ground that it has led to over-usage of available resources which has led to pollution and global warming. Also, not all the nations have benefitted from the phenomena, the inequality between the nations and people is on an ascent.
5. The recent macroeconomic events such as Covid pandemic and the conflict in Russia and Ukraine has immensely affected the globalisation and international trade. During the first quarter of Covid, the world output decline by 9 percent year on year. The world was dealing with the aftermath of Covid when the conflict between Russia and Ukraine escalated, which has put Europe under inflationary pressure and has a spillover effect on whole globe.

KEY WORDS

- International Financial Management
- Globalisation
- Geopolitics
- Covid Pandemic
- Russia Ukraine Crises

QUESTIONS

1. How international financial management differs from domestic financial management? Discuss.
2. Discuss the different phases of Globalisation.
3. What are the contemporary challenges of Globalisation?
4. What is the impact of current geopolitical tension on world trade?
5. Discuss the impact of Globalisation on Indian industries.

REFERENCES AND SUGGESTED READINGS

1. United Nations Conference on Trade and Development, Global Trade Update, February 2022.
2. https://www.weforum.org/agenda/2019/01/how-Globalisation-4-0-fits-into-the-history-of-Globalisation/

CHAPTER 2

International Business and Multinational Corporations

LEARNING OUTCOMES

After reading this chapter, the reader will be able to:

- Explain Necessity and Significance of International Business
- Interpret Theories of International Business
- Describe the Approaches to International Business
- Explain the Ways to enter International Market
- Discuss Benefits of Forming Multi-National Corporations
- Relate India's Position in Terms of Global Integration
- Interpret Theories of Competitive Strategies in International Business

2.1 INTERNATIONAL BUSINESS

The necessity for profit as well as ease of communication, travel and technological advances are driving a big number of commercial firms into international market places beyond their historical and customary bounds. Compared to firms operating within a country's borders, a global corporation is becoming more and more accepted in the business sector. The firms that operate beyond the borders of their domestic country come under the umbrella of international business. It consists of any exchange of value be it goods, services, technology, or intellectual property, between concerned parties across borders.

Although business has been conducted on an international scale for many years, international business has gained more significance only in recent years because of the emergence of multinational corporations in most part of the world.

Roger Bennet defines—International business involves commercial activities that cross national frontiers.

According to John D. Daniels and Lee H. Radebaugh, International business is all business transactions—private and governmental—that involve two or more countries. Private companies undertake such transactions for profits, governments may or may not do the same in their transactions.

2.2 THEORIES OF INTERNATIONAL BUSINESS

2.2.1 Mercantilism

Developed during the sixteenth century in England, theory of Mercantilism is the first theory of international Trade/business. As per this, the goal of foreign economic policy of any government is to increase the wealth of nation by accumulating gold and silver. This theory promotes protectionism in foreign trade, as it says nations should focus on promoting exports and try to minimize their imports.

A lot of countries like China, India, Taiwan, Japan, etc., still use some form of mercantilism as they promote exports from their respective countries through policies like subsidies and try to curb imports by imposing tariffs on foreign manufactured products.

Free-trade advocates highlight the fact that protectionist policies only favor few industries meanwhile hurting the consumers and other companies (as they have to pay extra for imported products and services) and taxpayers (it's their money which is used to pay subsidies to selected industries); whereas free-trade benefits the global community.

2.2.2 Absolute Cost Advantage

This theory was propounded by Adam Smith in 1770s. He reasoned that the wealth of nation is not determined by the value of gold and silver it has but by the lifestyle of its citizens. A nation should focus on goods that it can produce efficiently than the other nations rather than controlling the flow of trade. He emphasized that by focusing on few products only, a country will develop efficiencies in the same and so the other country and hence people in both the countries would benefit.

2.2.3 Comparative Cost Advantage

In 1817, David Ricardo proposed the theory of Comparative Cost Advantage which is an improvement over the theory of Absolute Cost Advantage. It states that it might be possible that an advanced nation might effectively produce all the goods than the other nations, but it should focus on the good which it can effectively produce than the other goods.

Theory of Comparative Cost Advantage focuses on the relative productivity differences between the products. Let's understand this with an example—Suppose an accountant can do both the work of keeping accounts and typewriting. So, should he take both the responsibilities and suffer in both areas or rather hire a typewriter at a lower wage, so that both can concentrate on their respective areas and have a greater overall productivity. The second option is what we call Comparative Cost Advantage.

2.2.4 Hecksher Ohlin Theory (Factor Proportion Theory)

Both the theory of Absolute Cost Advantage and Comparative Cost Advantage assumed that producers or countries would be able to ascertain the goods they can produce efficiently through market forces. The theory of Factor Proportion helps in determining what to produce by taking into consideration the availability and prices of factors of production (land, labor and capital). The factors that are present in abundance will be cheaper than the scarce factors and hence it would be cost effective to produce using such factors.

Leonteif Paradox

As per the factor proportion theory, the capital rich country like United States must export capital intensive products and import labor intensive products. But in 1950s, Wassily Leonteif, a Russian American economist, observed that the United States was importing capital intensive products and exporting labor intensive products, which was in clear contradiction to the existing theories of international trade. Later, Linder Hypothesis tried to explain this paradox situation by suggesting that countries with similar economic development, trade for similar but differentiated goods.

2.2.5 National Competitive Theory or Porter's Diamond

According to Michael E Porter, the determinants of national prosperity are neither the resources it has nor the value of its currency. Its competitiveness relies on the ability of innovation and upgradation. Companies perform globally because of the continuous pressure and challenge they get in their home country from their strong competitors, aggressive suppliers and demanding consumers. Ultimately countries gain success in selective industries because the domestic environment is challenging and progressive.

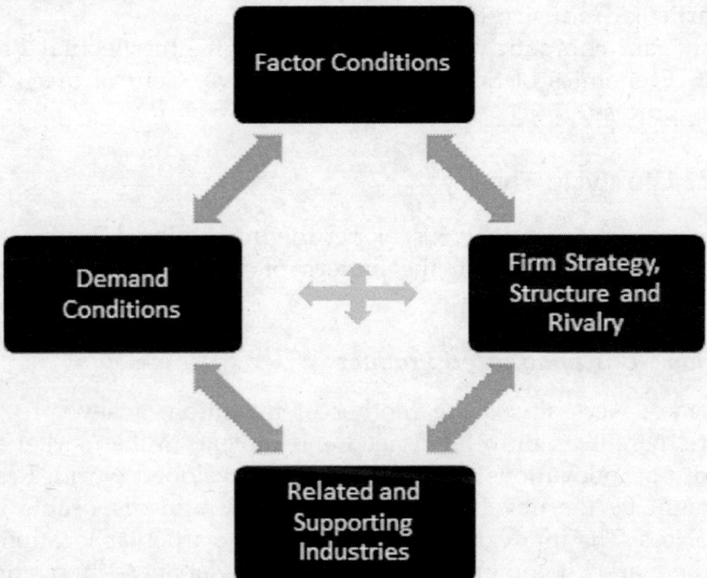

FIGURE 2.1 Porter's Diamond.

Previous theory insisted more on factors cost, value of currency and economies of scale as the stimulus of competitiveness. Porter explains that there are four factors responsible for the competitiveness of a country or an industry. He considers these factors as the "diamond of national advantage". The Porters diamond model includes:

Factor conditions: Factor conditions imply the effectiveness of a particular factor in the industry. Unlike factor proportion theory that only emphasizes on the availability of factors, the focus here is on the contribution of factor on product development.

Demand conditions: The nature of domestic demand for the industry's product or service influences the response of industry towards buyers. If the buyers are demanding and progressive, the firm will be able to create innovative products or services to satisfy them.

Related and supporting industries: The presence of related industries in the nation those are globally competitive is an important factor that influences an industry or company's competitiveness. The suppliers, who are globally competitive themselves, provide cost effective inputs in early and efficient ways.

Firm strategy, structure and rivalry: The conditions in the nation impact the way organizations are organized and managed and the nature of domestic rivalry. When the management and organizational structure of the company aligns with the modes preferred in the country, competitive advantage arises.

2.2.6 Global Strategic Rivalry Theory

Developed by Paul Krugman and Kevin Lancaster in the 1980s, this theory suggests that in order to dominate the international market, the firm must develop some competitive advantage over the other firms. The competitive advantage of the firm acts as a barrier to entry in that particular industry for the other firms.

A firm can gain competitive advantage through—Intellectual Property, Research & Development, Economies of Scale, Experience Curve, Control over raw materials and Unique business process.

2.2.7 Product Life Cycle Theory

Proposed by Raymond Vernon in 1960s, as per the International Product Life Cycle theory, there are three phases that explain the pattern of foreign direct investments of a firm. These are:

Early Introduction—Unstandardized Product

As the saying goes, Necessity is the mother of invention; a new product is developed when and where there is an unfulfilled need and the gap in the market arises. It has been seen that majority of innovations take place in the developed world. Reasons behind this phenomenon might be the developed industries and high disposable income of people living at such places. The innovations developed at a particular location are impacted by the features of the market it comprises of. For example, Japanese innovations are in general material, capital and resource saving.

The newly introduced product in the market undergoes a phase of modification. The producer has flexibility in tweaking and deciding the factors of production as per the need. Also, price elasticity is low (as the producer might be having monopoly in the early stages) resulting in low-cost consciousness from the producers' part (which means cost of factors of production is not a major consideration at this stage). Lastly, due to uncertainty in the beginning it is beneficial for the producer to stay in close touch with the market, suppliers and even competitors. All these factors affect the choice of producer to choose a location nearby base market in the early stages of product life cycle.

Once the local market for the product is developed, a demand in foreign market (having conditions similar to the base market) will also arise for the product. The Producer will start exporting the product to such markets and thus the internationalization of product begins.

The Maturing Product

As the product matures, the demand of product is firmly established in other developed nations as well. Some degree of certainty comes in terms of product design and standards, which results in a set procedure of production. The producer starts focusing on the cost of production. Now, taking other factors into consideration, if the overall cost of producing locally in the foreign market is less that the cost of exporting to the same, the producer will eventually set up a facility there.

Product Standardization and Streamlining of Manufacturing

Subsequently, if after achieving economies of scale in all the production facilities there exist a difference in cost of labour (so much so that it offsets the transport cost) then exporting back to the home market could be a consideration as well. Cost of labour in less developed countries is lower than the developed world, thus, for standardized product it is beneficial for the manufacturer to set up their plant there.

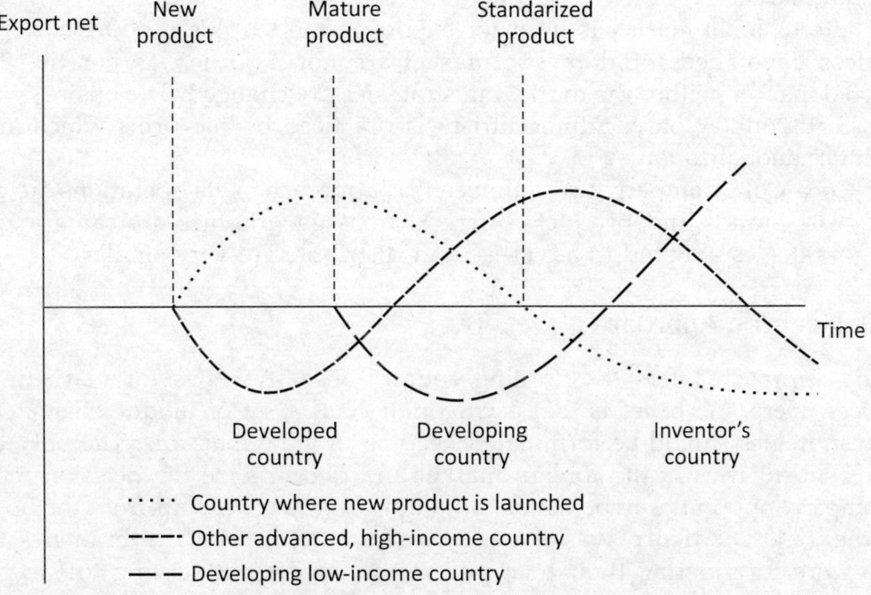

FIGURE 2.2 The Product Life Cycle.

At this stage, the demand for product in developed world is saturated but there is still a growing adoption of product in underdeveloped countries. By setting up the plant early in less developed countries, the producer enjoys an oligopolistic power there.

In developed world, a new product grabs the attention of market and residual demand for existing product is serviced through import from less developed countries. Then the cycle starts again.

The product life cycle theory was useful in the 1960s and 1970s to explain the business pattern of US industries. For example—the evolution of Personal Computers in the US.

2.3 APPROACHES TO INTERNATIONAL BUSINESS

If a company wants to grow and explore new opportunities in foreign markets, the approaches to international business they undertook can help them seize these opportunities, manage and organise their business affairs, manage their workforce needs, do strategic planning, and tell them how to run a profitable and sustainable company.

Approaches to international business simply refers to the way a firm defines its market and chose strategies accordingly to cater to the same. The various approaches used by firms in contemporary world are:

2.3.1 Ethnocentric Approach

Under this approach, foreign market is seen as an extension of the domestic market. The same practices and approach that worked or performed in the domestic market is used in international market as well.

The international market is used for exporting the surplus production. The product and services developed for domestic market are not modified as per the demand of international market neither the marketing strategies are changed. The business is operated from the head country only. Ethnocentrism is practiced by the firms which are in early stage of internationalization.

The Coca-Cola Company uses ethnocentric approach as its operations are centralised in nature. The brands and products offered across geographies are same and even the marketing strategies adopted to advertise and distribute are very similar.

2.3.2 Polycentric Approach

Polycentric approach refers to adopting country-wise strategies for marketing product and services. Here, the belief is that each country has a set of unique characteristics and hence the strategies should be formulated keeping in view the same. The polycentric firm establishes subsidiaries in the foreign market and decentralize the decision making. The parent company appoints key personnel who in turn hire other staff from the host country.

In the 1990s, **Citicorp** was using polycentric approach. Its branches at foreign countries were formulating their own policies and were not serving to the goal of the whole group. Eventually, the management decided to switch to geocentric approach.

2.3.3 Regiocentric Approach

After setting up the operations in a foreign country through subsidiary, if the firm realises that the neighbouring country share the similar market characteristics as that of host country, it may export its product to such countries as well. The product and marketing strategies are same in the whole region and hence this approach is referred as regiocentric approach.

General Motors is an interesting example of a company using regiocentric approach. Before 2010, the company used different strategies in different regions like Asia, Europe and America. Executives from different regions had considerable autonomy in designing product for their respective regions. One outcome of this orientation was that at one time there were 270 different types of radios installed in GM vehicles across the world.

2.3.4 Geocentric Approach

A firm following the geocentric approach considers the globe as a single country. It operates through various subsidiaries established in different part of the world. The parent company acts as a coordinator between different subsidiaries.

IBM is a true geocentric organization. Various subsidiaries of IBM act independently as far as the operations are concerned but broader strategies are formulated centrally.

2.4 ROUTES TO GO INTERNATIONAL

A company planning to expand its business beyond national borders has to decide the way to enter the international markets. The product development and marketing strategies of the company varies with the entry strategies it chooses. Following are some of the entry strategies to international business a firm may select as per its requirements.

2.4.1 Exporting

A firm in its early stage of internationalization should start with exporting its product to the foreign market as this strategy doesn't require any initial investment of capital apart from marketing and selling expenses. This also provides opportunity to the firm to explore the demand and market conditions of the unknown country. Exporting can be direct or indirect through a third party (distributor) in a foreign country.

Honasa Consumer Pvt Ltd (parent company of Mamaearth and The Derma Co) is an Indian unicorn founded in 2016. As the company is in growth phase, it has started exporting its products to other Asian countries via distributers and the share of exports in the company's operating revenue has grown to 1.8 percent in FY 2021.

2.4.2 Licensing

Licensing means giving rights to other parties to use your brand name or intellectual property right in turn of license fee or royalties. It's an easy way to enter into a new market without any investment. Also, it is beneficial for the firms that are selling products that may benefit from local production.

Nintendo Co. Ltd. is a Japanese video game company. It has created numerous popular franchises like Pokemon, Mario, The Donkey Kong and Metroid. It licenses other companies via licensing agencies to use its franchises. For example, a clothing company wanting to use Mario on its T-shirts, will have to enter into a licensing contract with Nintendo in order to do so.

2.4.3 Franchising

It refers to an arrangement between franchisor (owner of the business) and a franchisee where the latter would use the right of the business for a fee and the former would closely control the business processes. Franchising defers from licensing as the former deals with providing services whereas the latter deals with products.

Subway, an American fast food restaurant chain, operates as a franchise. Currently, its network consists of more than 20,000 franchisees (operated by entrepreneurs and small business owners). The product menu and services offered by different units are similar. In return Subway charges franchise fee and a share of revenue from the units.

2.4.4 Joint Ventures

A Joint Venture generally takes place between a foreign and a local firm to share the respective expertise and advantages. In less developed countries the foreign firm provides technical expertise, capital, capabilities and brand name whereas the local firm provides labour and manufacturing capabilities, local market expertise and connections.

BrahMos Aerospace is a joint venture between DRDO of India and NPO Mashinostroyenia of Russia, with core manufacturing concentrations in cruise missiles. The Company has become a role model by integrating public-private industries from India and Russia. Recently, it has signed a deal worth $374.9 million with Philippines to export a shore based anti-ship missile system acquisition project for its navy.

2.4.5 Manufacturing

A firm can establish a manufacturing facility in one or many of the foreign country, either for the consumption in host country or for exporting to other countries including the home country. A global firm manufactures in other countries to take advantage of cheap labour or other factors of production or to reduce the cost of transportation. Whereas the host country welcomes such initiative as the foreign firms bring investment, technical and managerial capabilities as well as generate employment in the host country.

Tesla, a leading Electric automotive company from US, takes advantage of expertise and lower cost of production by setting manufacturing plants outside US. It has plants in Germany that produces manufacturing equipment exclusively for Tesla, Canada that is specialized in Battery manufacturing equipment, China that manufactures supercharger, Netherlands which is an assembling plant catering to EU market, and many more under progress.

2.4.6 Assembly Operations

Assembly refers to joining/combining various components using permanent (welding, brazing, soldering and adhesive bonding) or semi-permanent (Screw, bolt and other threaded fasteners) methods to form a product. Under assembly operations, a firm produces various components in other countries (taking into account the comparative advantage) and then assembles it to further distribute. This method allows firm to by-pass tariffs and quotas in some cases by only assembling their product in the host country.

Apple Inc manufactures its flagship brand iphone in various countries like China, Malysia, Thailand, and South Korea among others. It has started iphone assembling facility at Foxconn and Wistron in India since 2017. This helps the company in catering the demand faster as well as save taxes.

2.4.7 Management Contract

Under this arrangement, the firm having management capabilities may enter into a contract with the firm in the host country to take up the production. It only manages the marketing and distribution of the product. The benefit here is that the firm doesn't have to invest anything in the host country and it may experiment with the product at a very low risk.

Garments, Footwears, Sports items are generally manufactured by small firms, the products are then supplied to MNCs. The MNCs sell such products to customers under their own brand name.

H&M, a leading fast fashion brand, sources ninety-nine percent of the products it sells from various suppliers who have their own manufacturing and processing units. It has its largest production market for clothing in China and Bangladesh.

One of the other examples is of German Airports operator **Fraport**. In 2008, Fraport entered into a management contract with the government of Saudi Arabia to operate two international airports in Riyadh and Jeddah for the period of six years.

2.4.8 Turnkey Operations

As the term itself suggests, turnkey operation refers to the business which is ready for operations, one has to just turn the key to unlock the door and start functioning. Under this system, the firm provides fully equipped production facility, technical know-how, training and sometimes even finance to the entity in the home country. This strategy is used by the established multi-national firm offering standard product or services. Construction of Highways or Airports are an example of turnkey operations.

Tata Projects, a leading infrastructure company in India, has expertise in executing large industrial and urban infrastructure projects. It provides turnkey solutions to set up oil & gas refineries, water and wastewater management solutions, rail & metro lines, airports, townships, power generation plants, power transmission & distribution systems, etc. It has executed various power generation, transmission and distribution projects across Africa as well.

2.4.9 Acquisitions and Mergers

Acquisition refers to the control of one entity over the other whereas the merger refers to the combination of two entities into the one. This strategy provides rapid growth in the foreign market to the acquiring country.

In the year 2007, **Hindalco Industries Limited** acquired US-based Novelis Inc in order to expand its global presence and became world's largest aluminium rolling entity at that time. Recently (in 2020), Hindalco acquired another American rolled products major Aleris Corporation via its wholly owned subsidiary Novelis Inc and strengthened its position as a giant aluminium company having footprint across Asia, Europe and North America.

FIGURE 2.3 Few Examples of Acquisitions and Mergers in India.

2.4.10 Wholly Owned Subsidiaries

A wholly owned subsidiary refers to the firm completely owned by the parent company. Establishing a subsidiary in a foreign country allows the parent company to take greater risk as well as have full control on the management. This strategy is suitable for the well-established company with deep pockets.

Reliance Industries Ltd (RIL) has a lot of wholly owned subsidiaries in foreign countries. At the beginning of year 2022, it has set up one such subsidiary named Reliance International Limited (RINL) at UAE for trading of crude oil, petroleum products, petrochemicals and agricultural commodities.

2.5 MULTINATIONAL CORPORATIONS

Multinational Corporation (MNC), is any corporation that is registered and operates in more than one country at a time or an enterprise which is having strategic presence in two or more than two distinct regions of the world. Generally, the corporation has its headquarters in one country and operates wholly or partially owned subsidiaries in other countries. Its subsidiaries report to the corporation's headquarters based in the home country.

The benefits of forming a multinational corporation for a business include increasing market share as well as vertical and horizontal economies of scale (cost savings that come from expanding output and consolidating management). Although cultural differences might provide unforeseen challenges as businesses set up offices and manufacturing facilities around the world, a company's technological know-how, experienced staff, and tried-and-true business models typically can be transferred from one nation to another. Multinational corporations are typically criticized for being an economic and frequently political tool of foreign dominance. Developing nations are particularly susceptible to economic exploitation since their economies are based on a small number of exports, frequently of basic items. Among the dangers facing host nations are monopolistic business practices, violations of human rights, and interference with more established economic growth strategies.

TABLE 2.1 World's Top 50 non-financial MNCs Ranked by Foreign Assets (Source: World Investment Report (2022), UNCTAD) (Figures in million dollars)

Ranking	*Company*	*Home Country*	*Industry*	*Foreign Assets*	*Total Assets*
1	Shell plc	United Kingdom	Mining, quarrying and petroleum	367 818	404 379
2	Toyota Motor Corporation	Japan	Motor Vehicles	319 475	522 471
3	Total Energies SE	France	Petroleum Refining and Related Industries	298 425	332 380
4	Volkswagen Group	Germany	Motor Vehicles	262 35	598 719
5	Deutsche Telekom AG	Germany	Telecommunications	259 466	318 979
6	Exxon Mobil Corporation	United States	Petroleum Refining and Related Industries	197 420	338 923
7	Stellantis NV	Netherlands	Motor Vehicles	194 548	194 548
8	BP plc	United Kingdom	Petroleum Refining and Related Industries	191 516	287 272
9	Anheuser-Busch InBev NV	Belgium	Food & beverages	179 313	217 627
10	British American Tobacco PLC	United Kingdom	Tobacco	172 480	185 153
11	Enel SpA	Italy	Electricity, gas and water	165 788	234 387
12	Chevron Corporation	United States	Petroleum Refining and Related Industries	161 158	239 535
13	EDF SA	France	Electricity, gas and water	160 091	408 841
14	Vodafone Group Plc	United Kingdom	Telecommunications	156 541	170 907
15	Honda Motor Co. Ltd.	Japan	Motor Vehicles	149 346	196 882

(Contd.)

Ranking	Company	Home Country	Industry	Foreign Assets	Total Assets
16	CK Hutchison Holdings Limited	Hong Kong, China	Retail Trade	147 640	155 598
17	Mercedes-Benz Group	Germany	Motor Vehicles	144 607	294 293
18	Siemens AG	Germany	Industrial and Commercial Machinery	139 302	161 329
19	Hon Hai Precision Industries	Taiwan Province of China	Electronic components	137 194	140 802
20	Microsoft Corporation	United States	Computer and Data Processing	135 685	333 779
21	BMW AG	Germany	Motor Vehicles	133 774	259 969
22	Johnson & Johnson	United States	Pharmaceuticals	133 432	182 018
23	RWE AG	Germany	Electricity, gas and water	130 133	161 184
24	China National Petroleum Corp. (CNPC)	China	Mining, quarrying and petroleum	129 200	625 390
25	Iberdrola SA	Spain	Electricity, gas and water	120 997	160 553
26	Eni SpA	Italy	Petroleum Refining and Related Industries	116 788	156 037
27	Nestlé SA	Switzerland	Food & beverages	115 109	152 551
28	Huawei Investment & Holding Co Ltd	China	Communications equipment	111 865	154 740
29	Bayer AG	Germany	Pharmaceuticals	109 553	136 189
30	Glencore PLC	Switzerland	Mining, quarrying and petroleum	104 703	127 510
31	Takeda Pharmaceutical Company Limited	Japan	Pharmaceuticals	103 498	108 226
32	Rio Tinto PLC	United Kingdom	Mining, quarrying and petroleum	102 739	102 896
33	Apple Inc	United States	Computer Equipment	100 005	351 002
34	ArcelorMittal	Luxembourg	Metals and metal products	99 794	102 517
35	Saudi Aramco	Saudi Arabia	Mining, quarrying and petroleum	98 915	576 717
36	Alphabet Inc	United States	Computer and Data Processing	98 628	359 268
37	Telefonica SA	Spain	Telecommunications	95 415	123 698

(Contd.)

Ranking	Company	Home Country	Industry	Foreign Assets	Total Assets
38	GlaxoSmithKline PLC	United Kingdom	Pharmaceuticals	92 915	106 622
39	Samsung Electronics Co., Ltd.	Korea, Republic of	Communications equipment	92 349	358 882
40	Tencent Holdings Limited	China	Computer and Data Processing	91 630	253 820
41	Medtronic plc	Ireland	Instruments and related products	90 052	93 083
42	Roche Group	Switzerland	Pharmaceuticals	89 426	101 214
43	Engie	France	Electricity, gas and water	88 817	255 219
44	AstraZeneca PLC	United Kingdom	Pharmaceuticals	88 748	105 363
45	Novartis AG	Switzerland	Pharmaceuticals	87 737	131 795
46	Mitsubishi Corporation	Japan	Wholesale Petroleum and Fuels	87 392	179 955
47	Amazon.com, Inc	United States	E-Commerce	86 143	420 549
48	Christian Dior SA	France	Textiles, clothing and leather	83 754	138 584
49	Nippon Telegraph & Telephone Corporation	Japan	Telecommunications	83 563	195 972
50	Mitsui & Co Ltd	Japan	Wholesale Metals and Minerals	83 249	122 559

As it can be seen from the Table 2.1, in the list of top 50 multinational enterprises (in terms of foreign assets) maximum countries are from the US, UK and Germany (7 each). Then there are 6 from Japan, 4 from Switzerland and 3 are registered in China.

2.6 INDIA'S POSITION IN TERMS OF GLOBAL INTEGRATION

As of 2021, India is the 6th largest economy in terms of Gross Domestic Product, producing goods and services worth $3.20 trillion in nominal terms, which is nearly 3% of the world GDP of $100 trillion (Figure 2.5) (World Bank data).

If we look into the data of merchandise exports (Figure 2.6), India is at seventeenth position in the year 2021. Taking into consideration the size of Indian economy it is quite low. It is twelfth largest importer, the number 150 economy in terms of GDP per capita (current US$) and the number 40 most complex economy according to the Economic Complexity Index (ECI).

The five largest exporters in the world, as of 2021, are China, United States, Germany, Netherlands and Japan (Figure 2.6).

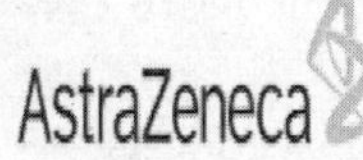

FIGURE 2.4 Few Examples of MNCs.

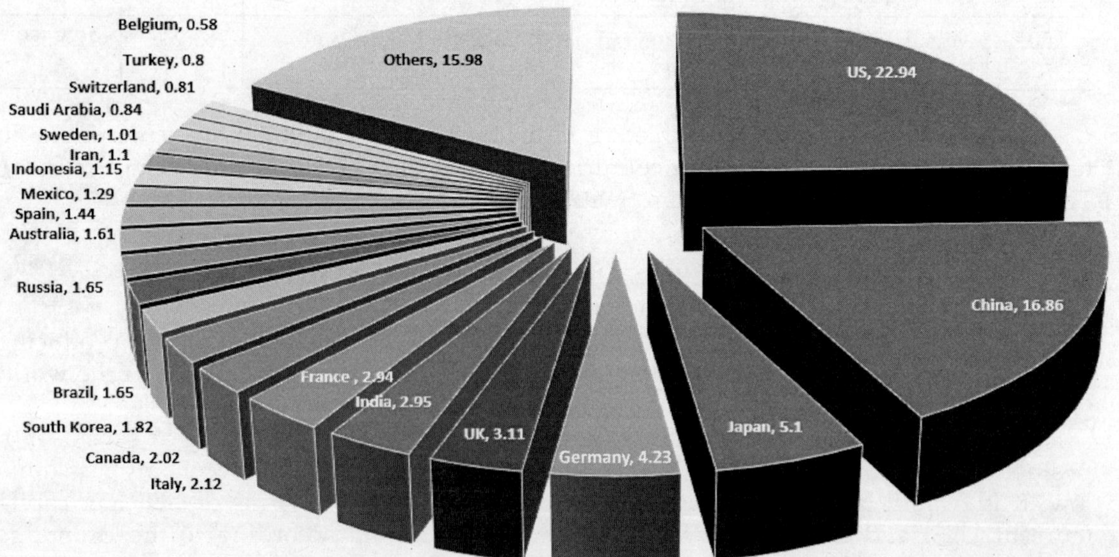

Figures are in Trillions of Dollar

Source: IMF (2021)

FIGURE 2.5 Global GDP.

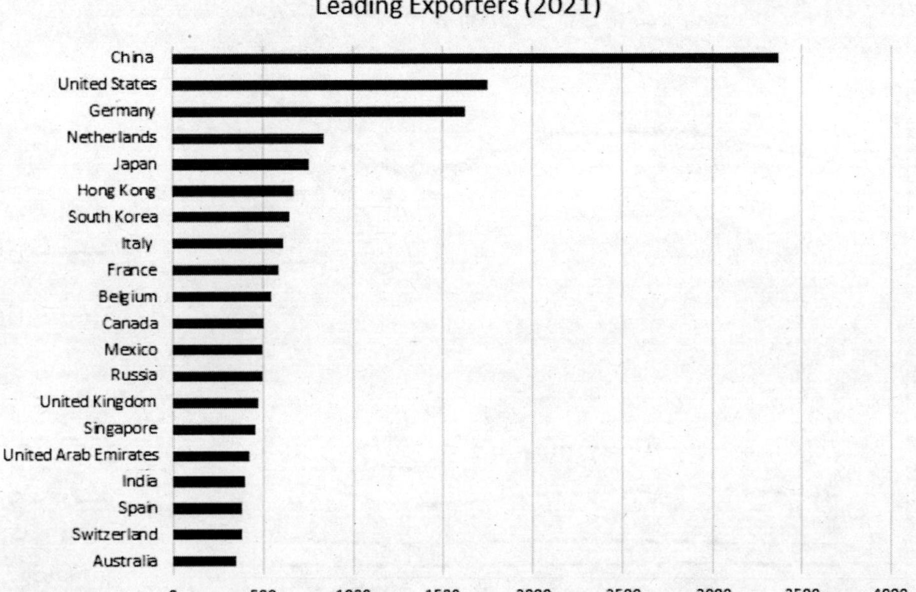

Figures are in Billions of US Dollar;
Source: World Bank (2021)

FIGURE 2.6 Leading Merchandise Exporters.

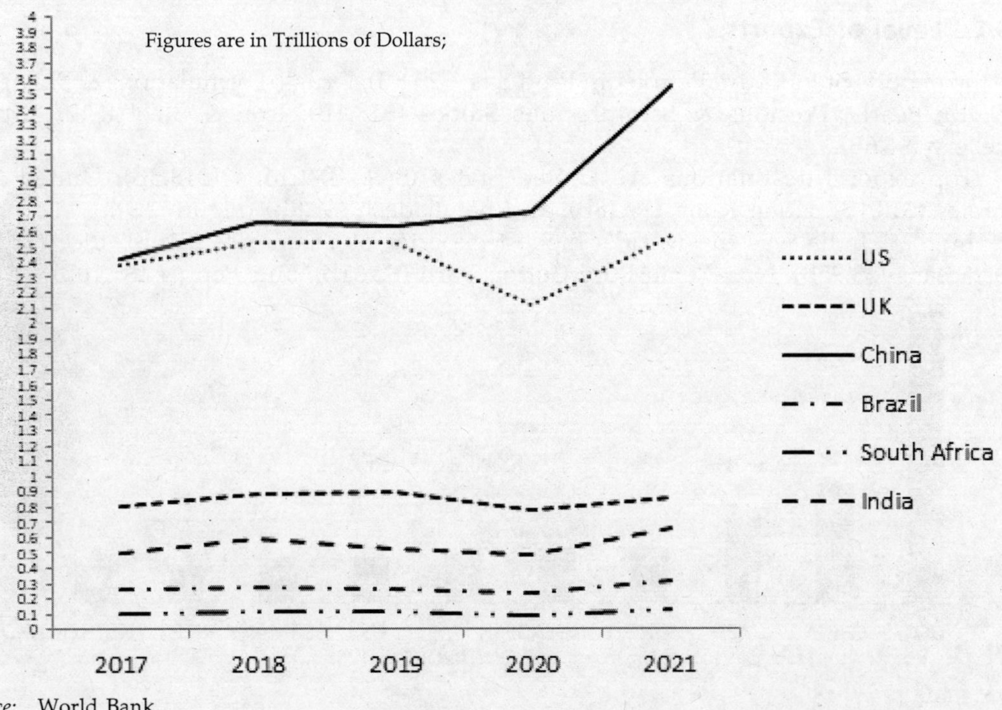

Source: World Bank

FIGURE 2.7 Total Exports.

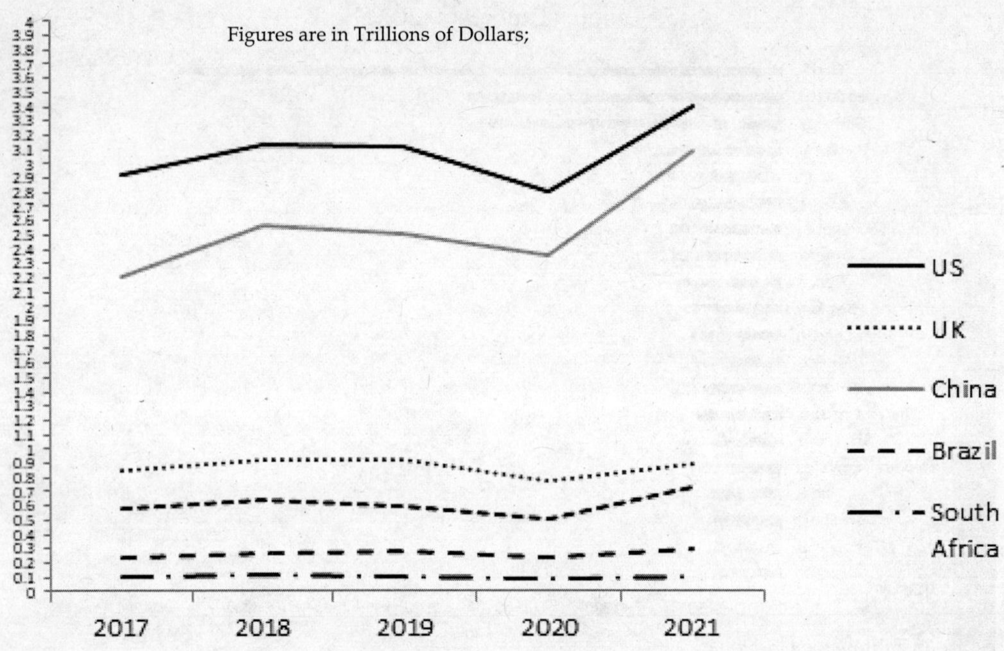

Source: World Bank

FIGURE 2.8 Total Imports.

2.6.1 Level of Exports

The top exports of India are Petroleum Products ($25.8B); Drugs, Formulations & Biologicals ($19.0B); Pearls, Precious & Semiprecious Stones ($18.1B); Iron & Steel ($12.1 B) and Jewellery ($6.6B).

Top exports destinations are United States ($49.7B) China ($18.5B), United Arab Emirates ($18.1B), Hong Kong ($9.18B), and Bangladesh ($8.8B) (Figure 2.9).

In 2021, India was the world's biggest exporter of Diamonds ($16B), Rice ($8.21B), Crustaceans ($3.95B), Non-Retail Pure Cotton Yarn ($2.61B), and Pepper ($1.16B)

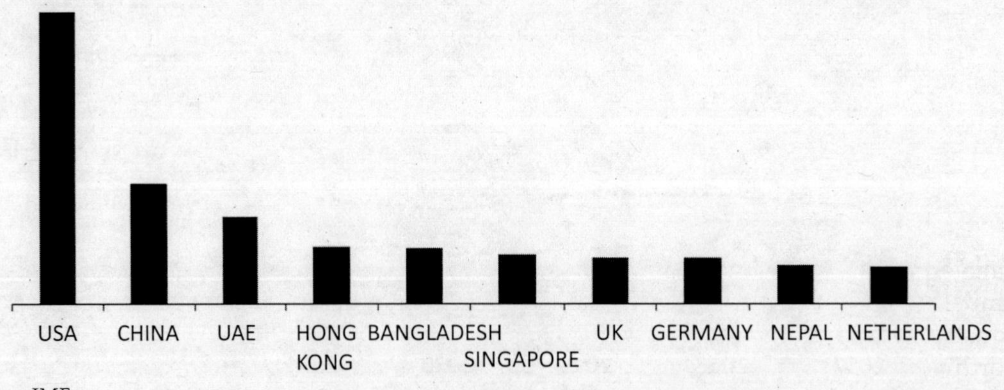

Source: *IMF*

FIGURE 2.9 Top Exports Destination of India (2021).

2.6.2 Level of Imports

In FY 2021, The top imports of India are Crude Petroleum ($59.5B); Gold ($34.6B); Petroleum Products ($23.2B); Pearls, Precious and Semiprecious Stones ($18.9B) and Coal, Coke and Briquittes ($16.3B).

India imported majorly from China ($64.2B), United States ($26.6B), United Arab Emirates, Switzerland and Saudi Arabia ($16.8B) (Figure 2.10).

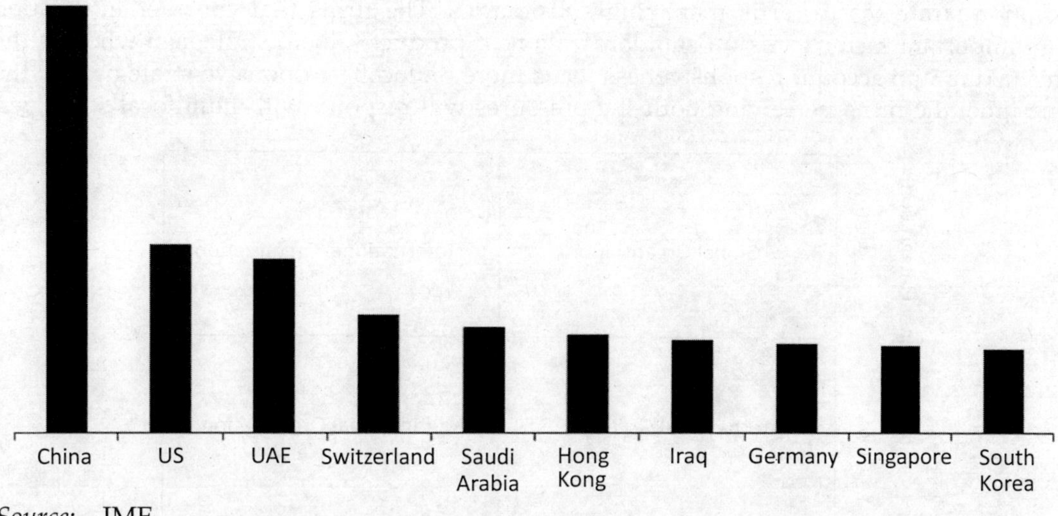

Source: IMF

FIGURE 2.10 Top Imports Destination of India (2021).

In 2021, India was the world's biggest importer of Coal Briquettes ($20.9B), Diamonds ($15.8B), Palm Oil ($5.04B), Soybean Oil ($3.02B), and Nitrogenous Fertilizers ($2.64B).

2.7 COMPETITIVE STRATEGIES OF INTERNATIONAL TRADE

The strategies that provide comparative advantage to a business or nation is termed as competitive strategies. Despite facing tough competition from other entities, if the business is able to earn higher than usual return on investment, it is said to have comparative advantage. There are two widely discussed theories of competitive strategies. The first is Porter's theory that is nation centric (already discussed) and the other is Prahalad & Doz's strategy model that focuses on industry.

2.7.1 Prahalad and Doz's Strategy Model

Prahalad and Doz in 1986 provided a framework to measure or understand the industry's competitiveness. As per the model, there are two aspects or dimensions upon which an industry can focus, which are Integration and Responsiveness. Integration refers to the coordination the firm establishes between different units located in different countries across the globe in order to efficiently manage operations and take advantage of the competitiveness of various locations. On the other hand, responsiveness stands for the ability of the firm to act on the local demand. The term "Think Global, Act Local" truly summarizes the IR (Integration & Responsiveness) model.

The Integration and Responsiveness grid categorizes the firm involved in international business into four varieties on the basis of these two strategies followed by the firm. They are—International, Global, Translational and Multinational.

The way a firm perceives its environment and takes pressure decides their resource allocation strategies towards managing subsidiaries. The firms that consider integration as an important factor focus on standardization of product (global strategies) whereas the firms taking into account responsiveness focus more on locally responsive strategies. At the same time, the firms perceiving both the pressures will respond with multifocal strategies.

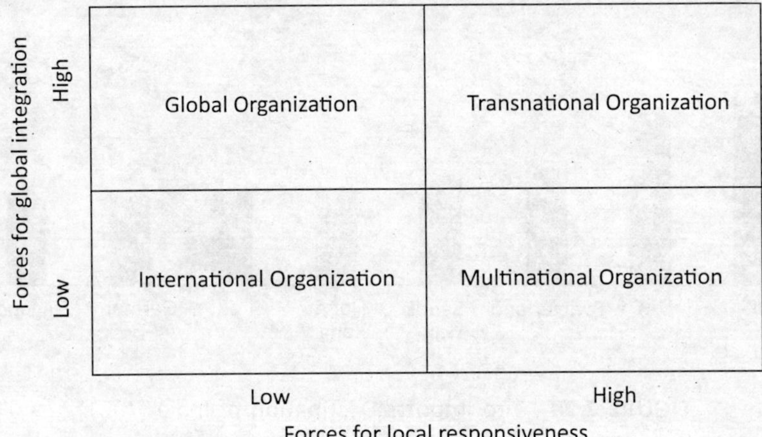

FIGURE 2.11 Prahalad and Doz's Strategy Matrix.

The Global firm follows the strategy of standardization, coordination, centralization and coordination in order to remain competitive. The international firm is neither globally integrated nor locally responsive. A multinational firm responding to local demands focuses on product diversification and adaptation. Transnational firm follows the strategy of both global integration and local responsiveness. The firm simultaneously seeks standardization, economies of scale, local responsiveness and product differentiation.

SUMMARY

1. International business denotes all those business activities which take place beyond the geographical limits of the country.
2. There are various theories that explain the motive of nation or businesses to go global. As per theory of Mercantilism, nation trade to accumulate wealth. Absolute cost advantage states that a nation can gain from international trade by producing products and services in which it is most efficient than others, whereas comparative cost advantage theory says the nation must focus its resources on few products as the resources are limited. According to factor proportion theory, a nation must

focus on the factor of productions rather than the product itself to decide what to produce. Later trade theories like global strategic rivalry theory and product life cycle theory started focusing on businesses rather than nations as the trader. Product life cycle theory describes the stages of a product from introduction, maturity to standardization.

3. Approaches to international business simply refers to the way a firm defines its market and chose strategies accordingly to cater to the same.
4. Under Ethnocentric approach foreign market is seen as an extension of the domestic market whereas polycentric firms consider each nation has a unique set of characteristics and cater them accordingly.
5. Regiocentric firms use clustering approach to cater to multiple nations. On the other hand, for a polycentric firm, whole globe is a single market. It produces standard products all around the globe.
6. Multinational Corporation (MNC), is any corporation that is registered and operates in more than one country at a time or an enterprise which is having strategic presence in two or more than two distinct regions of the world.

KEY WORDS

- International Business
- Comparative Cost Advantage
- Product Life Cycle Theory
- Ethnocentric
- Polycentric
- Geocentric

QUESTIONS

1. Differentiate between absolute cost advantage theory and comparative cost advantage theory.
2. Explain International Product Life Cycle with the help of a real-world example.
3. How ethnocentric approach of international business differs from polycentric approach? Explain with the help of an example of a firm that shifted its approach from ethnocentric to polycentric.
4. What are the various entry modes available to a firm trying to expand its operations beyond domestic borders?

REFERENCES AND SUGGESTED READINGS

1. Smith, A. (1887). *An Inquiry into the Nature and Causes of the Wealth of Nations...* T. Nelson and Sons.
2. Golub, S.S., & Hsieh, C.T. (2000). Classical Ricardian theory of comparative advantage revisited. *Review of international economics*, 8(2), 221–234.
3. Samuelson, P.A. (1948). International trade and the equalisation of factor prices, *The Economic Journal*, 58(230), 163–184.
4. Heckscher, E.F., & Ohlin, B. (1933). Factor-endowment and factor proportion theory.
5. Leontief, W. (1953). Domestic production and foreign trade; the American capital position re-examined, *Proceedings of the American philosophical Society*, 97(4), 332–349.
6. Porter, M.E. (1990). The competitive advantage of nations, *Harvard business review*, *73*, 91.
7. Krugman, P. (1983). New theories of trade among industrial countries, *The American Economic Review*, *73*(2), 343–347.
8. Vernon, R. (1979). The product cycle hypothesis in a new international environment, *Oxford bulletin of economics and statistics*, 41(4), 255–267.
9. 2022. The World Bank. https://data.worldbank.org/
10. Doz, Y. L., & Prahalad, C. K. (1981). Headquarters influence and strategic control in MNCs, *Sloan Management Review (pre-1986)*, 23(1), 15.

CHAPTER 3

Foreign Direct Investments

LEARNING OUTCOMES

After reading this chapter, the reader will be able to:

- Explain the Meaning of Foreign Direct Investment (FDI)
- Discuss the Trends in FDI
- Interpret Theories of FDI
- Describe Comparative Management
- Explain Cost and Benefits of FDI
- Discuss Cross-Border Mergers and Acquisitions

3.1 MEANING OF FOREIGN DIRECT INVESTMENT

An ownership stake in a foreign company or project is known as a foreign direct investment (FDI) and is made by a foreign investor, business, or government. It is strategic investment for a long period of time involving substantial amount in the host country.

Foreign Direct Investment into a country represents how much investment is coming into the country. It shows the competitiveness of the country. More flow of investment represents the preference of MNCs and investors for the country. They consider the country as competitive and growing.

The phrase typically refers to a corporate decision to buy a sizable portion of a foreign company or to buy it altogether in order to expand operations to a new area. The term is typically not used to refer to a stock purchase in an overseas firm only. FDI is a crucial component of global economic integration since it forges strong, lasting ties between national economies.

When businesses make international direct investments, they become multinational enterprises (FDI). FDI frequently entails the construction of new manufacturing facilities in foreign nations, as the Ohio plant for Honda. FDI may also include acquisitions of and mergers with existing foreign companies. Ford, a company that just gained actual control of Mazda, a Japanese automaker, serves as an illustration. Greenfield investments, or the construction of entirely new manufacturing facilities, as well as international mergers and acquisitions all provide multinational corporations (MNCs) a certain amount of influence. Thus, FDI is an example of MNC internal organisational growth.

In fact, FDI by MNCs today contributes significantly to the integration of national economies and the characterization of the growing global economy. Such MNCs have made an international presence and a reputation for themselves by engaging in FDI on a global scale. Regardless of national boundaries, they use their strong tangible and intangible resources to pursue profits and strengthen their competitive positions. In order to comprehend why businesses engage in FDI, we will analyse alternative FDI theories in this chapter. We also go into great detail about a type of FDI that is becoming more and more common: cross-border mergers and acquisitions.

3.2 TRENDS IN FOREIGN DIRECT INVESTMENT

For numerous reasons, FDI has increased more quickly than global output and trade. First off, businesses still worry about protectionist forces notwithstanding the broad fall in trade barriers over the previous three decades. FDI is viewed by executives as a way to get around potential trade restrictions. Second, a large portion of the increase in FDI has been driven by the political and economic developments that have been taking place in many of the developing countries of the world. FDI has been promoted by the general shift towards democratic political structures and free market economies. Economic growth, economic liberalisation, privatisation initiatives available to international investors, and the lifting of numerous FDI barriers have increased attractiveness of developing economies to foreign multinational corporations across a large portion of Asia, Eastern Europe, and Latin America.

As can be seen from Figure 3.1, foreign direct investment around the world reached to a new high in 2000 just before the dot com bubble. The investors gained confidence again after 2004, as the trade around the world grew at a faster pace and it peaked in 2007. The world again underwent a major shock during global financial crises. Another

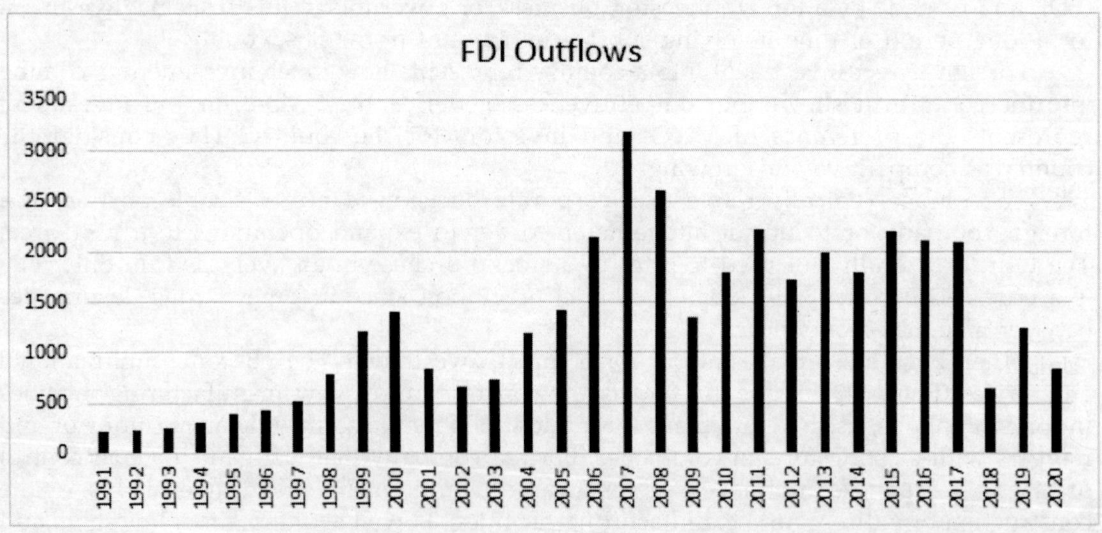

Source: UNCTAD

FIGURE 3.1 Foreign Direct Investment Outflows (World) (1991–2020) (Figures are in Billions of Dollars)

major dip can be seen in the year 2018. According to James Zhan, Director of UNCTAD's Investment Division in 2019, "the underlying FDI trend has demonstrated lacklustre growth since the global financial crisis and has been on a declining slope since 2013. The causes of this unfavourable trend, such as decreased foreign investment profitability and changes in global value chains, are not likely to change very soon. The macroeconomic environment is likewise getting worse", he claimed.

UNCTAD claims that the United States' corporate income tax overhaul is to blame for the drop in FDI in 2018. Multinational companies operating in the United States started a significant repatriation of accrued offshore earnings in 2017, which has had a negative impact on Europe.

Total FDI flows at the global level were nearly $1.6 trillion in the year 2021, an increment of 64% on year-on-year basis. In the Fiscal year 2021, the top sources of FDI were United States, Australia and United Kingdom, whereas the top recipients of FDI inflows were China, United States and Australia.

The sector mix of FDI has dramatically changed over the last three decades, moving away from manufacturing and extractive industries and towards services. Approximately 47% of FDI stock was in the service sector in 1990; by 2004–2006, this percentage had risen to 54%. Similar patterns may be observed in the cross-border mergers and acquisitions composition, where services are becoming significantly more important.

TABLE 3.1 Foreign Direct Investment Outflows and Inflows (Figures in Billions of Dollars)

Year		2017	2018	2019	2020	2021	*Annual Average*
World	Outflows	1610.11	941.29	1123.89	780.48	1707.59	1232.67
	Inflows	1632.64	1448.28	1480.63	963.14	1582.31	1421.40
France	Outflows	35.98	102.04	33.82	46.01	–2.84	43.00
	Inflows	24.83	41.83	28.36	4.87	14.19	22.82
Germany	Outflows	86.52	97.23	137.29	60.62	151.69	106.67
	Inflows	48.64	72.10	52.67	64.59	31.27	53.85
Netherlands	Outflows	25.66	–47.48	16.31	–191.40	28.86	–33.61
	Inflows	13.93	87.63	–14.14	–105.39	–81.06	–19.81
Switzerland	Outflows	21.94	43.60	–56.17	–36.15	–19.12	–9.18
	Inflows	111.20	–83.15	–105.81	–162.70	1.02	–47.89
United Kingdom	Outflows	142.37	82.96	–6.08	–65.36	107.74	52.33
	Inflows	96.35	87.84	45.45	18.19	27.56	55.08
United States	Outflows	327.78	–157.41	28.60	234.92	403.10	167.40
	Inflows	308.96	203.23	225.11	150.83	367.38	251.10
Australia	Outflows	7.80	7.14	9.86	9.94	9.22	8.79
	Inflows	46.11	68.32	39.41	16.73	25.09	39.13

(Contd.)

Year		2017	2018	2019	2020	2021	*Annual Average*
Japan	Outflows	164.59	144.98	232.63	95.67	146.78	156.93
	Inflows	9.36	9.96	13.76	10.70	24.65	13.69
China	Outflows	158.29	143.04	136.91	153.71	145.19	147.43
	Inflows	136.32	138.31	141.23	149.34	180.96	149.23
Singapore	Outflows	62.71	22.17	55.61	31.76	47.40	43.93
	Inflows	82.48	73.93	106.32	75.44	99.10	87.45
India	Outflows	11.14	11.45	13.14	11.11	15.52	12.47
	Inflows	39.90	42.16	50.56	64.07	44.74	48.29

Source: UNCTAD World Investment Report, 2021

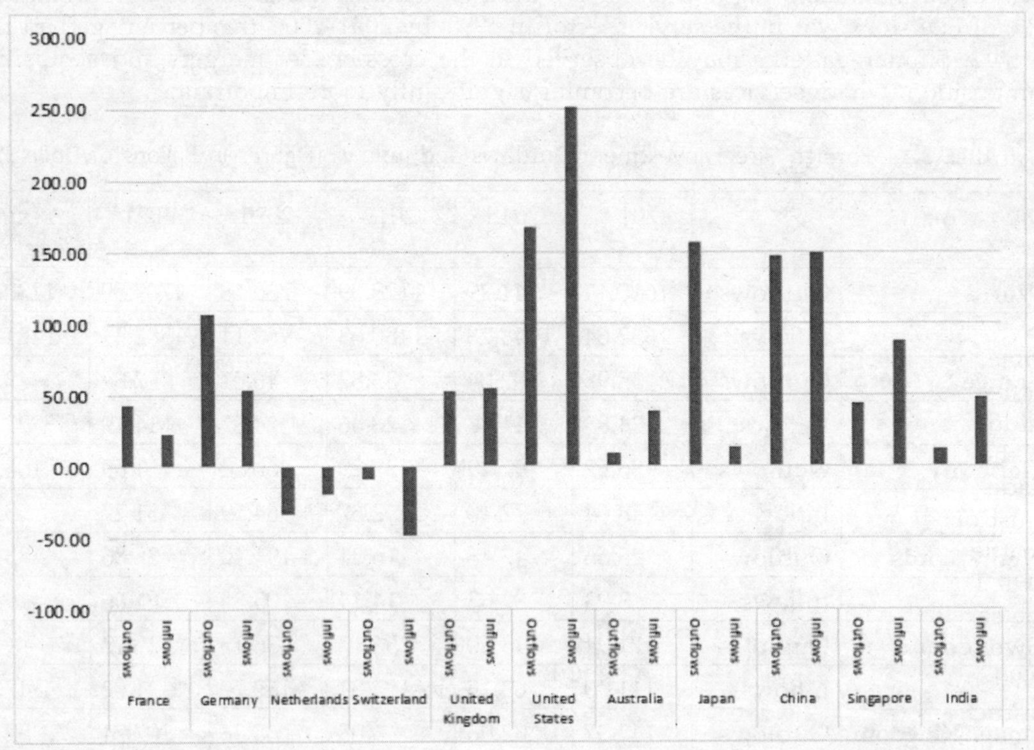

Source: UNCTAD World Investment Report

FIGURE 3.2 Average Foreign Direct Investment Inflows and Outflows between year 2017–2021.

Additionally, FDI in services has a different makeup now. It was mostly focused on trade and financial services up until recently. However, sectors including telecommunications, water, energy, and business services (like IT consulting services) are rising in importance.

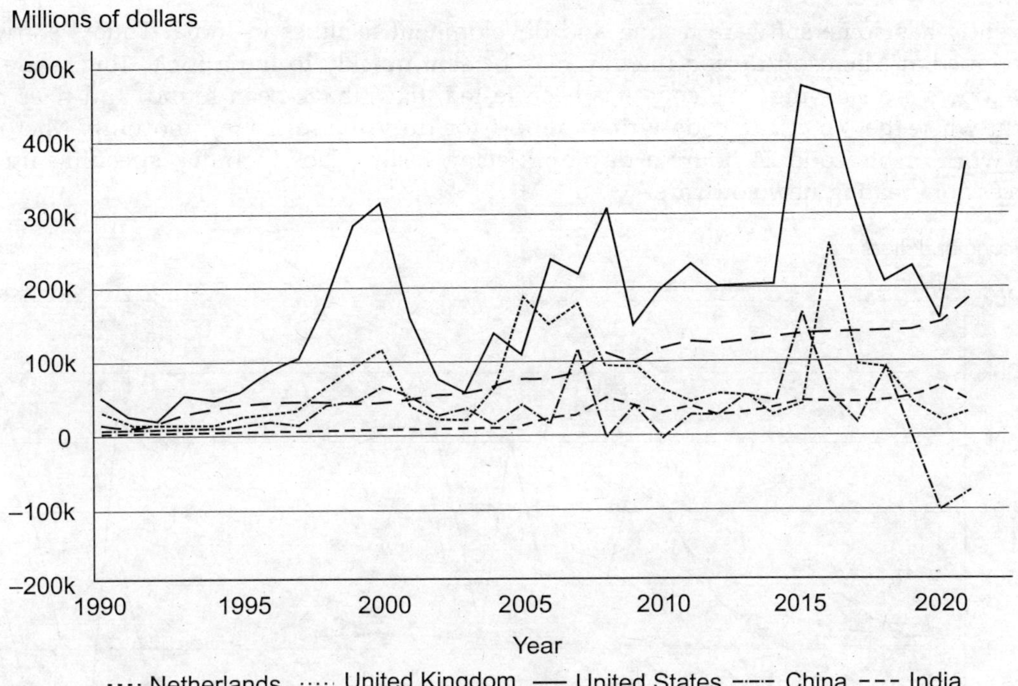

Source: UNCTAD World Investment Report 2022.

FIGURE 3.3 Foreign Direct Investment Outflows of Selected Countries.

Four elements that are driving the move to services are likely to continue for some time. In the first place, the change is a reflection of the broader trend in many industrialised economies away from manufacturing and towards service sectors. By the middle of the 2000s, services made up 52% of the GDP in developing countries and 72% of the GDP in developed countries. Second, a lot of services are not open to international trade. Where they are eaten is where they must be made. Starbucks, a service company, must open outlets in Japan in order to provide hot lattes to Japanese customers from its Seattle locations. The main method of introducing services to overseas markets is through FDI. Third, several nations have relaxed the rules governing foreign direct investment in the services sector (it was discovered that the WTO designed international agreements to lower barriers to FDI in the telecommunications and finance sectors throughout the late 1990s). This liberalisation has allowed for large inflows. After Brazil eliminated investment restrictions and privatised its state-owned telecommunications monopoly in the late 1990s, Brazilian telecoms had a substantial increase in foreign direct investment (FDI).

Finally, the expansion of Internet-based international telecommunications networks has given certain service businesses the opportunity to move some of their value-creation activities to other countries to benefit from lower factor costs. For instance, Procter & Gamble has moved part of its back-office accounting tasks to the Philippines where it can hire accountants with training in American accounting standards for a far lower salary. For the same reason, Dell has call-answering facilities in India. Similar to IBM, Microsoft currently has some software testing and development facilities in India. Today, software developed at Microsoft during the day may be sent quickly to India for testing while the developers are sleeping. The code has been tested, flaws have been found, and fixes may begin when the American code writers report for duty the following morning. Microsoft can work on its code 24 hours a day by placing testing labs in India, speeding up the process of creating new software.

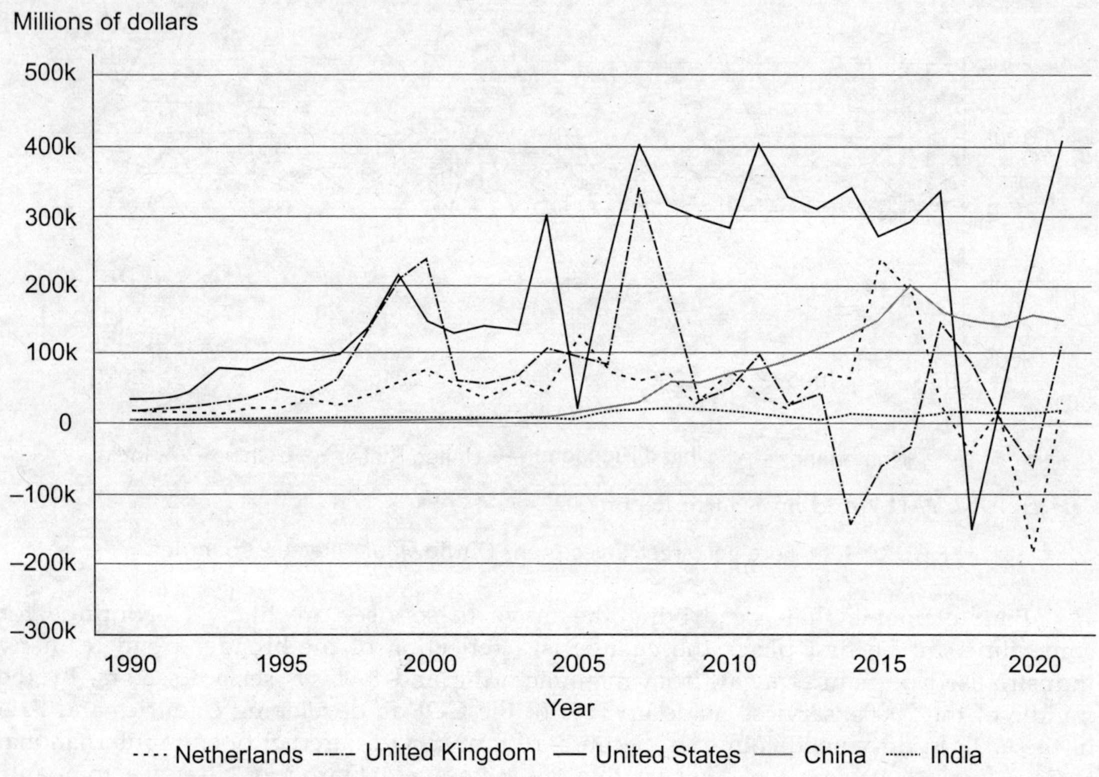

Source: UNCTAD World Investment Report 2022

FIGURE 3.4 Foreign Direct Investment Inflows of Selected Countries.

3.2.1 FDI Trends in India

As per the UNCTAD world investment report 2022, India has improved its position to 7th in the list of top host countries for foreign investments. Total FDI inflows in the year 2021 were $44.73B and the outflows were $15.52B. The top sources, from where the investments came, were Singapore, USA, Mauritius, Netherlands and Switzerland. If we look sectorally, highest investments from foreign were directed towards Computer Software and Hardware (24.60%). The other major recipients of FDI were Services Sector (financial and non-financial) (12.13%), Automobiles (11.89%), Trading (7.72%) and Infrastructure activities (5.52%).

TABLE 3.2 FDI Inflows and Outflows in million dollars (India) from 1990 to 2021 (Source: World Investment Report, UNCTAD)

Year	1990	1991	1992	1993	1994	1995	1996	1997	1998
FDI Inflow	236.7	75.0	252.0	532.0	974.0	2151.0	2525.0	3619.0	2633.0
FDI Outflow	6.0	–11.0	24.0	0.4	82.0	119.0	240.0	113.0	47.0

Year	1999	2000	2001	2002	2003	2004	2005	2006	2007
FDI Inflow	2168.0	3588.0	5477.6	5629.7	4321.1	5777.8	7621.8	20327.8	25349.9
FDI Outflow	80.0	514.4	1397.4	1678.0	1875.8	2175.4	2985.5	14285.0	17233.5

Year	2008	2009	2010	2011	2012	2013	2014	2015	2016
FDI Inflow	47102.4	35633.9	27417.1	36190.5	24195.8	28199.4	34582.1	44064.1	44480.6
FDI Outflow	21142.5	16057.8	15947.4	12456.2	8485.7	1678.7	11783.5	7572.4	5072.4

Year	2017	2018	2019	2020	2021
FDI Inflow	39903.8	42156.2	50558.3	64072.2	44735.1
FDI Outflow	11140.5	11446.9	13144.1	11109.2	15522.3

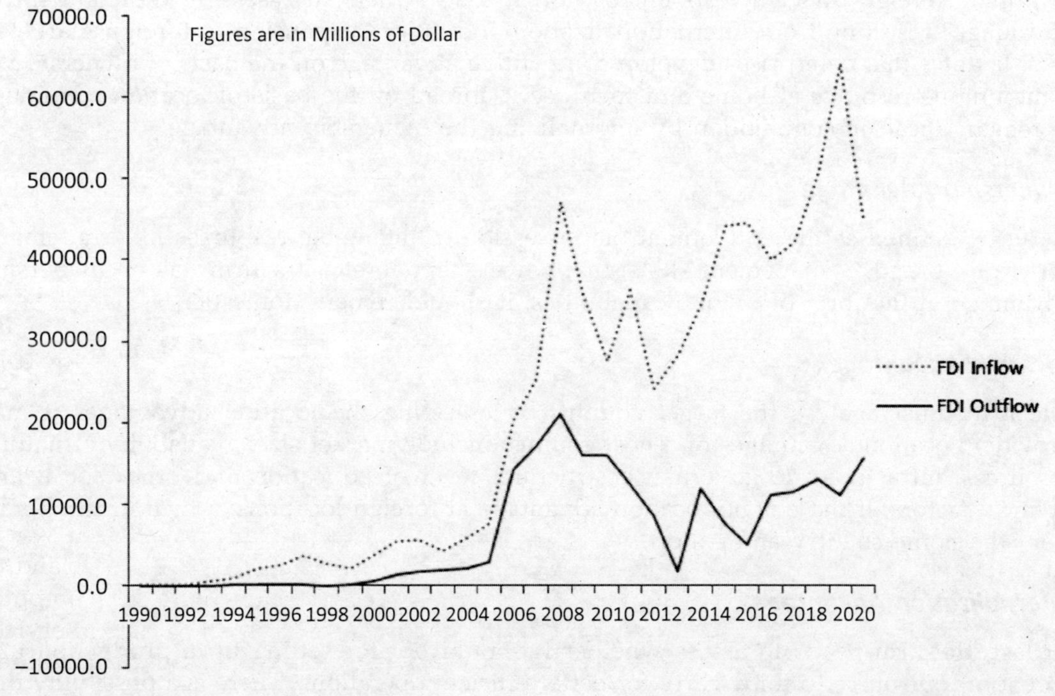

Source: UNCTAD

FIGURE 3.5 Foreign Direct Investment Inflows and Outflows from India (1990–2020).

3.3 THEORIES OF FDI

Why don't businesses export from their home country or licence production to a local company in the host nation instead of moving production overseas? In other words, why do businesses create multinational enterprises in order to expand their corporate influence abroad? We lack a thorough, well-developed theory of FDI, in contrast to theories of international trade and international portfolio investing. However, a number of ideas can explain some features of the FDI phenomenon.

The following are the main elements that influence business decisions to make investments abroad:

Trade restrictions, an imperfect labour market, intangible assets, vertical integration, the product life cycle, and services for diversified shareholder ownership are all factors.

3.3.1 Eclectic Paradigm Theory

Eclectic paradigm theory was propounded by John H Dunning in 1979. The theory is developed based on the Internalization theory developed by Buckley and Casson in 1976. The internalization theory together with eclectic paradigm theory provided the base for current theory of multinational enterprise given by Verbeke in 2009.

Dunning identified three factors that determine the international activities of multinational businesses. These are Ownership, Location and Internalization (also known as OLI framework). The framework explains whether it would be beneficial for firms to pursue foreign direct investment or not. It assists them in assessing the competitive advantages resulting from internationalization and guides expansion to foreign markets.

It states that enterprises develop competitive advantage on the basis of ownership of some unique resource at home and then use it abroad on the basis of location advantage to remain ahead in competition by internalizing the ownership advantage.

Ownership Advantage

It can be defined as the entitlement or possession of intangible resources like trademark, copyright, brand, management skills, manpower, capital, etc. If a firm has no ownership advantage in the form of unique capabilities, it should remain domestic.

Location Advantage

The firm must analyse the target country by assessing the location advantages it may provide. Location advantages of a host country include market size, availability of natural resources, infrastructure, governance structure, level of education and other social and political factors. If there is no location advantage at foreign locations, a firm must operate from the home country and export.

Internalization Advantage

At last, the firm needs to assess whether it should opt for setting up a production unit abroad or outsource to third party for better efficient operations. There is a possibility that the local partner at host country has the better understanding of the local market than the foreign player. In such cases the firm must go for licensing, franchising or outsourcing to remain competitively ahead. If the firm doesn't want to dissipate the ownership advantage it has, foreign direct investment through the subsidiaries is the best option, in this way, it would be able to internalize the ownership advantage it had at the first place.

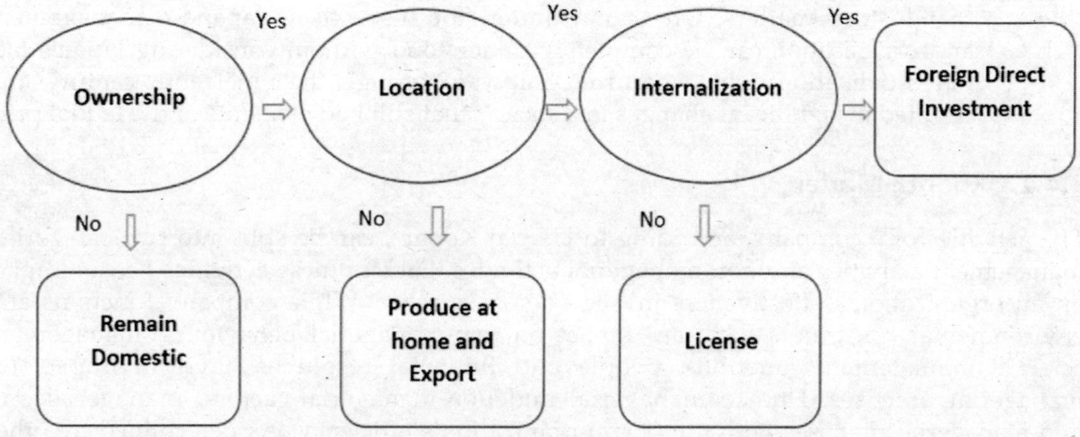

FIGURE 3.6 Ecletic Paradigm Theory.

3.4 COMPARATIVE MANAGEMENT

A new approach known as comparative management has arisen as a result of the emergence of multinational corporation all around the globe in the modern era. The study of managerial systems and practices in various cultural contexts and their variations and similarities can be referred to as comparative management. Understanding of the complexity, diversity, and influence of environmental factors on institutions is necessary.

Comparative management, according to Harold Koontz and Heinz Weihrich, is the measurement, identification, and interpretation of differences and similarities among distinct practises in various countries. The theories of comparative management focus on management and organisational variations that are brought about by nationally determinable factors and persist despite similarities in technology, environment, strategy, and other factors. They try to answer whether these disparities are likely to disappear or remain and how they might be explained.

The theories fall under two categories: Universalistic and Particularistic.

1. Under **Universalistic theory**, Cross-national variations in management and organisation, to the extent that they exist at all, are typically predicted to vanish in the future. Globalisation is a key driver behind this homogenization trend. Regardless of the nationality of the company, management, or employees, less effective management and organisational methods will be replaced by "best practises" as more and more markets are subjected to the pressure of global competition. Cross-national discrepancies now could be viewed as transient disequilibrium that will vanish once market restraints are eliminated.

2. Contrarily, **Particularistic theories** assert that cross-national variations in management and organisation will endure. For this reason, management and organisation must take into account varied national expectations and preferences. Furthermore, because national systems of management and organisation are path-dependent, particularistic interpretations of organisation and management indicate that history matters. One can wonder, for instance, if Japanese management and organisation can be completely understood without considering Japan's late industrialization, which occurred midway through the nineteenth century and resulted in significant changes in a society that still had elements of the feudal past.

3.4.1 Koontz Model

The activities of a company, according to Harold Koontz, can be split into two categories: management activities and non-managerial activities. Each of these activities has an impact on an organization's effectiveness in one way or another. While company functions and environmental constraints have an impact on non-managerial behaviours, management science, management functions, people and financial resources have an impact on managerial practises. Due to managerial and non-managerial factors, managerial and non-managerial practises both affect an organization's efficiency. As determined by other authors, the Koontz model essentially excludes managerial philosophy (managers' attitudes toward employees, partners, and other parties).

3.4.2 Farmer Richman Model

Farmer Richman's model can be seen as the first codified statement of comparative management and is widely accepted and used by researchers, educators, and management domain experts. It is a typical output of environment school. The model is based on four concepts: absolute managerial efficiency, exogenous constraints related to environment (including economic, educational, legal, and sociological variables), internal management regarding the process of human and material resource coordination, and relative managerial efficiency related to firm's activities coordination (generally speaking). Farmer and Richman justify their model on the methodological premise that approaches management as an environment dependent variable because the environment represents the primary component that influences management in a decisive way. Environment is the independent variable, according to Farmer and Richman, hence the other elements evolution is dependent on the changes in environment.

This theory is clearly supported by the directions of influences that are solely oriented from environment towards business efficiency. In this model, management feedback is completely disregarded. Undoubtedly, the model's design and functionality reflect a one-sided perspective on the phenomenon under study and undervalue the role of management. Due to this flaw, Schollhammer correctly categorised the model as a ecologist, a passive creature of external constraints.

Despite its limitations, Farmer and Richman's model is still useful since it is regarded as the first cogent structure based on comparative management methodology that was widely disseminated by management experts and served as a catalyst for their efforts. Additionally, the Farmer and Richman model has aided in the global re-evaluation of the significant role that the environment plays in management and knowledge processes.

3.5 BENEFITS AND COSTS OF FDI

To a greater or lesser degree, many governments can be considered pragmatic nationalists when it comes to FDI. Accordingly, their policy is shaped by a consideration of the costs and benefits of FDI. Here we explore the benefits and costs of FDI, first from the perspective of a host (receiving) country, and then from the perspective of the home (source) country. In the next section, we look at the policy instruments governments use to manage FDI.

3.5.1 Host-Country Benefits

The main advantages of inbound FDI for a host country come from effects on resource transfers, employment, balance of payments, competition, and economic growth.

Resource-Transfer

By providing capital, technology, and management resources to a host economy that would not otherwise be available, foreign direct investment can help that economy grow at a faster rate. Due to their scale and financial stability, many MNEs have access to funding sources that are not available to enterprises in the host country. These funds might be available from within the company itself, or maybe because of their renown, big MNEs find it simpler to access capital markets than local companies. Technology can promote economic growth and industrialization. There are two different types of technology, both of which have value. Technology can be used to create a product or it can be included into a manufacturing process (such as the technology used to find, extract, and refine oil) (e.g., personal computers). However, many nations lack the tools and resources for research and development necessary to create their own indigenous product and process technologies. Particularly in less developed countries is this true. These nations must rely on highly industrialised nations for the majority of the technology necessary to spur economic progress, and FDI can supply it.

According to research, multinational corporations frequently transfer a large amount of technology when they invest abroad. For instance, research on FDI in Sweden discovered that foreign companies enhanced the labour and total factor productivity of Swedish businesses they bought, indicating that sizable technology transfers had taken place (technology typically boosts productivity).

Additionally, a study on FDI by the Organization for Economic Cooperation and Development (OECD) discovered that foreign investors invested a sizable amount of money in R&D in the nations in which they had made investments, suggesting that they may have been doing more than just transferring technology to those nations. FDI leads to the creation of jobs. At Toyota's Valenciennes manufacturing facility, these French workers construct automobiles.

Foreign managerial expertise obtained through FDI could have significant advantages for the host nation. Foreign executives who have received the most recent management training can frequently contribute to enhancing the effectiveness of acquired or newly developed operations in the host nation. Local employees who have been trained to hold managerial, financial, and technical positions in the subsidiary of a foreign MNE may also have positive spin-off effects when they leave the company and support the creation of indigenous businesses. Similar advantages might result if a foreign MNE inspires local suppliers, distributors, and rivals to develop their own management capabilities.

Employment

Another positive benefit attributed to FDI is the creation of jobs in the host nation that would not have otherwise been possible. FDI has both direct and indirect effects on employment. When a foreign MNE hires numerous residents of the host country, it results in direct benefit. When jobs are created as a result of the investment in local suppliers as well as when employees of the MNE boost their local spending, there are indirect benefits. The indirect employment effects are frequently at least as significant as the direct employment benefits. For instance, predictions made when Toyota planned to establish a new auto plant in France indicated that the facility would generate 2,000 direct jobs and maybe an additional 2,000 jobs in service sectors.

Some cynics contend that not all of the "new jobs" produced by FDI constitute net increases in employment. Some contend that in the instance of foreign direct investment (FDI) by Japanese automakers in the United States, the employment gained by the investment have been more than offset by the jobs lost by American-owned automakers who have lost market share to their Japanese rivals. Due to these substitution effects, the overall number of new employments generated by FDI may not be as high as an MNE initially estimated. Between an MNE seeking to engage in FDI and the host government, the topic of the expected net increase in employment could be a key negotiating point.

As the multinational tries to restructure the operations of the acquired unit to increase its operating efficiency, employment may be immediately affected when FDI takes the form of the acquisition of an existing business in the host economy as opposed to a greenfield investment. Even in these situations, research reveals that after the first phase of restructuring is finished, businesses purchased by foreign firms frequently see quicker employment based growth than their local competitors. For instance, an OECD research discovered that international businesses created new jobs more quickly than their domestic rivals.

In America, foreign companies' workforces rose by 1.4 percent annually compared to local companies' 0.8 percent annual growth. While employment at domestic businesses decreased by 2.7 percent in Britain and France, the workforce of international companies expanded by 1.7 percent annually. The same study discovered that overseas enterprises frequently paid greater wages than domestic firms, indicating that the employment was of higher calibre.

Although employment decreased when an enterprise was acquired by a foreign firm, a different study that examined FDI in Eastern European transition economies discovered that many of those enterprises were in competitive problems and would not have survived if they had not been acquired. Additionally, following a preliminary period of retrenchment and adjustment, job downsizing was often followed by new investments, and employment either remained stable or increased.

Balance of Payments

For the majority of host governments, the impact of FDI on a nation's balance of payments accounts is a crucial policy concern. The balance of payments accounts of a nation keep track of both its transfers to and receipts from other nations. Governments typically express concern when their nation has a current account or balance of payments deficit. The export and import of commodities and services are tracked by the current account. A country experiences a current account deficit, often known as a trade deficit, when it imports more goods and services than it exports. A current account surplus is often preferred by governments over a deficit. Selling off assets to foreigners is the only way a current account deficit can be sustained over the long term. For instance, a consistent selling of American assets to foreign buyers (including stocks, bonds, real estate, and entire enterprises) has been used to finance the United States' ongoing current account deficit since the 1980s.

National governments like their country to have a current account surplus because they always loathe seeing their country's assets end up in foreign hands. FDI can assist a nation in accomplishing this objective in two different ways.

First, the effect of FDI may be to enhance the current account of the host country's balance of payments if it replaces imports of commodities or services. For instance, a large portion of the foreign direct investment (FDI) made by Japanese automakers in the United States and Europe might be considered as a replacement for imports from Japan. As many Japanese companies are now supplying the US market from production facilities in the United States rather than facilities in Japan, the current account of the US balance of payments has improved substantially. The United States has unquestionably profited from this as much as it has lessened the need to finance a current account deficit by selling assets to foreigners.

When the MNE employs a foreign subsidiary to export goods and services to other nations, a second potential benefit materialises. In the past ten years, a number of developing and established countries have experienced export-led economic growth as a result of inward FDI from international multinational corporations. For instance, exports from China surged from $26 billion in 1985 to over $250 billion in 2001 and $969 billion in 2006. The presence of foreign multinational corporations that made significant investments in China during the 1990s was a major factor in this remarkable export rise. In 2001, 50 percent of all exports from that nation were produced by subsidiaries of foreign multinational corporations, up from 17 percent in 1991. For instance, 95% of China's exports of mobile phones came from its Chinese subsidiaries of foreign multinational corporations, including Nokia, Motorola, Ericsson, and Siemens.

Competition and Economic Growth

Economic theory tells us that the efficient functioning of markets depends on an adequate level of competition between producers. When FDI takes the form of a greenfield investment, it results in establishing a new enterprise, thus increasing the number of players in a market and consumer choices. As a result, there may be more competition on a national level, which could lower costs and improve consumer prosperity. Growing rivalry tends to encourage businesses to invest in plant, equipment, and R&D as they fight for a competitive advantage. Long-term outcomes could include stronger economic growth, product and process innovations, and increased productivity growth.

After the FDI laws were loosened in 1996, for instance, the South Korean retail industry appears to have benefited from such favourable consequences. FDI from major Western discount retailers like Wal-Mart, Costco, Carrefour, and Tesco appears to have pushed local discounters like EMart to increase the effectiveness of their own businesses. More competition and cheaper pricing as a result have benefited South Korean consumers.

When it comes to services like telecommunications, retail, and many financial services, where exporting is frequently not a possibility because the service must be created where it is supplied, FDI's impact on competition in domestic markets may be very significant. For instance, as part of a 1997 World Trade Organization-sponsored agreement, 68 nations representing more than 90% of global telecommunications revenues agreed to begin opening their markets to foreign investment and competition as well as to follow standard guidelines for fair competition in the sector. In most nations, the telecommunications market was monopolised by a single carrier, which was frequently a state-owned firm, and was closed to international rivals prior to this agreement. Two key advantages have resulted from the agreement's considerable increase in competition in many national telecoms markets. First, foreign direct investment has boosted competitiveness and encouraged spending on the global modernisation of telephone networks, improving service. Additionally, the heightened competition has led to lower prices.

3.5.2 Host-Country Costs

Host countries are concerned about three FDI costs. They result from perceived loss of national sovereignty and autonomy, negative consequences on the balance of payments, and potential negative effects on domestic competition within the host country.

Competition

Sometimes, host governments are concerned that the subsidiaries of foreign MNEs may be more powerful economically than local rivals. The foreign MNE may be able to use money made elsewhere to subsidise its costs in the host market if it is a part of a larger multinational organisation. This could force local businesses out of business and allow the firm to dominate the market. Once the market is monopolised, a foreign MNE may increase prices above those that would apply in markets that are competitive, which would be detrimental to the host country's economic welfare. This worry is typically more prevalent in nations with fewer large domestic corporations (generally less developed countries). In the majority of highly industrialised countries, it is typically a minor concern. While foreign direct investment (FDI) in the form of greenfield investments should generally increase competition, it is less certain that this is the case when FDI is in the form of the purchase of an existing business in the host country. The impact on competition may be neutral since an acquisition does not lead to a net increase in market participants. When a foreign investor buys two or more local businesses and then merges them, it can lessen competition in that market, give the foreign company monopoly power, limit consumer choice, and raise prices.

For instance, Hindustan Lever Ltd., the Unilever subsidiary in India, purchased Tata Oil Mills, the primary local competition, to gain a strong position in the bath soap (75%) and detergents (30%) sectors. Additionally, Hindustan Lever purchased a number of regional businesses in various countries, including the ice cream producers Dollops, Kwality, and Milkfood. By integrating these businesses, Hindustan Lever increased its market share for ice cream in India from 0% in 1992 to 74% in 1997.

Although these incidents are obviously concerning, there isn't much proof that these trends are pervasive. In many countries, national competition authorities have the power to examine and halt any mergers or acquisitions that they believe may harm competition. If these organisations are operating efficiently, it should be sufficient to make sure that foreign entities do not monopolize a country's markets.

Balance of Payments

The host country's balance of payments may suffer from FDI in two different ways. First, the eventual outflow of earnings from FDI must be compared to the initial capital intake from the parent firm to the overseas subsidiary. Such outflows are recorded on balance of payments accounts as capital outflows. In response to these outflows, several countries have capped the amount of profits that can be sent back to the nation where a foreign subsidiary is headquartered. When a foreign subsidiary imports a sizable portion of its inputs from outside, the host country's balance of payments experiences a debit on the current account, which raises a second issue. For instance, Japanese-owned auto assembly plants in the United States have come under fire as they tend to import many components from Japan.

The positive effect of this FDI on the current account of the US balance of payments may not be as significant as first thought. In response to these accusations, the Japanese automakers promised to source 75% of their component parts from US based producers (but not necessarily US owned manufacturers). When the Japanese automaker Nissan made an investment in the UK, it promised to boost the percentage of local material to 60% and later increased it to more than 80% in response to worries about local content.

National Sovereignty and Autonomy

Some host governments are concerned that some economic independence is lost as a result of FDI. The worry is that a foreign parent, over whom the host country's government has no real authority and who has no real commitment to the host country, will make important decisions that could have a negative impact on the host country's economy. Most economists consider such worries as illogical and without foundation. According to political scientist Robert Reich, such worries are the result of outdated thinking since they neglect to take into account the expanding interdependence of the global economy. It is impossible for one country to "hold another to economic ransom" in a world where businesses from all advanced nations are progressively investing in each other's marketplaces without hurting themselves.

3.5.3 Home-Country Benefits

Three factors contribute to FDI's advantages for the home (source) country. First, the inflow of foreign revenues helps the home country's balance of payments. If the foreign subsidiary generates demand for home-country exports of capital goods, intermediate goods, complementary items, and the like, FDI can also help the home country's balance of payments.

Second, the employment consequences of FDI abroad bring advantages to the home country. Positive employment benefits happen when the foreign subsidiary generates demand for exports from the home nation, much like with the balance of payments.

Toyota imports some component parts for its European-based auto assembly operations straight from Japan, therefore their investment in auto assembly activities in Europe has benefited both the Japanese balance of payments position and employment in Japan.

Third, advantages occur when the home-country MNE gains useful knowledge from its exposure to overseas markets that can then be used back home. This has the same effect as a reverse resource transfer. An MNE can learn about superior management practises and superior product and process technology by being exposed to a foreign market. When these resources are returned home, the economic growth rate of the original country is boosted. For instance, learning about their manufacturing procedures was one of the reasons General Motors and Ford invested in Japanese automakers (GM owns a portion of Isuzu, and Ford owns a portion of Mazda). The outcome might be a net gain for US economy, if GM and Ford are successful in bringing this knowledge back to their US operations.

3.5.4 Home-Country Costs

It is necessary to weigh the apparent costs of FDI for the home (source) country against these advantages. The impacts of FDI on the balance of payments and employment are of utmost importance. The balance of payments for the nation could suffer in three ways. First, the initial capital outflow needed to finance the FDI hurts the balance of payments. However, the ensuing inflow of foreign earnings typically more than makes up for this effect. Second, if the goal of the foreign investment is to supply the domestic market from a low-cost production location, the current account of the balance of payments suffers. Thirdly, if direct exports are replaced by FDI, the current account of the balance of payments suffers. Consequently, as far as Toyota's manufacturing processes in the US substitutes exports from Japan, the current account position of Japan will deteriorate.

The most significant issues with regard to job effects occur when FDI is viewed as a replacement for indigenous output. Toyota's investments in the US and Europe were similar to this. A clear outcome of such FDI is less employment within the home country. This problem would not be as pressing if the labour market in the home nation is already competitive and there is little unemployment. However, if unemployment is a problem in the home country, worries about job exports may surface. For instance, American labour leaders regularly argue that the United States will lose hundreds of thousands of jobs when American businesses invest in Mexico to benefit from the free-trade agreement between the United States, Mexico, and Canada.

3.6 CROSS-BORDER MERGERS AND ACQUISITIONS

As was already explained, FDI can occur through greenfield investments, which entail the construction of new industrial facilities in a foreign nation, or through cross-border mergers and acquisitions that accounts for more than half of FDI flows in terms of dollar. For instance, British Petroleum paid $48 billion to acquire the American oil company Amoco in 1998. For $40.4 billion, the French conglomerate Vivendi purchased the significant Canadian corporation Seagram in 2000. And Rhone-Poulenc SA (Life Sciences), a French firm, purchased Hoechst, a significant German pharmaceutical corporation, for

$21.9 billion. Reuters, a British news organisation, was purchased by Thomson Corporation, a US information services company, for $17.6 billion in 2008. 2009 saw Roche, a Swiss pharmaceutical giant, paid $46.7 billion to acquire Genentech, a highly successful US biotech firm. In 2010, Kraft Foods, a US firm, acquired Cadbury, a British confectionery producer, for $18.8 billion.

To top it all off, in 2000, a British telecommunications corporation named Vodafone spent $203 billion to purchase Mannesmann, a significant German business. The continuing liberalisation of the capital markets and the integration of the global economy are to blame for the sharp rise in cross-border M&A transactions. Businesses may be driven to participate in cross-border M&A transactions in order to improve their competitive positions in the global market by acquiring unique assets from other businesses or by making more extensive use of their own assets. Cross-border M&As have two major advantages over greenfield investments as a means of FDI entry: speed and access to proprietary assets.

By selling off divisions that lie beyond the purview of their core competencies and acquiring strategic assets that boost their competitiveness, mergers and acquisitions are a common strategy of investment for companies looking to protect, consolidate, and improve their worldwide competitive positions. For those companies, "ownership" assets obtained from another company, such as technical expertise, well-known brand names, and existing supplier networks and distribution systems, can be used right away to improve global customer service, boost profits, increase market share, and boost corporate competitiveness by more effectively utilising global production networks. Companies can strategically leverage cross-border M&A transactions to access the brand strength, technological know-how, and managerial expertise found in target companies thanks to open capital markets. Deals for cross-border M&A don't always succeed as expected.

Since most nations desire to maintain local control of domestic firms, cross-border corporate acquisitions are a politically delicate topic. Therefore, whereas nations may welcome greenfield investments because they are seen as providing new investment and employment prospects, efforts by foreign corporations to buy indigenous firms are frequently received with resistance and perhaps even resentment. Thus, from the standpoint of shareholder welfare and public policy, it is crucial to consider whether or not cross-border acquisitions result in synergistic gains and how such gains are allocated between acquiring and target enterprises. When the combined firm's worth exceeds the individual (target and acquiring) firms' stand-alone valuations, synergistic gains are realised.

One may argue that cross-border acquisitions are mutually advantageous and shouldn't be hindered both from a national and global perspective if they result in synergistic gains and both the acquiring and target shareholders become wealthier at the same time.

Depending on the goal of the acquiring firms, cross-border acquisitions may or may not result in synergistic profits. Gains will typically occur when the acquirer is motivated to profit on the aforementioned market flaws. In other words, businesses may seek to purchase foreign companies in order to benefit from under-priced production inputs and circumvent trade restrictions. As was already established, market flaws for intangible assets can significantly influence whether businesses decide to make cross-border acquisitions.

According to the internalisation theory, a company with intangible assets that have a public good property, such as managerial and technical know-how, may acquire foreign firms as a platform for using those assets on a larger scale while avoiding potential misappropriation that may happen while transacting in foreign markets through a market mechanism. The desire of the acquirer to obtain and absorb the intangible assets of the target company may also serve as a driving force for cross-border acquisitions. The acquirer aims to build wealth in this backward internalization instance by capturing the rent produced by the economies of scale gained from employing the target's intangible assets on a global scale. Thus, the internalisation may move ahead to internalise the assets of the acquirer or backward to internalise the assets of the target.

SUMMARY

1. An ownership stake in a foreign company or project is known as a foreign direct investment (FDI) and is made by a foreign investor, business, or government. It is strategic investment for a long period of time involving substantial amount in the host country.
2. Eclectic paradigm theory uses three variable framework that explains whether it would be beneficial for firms to pursue foreign direct investment or not. The three variables are Ownership advantages, location advantages and internalization advantages.
3. Comparative management, according to Harold Koontz and Heinz Weihrich, is the measurement, identification, and interpretation of differences and similarities among distinct practises in various countries.
4. Universalistic theories say that, Cross-national variations in management and organisation, to the extent that they exist at all, are typically predicted to vanish in the future, whereas particularistic theories assert that cross-national variations in management and organisation will endure.
5. The main advantages of inbound FDI for a host country come from effects on resource transfers, employment, balance of payments, competition, and economic growth.
6. Host countries are concerned about three FDI costs. They result from perceived loss of national sovereignty and autonomy, negative consequences on the balance of payments, and potential negative effects on domestic competition within the host country.

KEY WORDS

- Farmer Richman Model
- Koontz Model
- Comparative Advantage
- Cross-Border Mergers and Acquisitions

QUESTIONS

1. How eclectic paradigm theory guides a firm whether it should venture into FDI or not? Elucidate.
2. Why is it important for managers to undertook comparative management approach while operating in global business environment?
3. What are the costs and benefits of FDI for Host and Home countries? Discuss.
4. How Cross-Border Mergers and Acquisitions are different from Green Field Investments?

REFERENCES AND SUGGESTED READINGS

1. UNCTAD (2022). *World Investment Report.*
2. Dunning, J.H. (2001). The eclectic (OLI) paradigm of international production: past, present and future, *International journal of the economics of business*, 8(2), 173–190.
3. Koontz, H., O'Donnell, C., & Weihrich, H. (1986). *Essentials of management* (Vol. 18), New York: McGraw-Hill.
4. Koontz, H. (1969). A model for analyzing the universality and transferability of management, *Academy of Management Journal*, 12(4), 415–429.
5. Farmer, R.N., & Richman, B.M. (1964). A model for research in comparative management. *California management review*, 7(2), 55–68.
6. Schollhammer, H. (1969). The comparative management theory jungle, *Academy of management Journal*, 12(1), 81–97.

CHAPTER 4

International Monetary System

LEARNING OUTCOMES

After reading this chapter, the reader will be able to:

- List and Explain Global Economic Institutions and their Roles and Governance
- Explain the Evolution and Functioning of International Monetary System
- Explain the Role of European Monetary System
- List the Countries Accepted the Unified Currency—The Euro and European Monetary Union
- Explain difference between Fixed versus Flexible Exchange Rate Regimes

4.1 GLOBAL ECONOMIC INSTITUTIONS

International institutions like World bank, IMF and WTO among others play a very major role in monitoring as well as governing the global economic scenario.

4.1.1 International Monetary Fund (IMF)

After the World War II, in July 1944 at Bretton Woods, New Hampshire, USA, an international conference took place to promote global economic stability and prosperity. The participating countries created two global organizations, the IMF and the World Bank, to establish a framework of economic cooperation among member countries.

The goal of the IMF and the World Bank is to raise the living Standards of people in their member countries. Both the organization works in complementary fields. While the concentration of IMF is on macroeconomic and financial stability, the World Bank focuses on poverty alleviation and long-term economic development. The IMF and the World Bank coordinate routinely in order to assist member countries. The governors, management and staff of both the organizations coordinate and collaborate in various arenas (like financial stability, sustainable development, climate change) to further their respective mandates.

The IMF promotes macroeconomic and financial stability of the member countries and dispenses policy advice to assist them in building and maintaining strong economies.

It primarily provides short-term and medium-term loans to countries facing financial liquidity and default issues.

The challenge of policy makers is to safe guard their own country from economic and financial instabilities while raising the living standards of people through rising employment, productivity and sustainable growth. The economic and financial stability of a country is both national and global concern as in the globalized world, the countries have become more vulnerable to economic and financial instability of other countries. For example, the 1997–98 Asian crises that began in Thailand and quickly spread to neighbouring economies like Indonesia, Malaysia, South Korea and then to Russian and Brazilian economies.

Role of IMF

1. **Surveillance:** The IMF monitors the international monetary and financial system as well as economic and financial policies of its member countries, identifies economic trends and developments at global, country and regional level to recognise the potential threats to economic and financial stability. It recommends needed policy adjustments to the countries to sustain growth and stability.
2. **Capacity Building:** The IMF provides technical assistance and training to countries to develop sound institutions and policies.
3. **Lending:** It provides short-term and medium-term loans to countries facing balance of payment crises or are at the verge of defaulting their international monetary obligations.

The IMF is accountable to its 190 member countries.

Governance Structure

Board of Governors: Board of Governors consists of a governor and an alternate governor form each member country. It delegates most of its powers to the executive board but retains the power to amend the articles of agreement and by laws, admittance of new members, compulsory withdrawal of members, approve quota increases and allocate or cancel special drawing right (SDR). The Board of governors of the IMF meet once a year to discuss the working.

Ministerial Committees: There are two ministerial committees, the International Monetary and Financial Committee (IMFC) and the Development Committee that advice the board of governors. The IFMC comprises of 24 members and the development committee consists of 25 members.

Executive Board: The day-to-day business of the IMF is overseen by the 24-member executive committee. It acts on behalf of the board of governors.

IMF Management: The IMF's Managing Director is the chairman of IMFs executive body as well as the head of staff. He is appointed by the executive board for a term of five years and is assisted by first deputy managing director and three deputy managing directors.

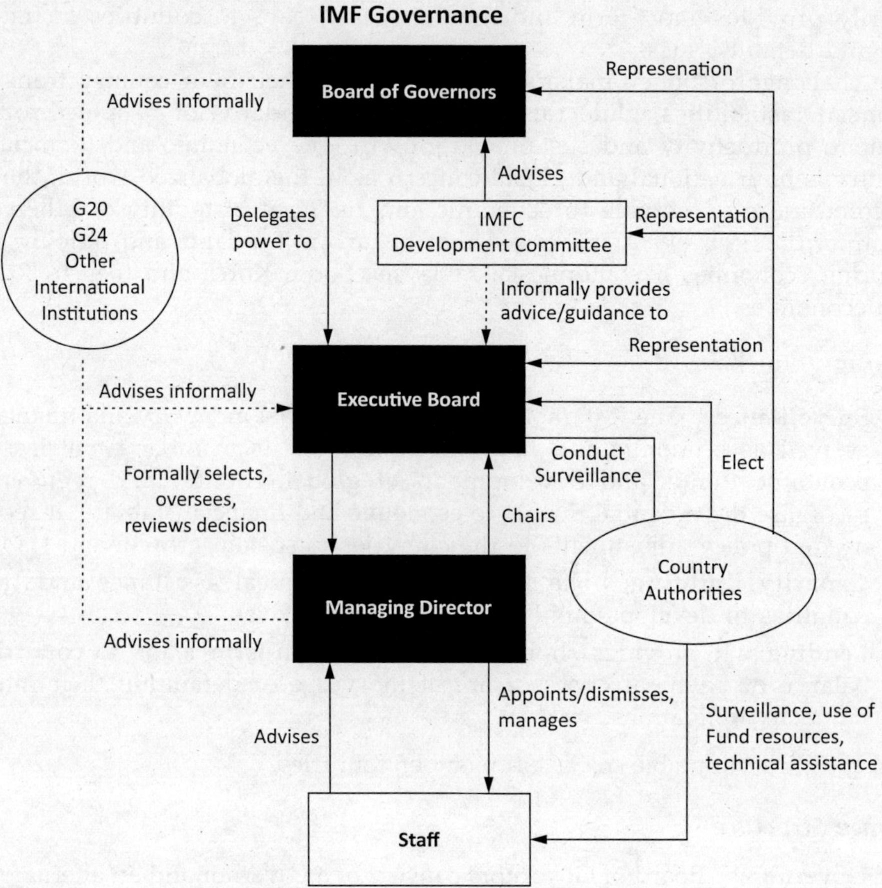

Source: IMF, Secretary's department

FIGURE 4.1 IMF Governance Structure.

Monetary Policy and Central Banking: Central banks play a crucial role in maintaining economic and financial stability. They use the monetary policy to control inflation. In the wake of Covid 19 pandemic, central banks have expanded their toolkit and used conventional and non-conventional methods to ease monetary policy, support liquidity in key financial markets and maintain flow of credit. The IMF supports its member countries by providing policy advisory and technical assistance. The IMF and the World Bank help less developed and underdeveloped countries by providing financial and technical assistance.

4.1.2 World Bank

The mandate of the World Bank is to promote long-term economic development and poverty alleviation by providing financial and technical assistance to reform projects (like providing electricity and water, building schools, fighting disease) of developing and underdeveloped countries.

The World Bank, in the initial year of its establishment, focused on rebuilding the economies devastated by World War and accelerate the economic growth of developing countries. In the subsequent years, as per the needs of member countries, the Bank started providing training to officials from member countries (Economic Development Institute) as well as mediated in international disputes that had an economic element. By the 70s, the Bank confronted absolute poverty in the developing world, and hence shifted its focus towards poverty eradication as well as economic growth (world development report, 1978). The World Bank re-entered the conflict prevention, post-war reconstruction, and aid for nations to reorient their economies after significant political transition during the late 1990s. The concept of the World Bank as a knowledge institution was introduced in the middle of the 2000s, and by 2010, the Open Agenda had prompted the Bank to adopt a more open strategy for development. The World Bank ushered in the new century by collaborating with the United Nations on the Millennium Development Goals in 2000 and the Sustainable Development Goals in 2015, placing an emphasis on community-driven development and aid coordination, working to protect vulnerable groups, and reducing the effects of climate change.

Sources of Funds

There are several ways to fund the World Bank. The wealthier member states' contributions served as the first source of revenue. The World Bank has started to raise money on the capital markets more lately.

Since it has a AAA credit rating, the World Bank can easily raise money at low interest rates. As a result, it can offer finance to underdeveloped countries at reduced rates. Return on investments and fees from advisory services rendered are some additional funding sources.

Organizational Structure

With 189 member nations, the World Bank resembles a cooperative. The Board of Governors, who are the top decision-makers of the World Bank, represents these member nations, or shareholders. The governors are typically the finance or development ministers of the member nations. They get together once a year during the World Bank Group and International Monetary Fund Board of Governors' annual meetings.

The governors delegate some specific duties to 25 Executive Directors, who are located at the Bank. An Executive director is appointed by the five largest shareholders whereas the elected executive directors represent other member nations. The President of the World Bank Group is in charge of the general management of the Bank and presides over meetings of the Boards of Directors. The Board of Executive Directors elects the President to a five-year term with the option of renewal.

The World Bank Boards of Directors are composed of Executive Directors. In order to manage the Bank's operations, including the approval of loans and guarantees, new policies, the administrative budget, nation aid programs, and borrowing and financial choices, they often meet at least twice per week.

The operations of World Bank are divided within its five institutions, namely:

International Bank for Reconstruction and Development (IBRD)

The entity that came before the World Bank was called the International Bank for Reconstruction and Development (IBRD). It was established in 1944 to aid in the Second World War's post-war reconstruction. The IBRD gave loans to the European warring nations to aid in the reconstruction of their infrastructure and economies, which were destroyed during the conflict.

It was later combined with the recently established IDA to become the World Bank. It concentrates on providing credit to low- and middle-income nations with strong credit ratings. It promotes infrastructure and capacity-building initiatives that are consistent with the Sustainable Development Goals through its lending (SDGs).

International Development Association (IDA)

The International Development Association (IDA) and the IBRD were founded in 1960, creating the current World Bank. The IDA offers financial aid to underdeveloped nations that are at a high risk of experiencing debt difficulties. Through IDA credits, they offer the help. Grants or loans with zero or low interest rates are two ways that the credits are provided. With grace periods of five to ten years, loan repayments may take up to 38 years to complete.

International Finance Corporation (IFC)

The International Finance Corporation (IFC), established in 1956, is a subsidiary of the World Bank. Only the private sector is supported in developing nations. They achieve this by making both debt and equity investments in private enterprises.

The South Korean company LG Electronics and the Indian company HDFC are two of the IFC's more well-known investments. In addition to the financial investment, they also offer technical advising services to the target enterprises to aid them in overcoming any operational issues.

Multilateral Investment Guarantee Agency (MIGA)

In order to protect investors from the political risk associated with making investments in emerging and frontier markets, the Multilateral Investment Guarantee Agency (MIGA) was established. They offer protection from terrorism and civil war as well as from contract violations and debt default. The MIGA guarantees are valid for a minimum of three years and a maximum of 20 years.

By assisting investors to manage their risk, MIGA also seeks to encourage foreign direct investment (FDI) in developing nations. With the exception of goods that are banned in either the host or investment country, weapons, and environmentally hazardous goods, they insure the majority of firms.

International Centre for Settlement of Investment Disputes (ICSID)

It helps in establishing a legal framework for the resolution of disputes resulting from investment contracts. It is comparable to WTO dispute resolution. In order to maintain a unified rule that regulates investment activity between member states, it applies international law to dispute resolution.

In addition, the ICSID offers arbitration and mediation services that can be used to settle disputes without a hearing. The major goal is to make the investment procedure as simple as possible so that the World Bank can continue to finance global development initiatives.

4.1.3 United Nations Conference on Trade and Development (UNCTAD)

The motto of free-trade and non-discrimination in international trade was followed by the Bretton Woods system. The policies of IMF and GATT which promoted the above motto, it was realised, were working only in favour of the developed world. Their policies were similar for all the countries whether developed or not on the basis of the assumption that all the countries have started from the same point. The less developed countries argued against this as in the industrial era not all the countries have same technologies and resources and hence shouldn't be treated the same way. The developing countries in July 1962, under Cairo declaration demanded from United Nations to call an international conference on trade and development.

In 1963, the Economic Council of United Nations recommended convening such a conference and the United Nations Conference on Trade and Development was set up.

A permanent intergovernmental body of United Nations, UNCTAD was founded in 1964 at Geneva, Switzerland. Its objective is to reduce poverty and achieve sustainable development goals. Currently, 195 countries are member of UNCTAD.

Functions

The primary function of UNCTAD is to accelerate the growth in less developed region of the world by focusing on promotion of trade, balance of payment deficits, burden of debt, etc.

Macro level challenges in development: UNCTAD monitors the macro-economics of each country and suggests policy measures accordingly.

Integration into the Global Trading System: It suggests policy measures to member nations so that they can better integrate their economy to the global economy. It assists developing nations in decoding the complexities of multilateral trade negotiations and formulating their positions better. It also acts as a negotiator of trade agreements between different countries.

Limit Exposure of Countries to Financial Volatility and Debt: UNCTAD annually prepares the report on debt sustainability of developing countries and suggests measures to be considered.

Attract Investment for Development: To make developing countries more development friendly, UNCTAD suggests policy measures as well as acts as a mediator and sources funds for the development projects in less developed and underdeveloped countries.

Increase Access to Digital Technologies: The developing and less developed countries are technologically backward in comparison to developed countries. To address this, UNCTAD provides training and support to such countries.

Promote Innovation and Entrepreneurship: Through various schemes, it promotes innovation and entrepreneurship.

Reduce Commodity Dependence by Diversifying the Economies: Commodities are the primary goods obtained from agricultural or mining activities that have not been processed. As per UNCTAD's State of Commodity Dependence 2021, 101 nations are now dependent on commodity trade which means more than 60% of their trade is made up of primary goods. Commodities being primary goods are highly volatile and can leave economies that are highly exposed to shocks. They are currently driving economies of more than 50% countries in the world.

Promote Competition and Protect Consumer: Competition improves productivity and stimulates innovation, contributing to an effective business environment. Whereas protected and empowered customers make informed choices which directly improves their welfare while contributing to level playing field for businesses. The purpose, here, of UNCTAD is to improve markets functioning through strengthened competition and consumer protection.

Sustainable Development: UNCTAD promotes sustainable development by funding various sustainable projects as well as by creating awareness among member countries.

Removing Trade Barriers: UNCTAD promotes free-trade practices among member nations. It suggests policy measures to them that stimulate global trade.

4.1.4 World Trade Organization

The WTO is successor of Generalized Agreements of Tariffs and Trade (GATT) which was established after the Second World War.

It is an international organization that deals with rules of trade between nations. Its roles comprise of operator of global system of rules of trade, mediator for negotiation of trade agreements and trade disputes and supporter of the requirements of under-developed countries.

As per the world trade organization—The primary purpose of the WTO is to open trade for the benefit of all.

In total the World Trade Organization currently has 160 plus (164 as in 2022, another 25 countries are negotiating membership) member countries. To join WTO a country has to align its financial and economic policies in line with WTO rules.

Organizational Structure

The decisions are made by consensus of the entire membership. Although there is the provision of decision by majority votes, it has never been used (very rarely used during WTOs predecessor the GATT). The agreements are then ratified in the parliaments of all the member countries.

The top decision-making body of the WTO is the Ministerial Conference that meets usually every two years and the day-to-day decision-making body is the General Council that meets multiple times in a year at Geneva.

Generally, the General Council consists of ambassadors and heads of delegations (representing their respective country) based in Geneva but sometimes the officials sent by member countries. It also acts as the Dispute settlement body and the trade policy review body. Then there are various other councils, committees and groups dealing with other areas.

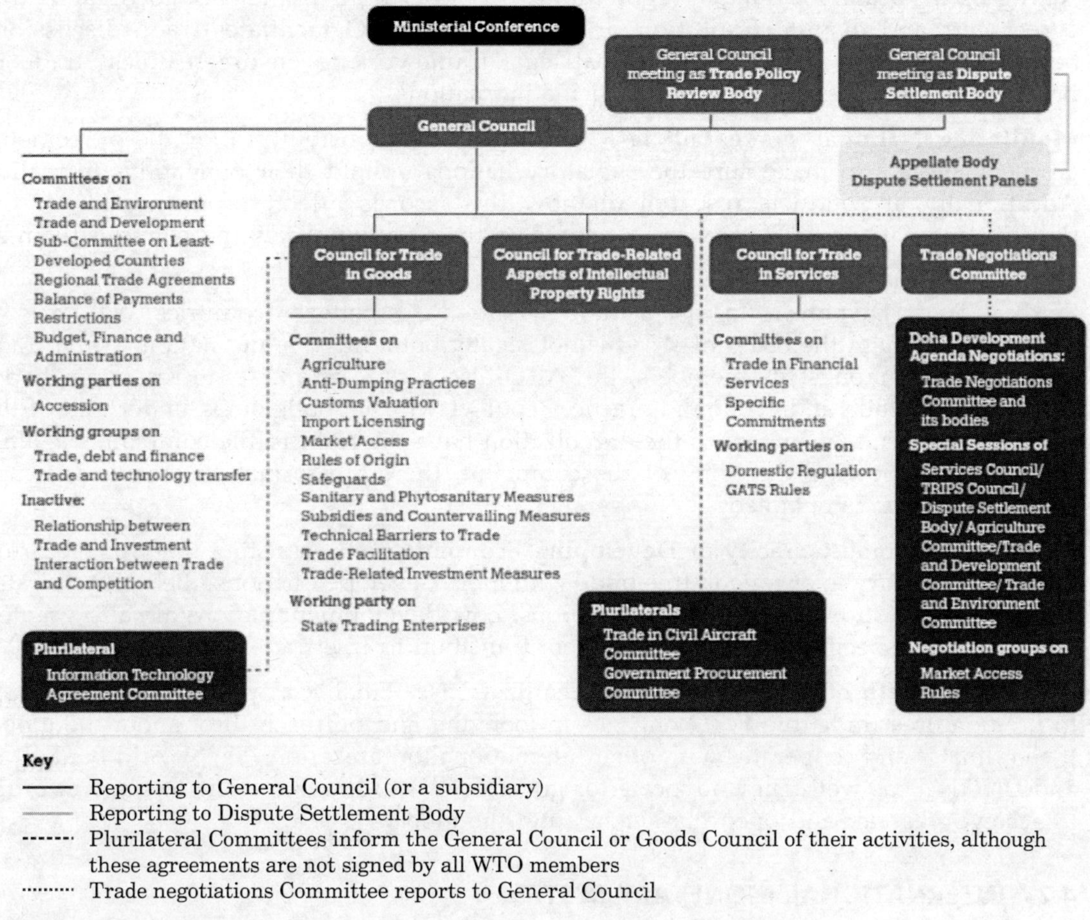

Source: WTO

FIGURE 4.2 Organizational Structure of World Trade Organization.

Sources of Fund

The major source of income of WTO is the contributions from member countries. The amount of contribution depends upon the share of respective country in the international trade. It also earns from print and electronic publications and rental fees. It manages a number of trust funds as well which are used to support various training and technical assistance program aimed at enabling the under developed countries to make better use of WTO.

Functions of the World Trade Organization

Administering Trade Agreements: World trade organization acts as a mediator between different countries and administers trade agreements between them. The primary role of WTO is to promote free trade and reduce trade barriers across the globe.

Acting as a Forum for Trade Negotiations: By offering a framework to organize the agreements and dispute resolution procedures, the WTO facilitates trade discussions between nations. It establishes a global legal framework to ensure seamless trade in products and services between the participating nations.

Monitoring National Trade Policies: The WTO's responsibility after the agreements are negotiated is to make sure the signatory nations uphold their obligations in reality. Additionally, it conducts research on how the accords affect the economies of the participating nations. WTO advises countries on their trade policies and counsels them so that they can move towards free trade.

Settling Trade Disputes: In case a trade dispute arises between countries, WTO acts as a mediator, though the order of WTO is not legally bounding on any nation. When trade disputes arise amongst its members, the WTO also serves as a dispute resolution body. If a country's trade and economic practices conflict with its obligations under one of the WTO's agreements, members of the organization have the right to file complaints against that nation. Following the filing of the complaint, there are formal court-style hearings until a resolution is obtained.

Building the Trade Capacity of Developing Economies: By assisting them in acquiring the skills necessary to engage in free trade with more developed nations, the WTO operates special initiatives to support emerging nations. Low-development nations are also granted benefits under specific accords to help them transition to free trade with other nations.

Cooperating with other International Organizations: Finally, as part of its larger goals to promote free trade, the WTO engages in lobbying and outreach throughout the globe. It coordinates and cooperates with other international organizations like, World Bank, IMF and UNCTAD as well. They advocate for governments to lower barriers to trade in order to achieve free, fair and open markets around the globe.

4.2 INTERNATIONAL MONETARY SYSTEM

The international monetary system can be defined as the system that determines the exchange rates between various currencies across the globe as well as that facilitates trade and investment effectively.

An exchange rate is the value of one currency in terms of another.

The term exchange rate regime refers to the mechanism, procedures and institutional framework for determining exchange rates at a point in time and changes in them over time, including factors which induce the changes.

4.2.1 Evolution of International Monetary System

The Gold Standard

At the beginning, the gold coins containing fixed amount of gold was used as currency in circulation (Gold Specie standard). Later, the gold coins were replaced by paper notes but they were backed by the fixed gold content and the monetary authorities (the central bank of the country) ready to convert the notes into gold on demand at a fixed conversion rate (Gold Bullion Standard).

Under the gold exchange standard, the currency of one country could be converted into the currency of other country on the basis of their conversion rate with the gold. This was also known as "mint parity" exchange rate. Following conditions must be obeyed by the monetary authorities of a nation under the true gold standard:

1. The rate of conversion of paper money into gold must be fixed forever.
2. The gold must flow freely between countries on gold standard.
3. The money in circulation must be tied to the gold reserves in the country. If the gold reserves decrease, the money supply must also contract and vice-versa.

The monetary authorities had to follow strict monetary and credit policies in order to operate under the gold standard. For this reason, the gold standard was abandoned during the great depression by all the nations.

The Bretton Woods System

After the second World War, the two new international organizations, the World Bank and the International Monetary Fund, were set up by the Allied nations to revamp the global monetary system. The features of the resulting exchange rate regime were:

1. The US dollar was fully convertible to gold at the fixed rate of $35 per ounce, as undertook by the US government.
2. All the other member nations of the IMF, consented to maintain their currencies within the limit of 1% to the parity fixed vis a vis the dollar.

The IMF guaranteed the nations to provide credit facilities in case they need to buy or sell their currencies in order to maintain the currency exchange rate within the consented limits.

This regime was adjustable rather than rigid like the gold standard as the nations were allowed to change the parity of their currency against the dollar in case of fundamental disequilibrium. A fundamental disequilibrium is a situation, in which, a country faces continuous balance of payment deficits and it becomes necessary for the country to revalue its currency. The member nations could revalue their currency up to ten percent in either direction, however for revaluation more than the said limit could be executed only after the consent of the IMF. This flexibility was not available to the USA, it had to maintain its value of currency vis-a-vis gold.

Under this system, the US dollar became international money as countries would use dollars for international trade and also store it as reserves. The system was perfect until the other countries were confident about the stability of US dollar and the USA was able to convert dollars into gold on demand at a fixed rate of $35 per ounce. As this confidence began to wane beginning in the middle of the 1960s as a result of some political and economic circumstances, the system came under pressure and ultimately collapsed. The currencies around the globe went on a float on August 15, 1971, when the US government backed down on its promise to exchange dollars for gold at the pre-determined rate. By raising the price of gold and enlarging the bands of allowable variation around the central parity, an effort was made to revive the system. The so-called Smithsonian Agreement was this. Early in 1973, the world switched to a system of floating rates after the new arrangement too failed to keep the system in place.

Following a period of wildly fluctuating exchange rates, which were worsened by severe shocks like the 1973 oil price crisis, policy makers in several nations began experimenting with exchange rate system that were a blend of fixed and floating rates. By 2000s, the world had a wide variety of exchange rate regimes in place.

4.2.2 Current Exchange Rate Regimes

In accordance with the currency rate system each member country has chosen, the IMF divides its members into seven categories. Below is a description of the exchange rate arrangements under various categories. The data was taken from the IMF's "Annual Report on Exchange Arrangements and Exchange Restrictions 2021" publication. Figure 4.3 shows a graphic representation of the number of nations in 2021 that adhered to various regimes.

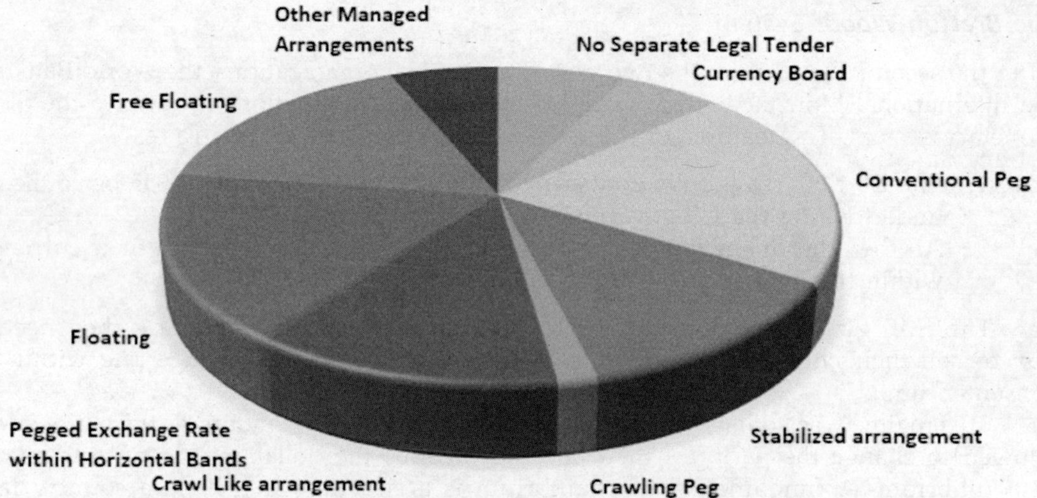

Source: Annual Report on Exchange Arrangements and Exchange Restrictions, 2021 (IMF).

FIGURE 4.3 Exchange Rate Arrangements.

No Separate Legal Tender

Under this arrangement the nations adopt currency of another nation as their legal tender or they become part of a group of nations that share common currency. Implementing such system obviously means that the monetary authorities lose the independent control over domestic monetary policy. Countries like Puerto Rico, Zimbabwe, Panama, etc. have adopted US dollar as their currency. Whereas European Union is a prominent example of nations accepting a single currency, Euro, as their legal tender.

Currency Board

Currency board is a regime in which money supply in the nation is fully backed by a foreign currency acting as reserve and the monetary authority is committed to exchange the domestic currency with foreign currency at a fixed rate. It is similar to the gold standard.

The central authority loses the right to control monetary policy. The monetary policy of foreign country (the country that issues the reserve currency) becomes effective. In general, the system works fine but if the economic condition of foreign country and domestic country are contradictory, the currency board can create adverse effects. For example, if there is recession in the foreign country, its monetary authority would lower down the interest rates to motivate people to borrow more and spend. On the contrary, the domestic country is going through inflation, the lower down of interest rates could accentuate the inflationary pressure in the economy.

Countries like Estonia, Latvia and Bosnia has fully pegged their respective currencies to the Euro. Similarly, Hong Kong dollar (Currency of Hong Kong which is an independent tertiary of China) is fully pegged to US dollars.

Conventional Pegs

The nation (formally or de facto) pegs its currency to another currency or a basket of currencies at a fixed rate, with the weights of the basket reflecting the geographic distribution of trade, services, or capital flows. The basket is made up of the currencies of major trading or financial partners. Standardization of currency composites is another option, as seen with the SDR. There is no need to maintain the parity permanently. The currency rate may fluctuate for at least three months within small margins of less than 1% around a central rate, or the highest and minimum value of the exchange rate may stay within a small margin of 2%.

The monetary authority is prepared to maintain the fixed parity either directly (by selling or buying foreign currency in the market) or indirectly (e.g., via aggressive use of interest rate policy, imposition of foreign exchange regulations, exercise of moral suasion that constrains foreign exchange activity, or through intervention by other public institutions). Because traditional central banking activities are still viable and the monetary authority can vary the level of the exchange rate, albeit sparingly, there is more flexibility in monetary policy than in exchange systems without separate legal tender and currency boards.

Crawling Pegs

The exchange rate is changed on a regular basis in small amounts at a fixed rate or in response to changes in certain quantitative indicators, such as differences in past inflation rates relative to important trading partners, differences between the inflation target and expected inflation in important trading partners, and so on. The rate of crawl can be set to produce changes in the currency rate that are inflation-adjusted (backward looking), or it can be set at a preannounced fixed rate and/or below the anticipated inflation differentials (forward looking). Keeping a crawling peg in place places restrictions on monetary policy akin to a fixed peg regime.

Pegged within Bands

The difference between the exchange rate's maximum and minimum value is greater than 2 percent, or the value of the currency is maintained within specified margins of fluctuation of at least 1% around a fixed central rate. It also covers agreements made by nations participating in the European Monetary System's (EMS) exchange rate mechanism (ERM), which was replaced by the ERM II on January 1, 1999. Depending on the band width, monetary policy has some restricted flexibility.

Pegged within Crawling Bands

The central rate or margins are adjusted periodically at a fixed rate or in response to changes in specific quantitative indicators. The currency is maintained within certain fluctuation margins of at least 1% around a central rate, or the margin between the maximum and minimum value of the exchange rate exceeds 2%. The band width influences how flexible an exchange rate is. Bands either gradually spread with an asymmetric choice of the crawl of upper and lower bands or are symmetric around a crawling centre parity (in the latter case, there may be no preannounced central rate). The obligation to keep the exchange rate within the band sets restrictions on monetary policy, with the degree of independence of the policy being a function of the band width.

Managed Floating

Without having a pre-determined aim or route for the exchange rate, the monetary authority makes an effort to affect it. The rate may not adapt automatically since the indicators for managing the rate are mostly subjective (such as the balance of payments situation, foreign reserves, and parallel market movements). A direct or indirect intervention is possible.

Free Floating

The exchange rate is established by the market, and any state involvement in the foreign currency market aims to moderate the rate of change and prevent excessive swings in the exchange rate rather than to set a fixed level for it.

As of April 30, 2021, 92 countries were using soft peg to determine their exchange rates. Of which 24 were into crawl-like arrangements, stabilized arrangements were adopted by 24 countries, Conventional peg by 4 and pegged exchange rates with horizontal bands by 1 (Morocco).

Other managed arrangements are used by 12 countries. Whereas Floating arrangements and Free-floating method is adopted by 32 countries each to determine their exchange rates.

Hard Pegs was used by 25 countries including Caribbean islands like Aruba, Bahamas, Barbados, and Bermuda who have pegged their respective currencies to US dollars as well as Many African countries who have pegged their currencies to the euro (exception Djibouti and Eritrea whose currencies are pegged to US dollars) and Middle eastern nations like Saudi Arabia, Qatar, Oman who again have pegged their currencies to the US dollars.

4.3 EUROPEAN MONETARY SYSTEM

After the collapse of Bretton Woods Agreement, the value of several currencies started fluctuating freely due to the lack of any anchor. European Monetary System was established in 1979 by countries of Europe to promote economic cooperation. It was an adjustable exchange rate regime aimed at stabilizing the currencies and control inflation. It allowed its member nation to appreciate or depreciate their currency when necessary.

In 1971, as per the Smithsonian agreement, the currencies were allowed to move within a band of plus/minus 2.25% from the agreed exchange rate. However, the members of EEC (European Economic Community) agreed on a narrow band of plus/minus 1.25 percent for their currencies. This arrangement was succeeded by EMS (European Monetary System). The two main instruments of EMS were ECU (European Currency Unit) and ERM (Exchange Rate Mechanism).

The European Currency Unit (ECU) is a "basket" currency created by weighing the currencies of the European Union's member nations (EU). The weights are determined by the relative GNP and intra-EU trade shares of each currency. The ECU functions as the EMS's accounting unit and is crucial to how the exchange rate system operates. The method by which EMS member nations collectively manage their exchange rates is known as the Exchange Rate Mechanism (ERM). The "parity grid" system, which establishes par values between ERM currencies, is the foundation of the ERM. By initially establishing the par values of EMS currencies in terms of the ECU, the par values in the parity grid are computed.

A currency could only depart from the parities with other currencies by a maximum of 2.25 percent when the EMS was first introduced in 1979, with the exception of the Italian Lira, which could stray by a maximum of 6 percent. However, the range was expanded to a maximum of plus or minus 15% in September 1993. The central banks of both nations must interfere in the foreign exchange markets to keep the market exchange rate within the band when a currency is at either its lower or upper bound. The member nations contribute gold and foreign reserves to a credit fund, to which the central banks can borrow, allowing them to interfere in the exchange markets.

However, the EMS member nations were not able to coordinate fully in terms of economic policies, and hence the EMS went through multiple adjustments. For example, the Italian lira was devalued multiple times (1985 and 1990 by 6 percent and 3.7 percent respectively). Then, in 1992, the UK and Italy moved out of the ERM because of the misalignments in their policies vis-a-vis Germany.

Despite the ongoing turmoil in EMS, Members of the European Union convened in Maastricht (Netherlands) in December 1991 and signed the Maastricht Treaty. The agreement stated that by January 1, 1999, the EMS would permanently fix exchange rates between the member currencies. After that, a unified European currency would be introduced to replace separate national currencies. The issuance of common currency and the formulation of monetary policy in the euro zone would be the sole purview of the European Central Bank, which would have its headquarters in Frankfurt, Germany. Then, the national central banks of many nations would operate very similarly to the regional member banks of the American Federal Reserve System.

The European Monetary System's member nations decided to tightly coordinate their fiscal, monetary, and exchange rate policies and bring their economies into line in order to lay the groundwork for the EMU (European Monetary Union). In particular, each member nation shall work to: (i) maintain its currency within the established exchange rate ranges of the ERM; (ii) keep its gross public indebtedness below 60% of GDP; (iii) attain a high level of price stability; and (iv) keep the ratio of government budget deficits to GDP below 3%.

4.4 EURO AND EUROPEAN MONETARY UNION

An historic event occurred in the world of international finance on January 1, 1999. A unified currency known as the Euro was accepted by 11 of the 15 EU nations, which voluntarily gave up their monetary independence. Austria, Belgium, Finland, France, Germany, Ireland, Italy, Luxembourg, the Netherlands, Portugal, and Spain make up the original Euro-11. Denmark, Greece, Sweden, and the United Kingdom were the other four European Union members who chose not to participate in the initial wave. Greece, however, only became a member of the eurozone in 2001 after being able to meet the convergence requirements. Slovenia followed suit in 2007, followed by Cyprus and Malta in 2008. In 2009, Slovakia embraced the Euro, and in 2011, Estonia followed suit. Then, Lithuania and Latvia both accepted the Euro in 2014. Lastly, in January 2023, Croatia became the twentieth nation to adopt Euro as its currency.

4.5 FIXED VERSUS FLEXIBLE EXCHANGE RATE REGIMES

Arguments in favour of flexible exchange rate regimes are: (1) It provides autonomy to the central bank of the nation; (2) External adjustments are easier. As in the flexible exchange rate regime, the rates are determined by market forces, whenever there is a deficit in countries balance of payments, the supply of the currency will exceed than its demand in the foreign market at the prevailing rate. Due to market forces, the value of currency will depreciate and the equilibrium will be achieved. Hence, under flexible exchange rate regime, government/central bank does not have to intervene and can use its fiscal and monetary policy to pursue its economic goals.

On the other hand, under fixed exchange rate regime, the central bank has to formulate its economic and monetary policies as per the balance of payments deficit or surplus situation and thus it is not free to formulate policies as per its economic objectives.

4.6 IMPOSSIBLE TRINITY

The theory of Impossible Trinity was proposed by Fleming (1962) and Mundell (1963). As per the theory, it is impossible for any central bank to achieve all the three monetary policy goals simultaneously, the three goals are—Independent monetary policy, free capital flow, and exchange rate stability.

If a country chooses side A, which is free movement of capital and independent monetary policy, the exchange rate wouldn't be stable. The differential in interest rates between countries will result in movement of capital which in turn would cause the volatility in exchange rates. Similarly, fixed exchange rate with a free hand in changing the monetary policy demands for a restricted capital flows in and out of the national border. Choosing side B implies that there would not be free capital flow. Side C, combination of stable exchange rate and free flow of capital, will again stress the currency pegs if interest rates are not allowed to fluctuate.

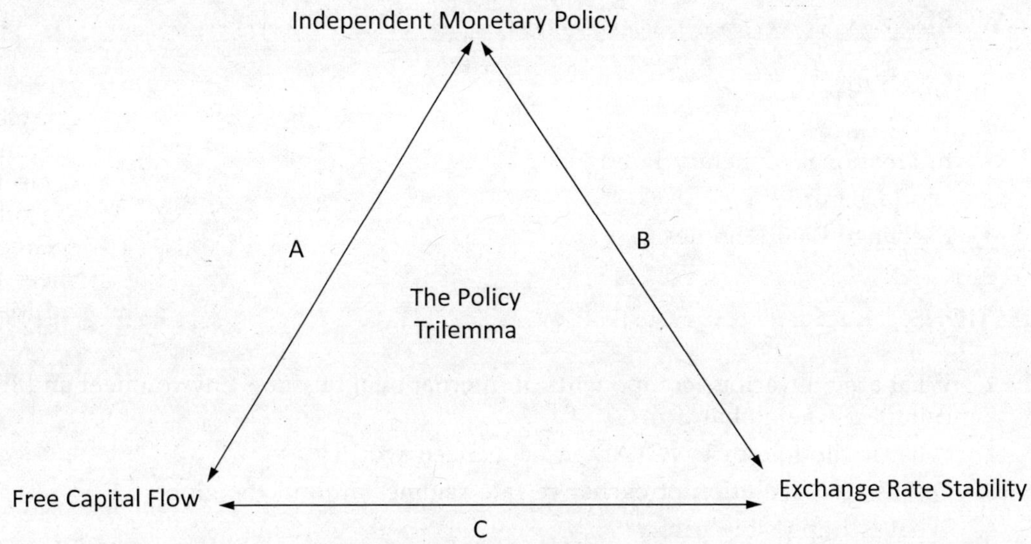

FIGURE 4.4 Impossible Trinity.

SUMMARY

1. An International Business Environment refers to the surroundings in which international companies carry on their businesses.
2. International Business Environment consists of political, economic, socio-cultural and technological environment.
3. Political environment consists of the overall approach, attitude, and actions of the government of the country towards the foreign companies and the respective country.
4. A cultural environment basically encompasses the general beliefs and values of the people in a country. These values and beliefs, in turn, depend on the history, language, and religion of the country.
5. Economic Environment consists of the economic and financial conditions of a country as well as the economic environment around the globe. It also includes the global financial and economic institutions.
6. Technological environment means the development of technologies as well as infrastructure across nations.
7. UNCTAD is a permanent intergovernmental body of United Nations, UNCTAD was founded in 1964 at Geneva, Switzerland. Its objective is to reduce poverty and achieve sustainable development goals.
8. WTO is an international organization that deals with rules of trade between nations. Its roles comprise of operator of global system of rules of trade, mediator for negotiation of trade agreements and trade disputes and supporter of the requirements of underdeveloped countries.

KEY WORDS

- UNCTAD
- WTO
- International Monetary Fund
- World Bank
- Exchange Rate Regimes

QUESTIONS

1. What are the various components of international business environment and how it impacts the global firm?
2. What is the role of UNCTAD in Globalized world?
3. Discuss the evolution of exchange rate regimes around the globe.
4. What is Impossible trinity?

REFERENCES AND SUGGESTED READINGS

1. https://unctad.org
2. https://unctad.org/news/strengthening-resilience-commodity-dependent-countries
3. https://www.economicsdiscussion.net/unctad/unctad-organisation-functions-and-meetings-economics/30512
4. https://www.worldbank.org/en/home
5. https://www.imf.org/en/Home
6. https://www.wto.org/
7. Annual Report on Exchange Arrangements and Exchange Restrictions, 2021, IMF.
8. Classification of Exchange Rate Arrangements and Monetary Policy Framework, 2004, IMF.

CHAPTER 5

Balance of Payment

LEARNING OUTCOMES

After reading this chapter, the reader will be able to:

- Define Balance of Payment
- Explain Significance and Structure of Balance of Payment
- Differentiate Equilibrium, Disequilibrium and Adjustment
- Explain Different Approaches to Adjustment
- Compare and Explain Capital Account Convertibility
- Discuss Balance of Payments Trends in Major Countries

5.1 INTRODUCTION

All contemporary economies compile and publish thorough statistics regarding their transactions with the rest of the world. A nation's national accounts include a systematic accounting record of its economic transactions with the residents of foreign countries. Additionally, it may be seen as a list of all the elements that influence the supply and demand of the nation's currency. The following is a precise definition of a country's balance of payments (BOP):

"The Balance of Payments is a systematic accounting record of all economic transactions during a given period of time between the residents of the country and the rest of the world."

Economic transaction means a transfer of economic value, i.e., transfer of title, ownership of goods and services, money, and assets from one economic agency (such as a person, company, government, etc.) to another. The transfer could be requited, in which case the transferee or recipient provides the transferor or giver with something of equal economic value in exchange, or it could be unrequited which means unilateral gift.

5.1.1 Significance of Balance of Payment

First, it offers comprehensive data on the supply and demand for a nation's currency.

Second, information on a nation's balance of payments may indicate that it has potential to be a trading partner for the rest of the globe. A nation may not be able to increase its imports from abroad if it is experiencing severe balance-of-payment problems. Instead, the nation might implement policies that limit imports and deter capital flight in an effort to repair the balance of payment situation. On the other side, a nation with a sizeable balance of payments surplus would be more inclined to increase imports, providing chances for marketing for international businesses, and less inclined to enact foreign exchange restrictions.

Third, information on the balance of payments can be used to assess how well a nation is performing in the global economy. Imagine a nation that consistently has a trade deficit. The lack of international competitiveness of the nation's domestic sectors may then be indicated by these trade data. Understanding the balance of payments account's structure is important in order to properly evaluate balance of payments data.

Any transaction that involves paying foreigners is recorded in the balance of payments accounts as a debit and is denoted with the minus sign (–). Any transaction that generates a receipt from a foreigner is recorded as a credit and is denoted by a plus sign (+). A rising trade deficit slows down the expansion of the economy as a whole. According to economists, the government will need to update its projection of the country's fourth quarter gross domestic product to reflect a somewhat slower expansion in light of the new figures.

5.2 STRUCTURE OF BALANCE OF PAYMENT

BOP is a collection of accounts that are traditionally divided into three main categories, each with subdivisions. The three major categories are as follows:

1. *The Current Account:* The current account keeps track of transactions that fall into three categories. This includes imports and exports of goods (e.g., machinery, agricultural products, vehicles, chemicals) and services (e.g., intangible products such as copyright, trademarks, banking and insurance services), as well as unilateral transfers of goods and services. The third category, income receipts and payments, includes income from foreign investments as well as payments owed to foreigners who invest in a country.
2. *The Capital Account:* Transactions affecting the country's foreign assets and liabilities are included under this account.
3. *The Reserve Account:* This account is essentially identical to the capital account as it also refers to assets and liabilities. However, only "reserve assets" are listed in this category. The monetary authorities of the trading nations hold and trade reserve assets, these are the assets that the nation's monetary authority employs to balance the surpluses and deficits that result from the other two categories combined. They include assets with a foreign currency equivalent, special drawing rights, monetary gold and IMF reserve positions.

The primary categories and subcategories listed above will all be looked at in some detail in the sections that follow. Our goal is to comprehend the BOP account's overall structure and the types of connections between its many sub-groups.

5.2.1 The Current Account

1. *Merchandise*

In general, all transactions involving moveable goods should fall under the purview of merchandise trade, with a few exceptions, where ownership of goods changes from residents to non-residents and from non-residents to residents during export or import. In order to recognise international freight and insurance as separate services that are being exported and prevent their value from being added to the value of the products themselves, the valuation should be done on a free on board (FOB) basis.

Exports are credit entries that are valued on a FOB basis. This data is collected from the forms that exporters are needed to fill and submit to the appropriate authorities. The debit entries include imports valued at cost, insurance and freight (CIF). Despite being improper, valuation at CIF was forced owing to insufficient data. The "Net" column displays the difference between the sum of credits and debits. This is the balance on the merchandise trade account, which is either in deficit or in surplus. When American consumer imports ceramic pots from India, then, the transaction will enter the balance of payments account of India as a credit on the current account.

2. *Invisibles*

The invisibles account comprises payments and receipts for factor services, such as labour and capital, unilateral transfers, as well as services like transportation and insurance. Services provided by residents to non-residents, income earned by residents from their ownership of foreign financial assets (interest, dividends), income earned from the use by non-residents of non-financial assets like patents and copyrights owned by residents, and offset entries to the cash and in-kind gifts received by residents from non-residents are all considered credits under invisibles.

The same goods are included in debits, but the roles of residents and non-residents are switched.

A. Current Account	**Credit**	**Debit**	**Net**
1. Merchandise			
2. Invisibles (3+4+5)			
3. Services			
i. Travel			
ii. Transportation			
iii. Insurance			
iv. Government not elsewhere classified			
v. Miscellaneous			
4. Transfers			
vi. Official			
vii. Private			
5. Income			
viii. Investment Income			
ix. Compensation to employees			
Total Current Account (1 + 2)			

FIGURE 5.1 Structure of Current Account in India's BOP Statement.

3. *Income Receipts and Payments*

The payments and receptions of interest, dividends, and other income on prior foreign investments make up the majority of the third category of the current account. For instance, interest received by Indian investors on their foreign bond holdings will be recorded as a credit in the balance of payments. The opposite will occur with interest payments made by Indian borrowers to overseas creditors, which will be reflected as debits.

4. *Unilateral Transfers*

In this category of current account "Unrequited" payments are included. Foreign aid, compensation, grants from the public and private sectors, and gifts are a few examples. Unilateral transfers are different from other balance of payments accounts as it has a one-way flow without any compensating flow. Unilateral transfers are viewed as an act of purchasing goodwill from the beneficiaries for the sake of maintaining the double-entry bookkeeping norm. Therefore, a nation that provides foreign help to another nation may be seen as importing goodwill from the recipient nation.

5.2.2 The Capital Account

Credit and debit transactions under non-produced non-financial assets, as well as capital transfers between residents and non-residents, are included in the capital account. Thus, acquisitions and dispositions of non-produced non-financial assets, such as land sold to embassies and lease and licence sales, as well as capital transfers, are recorded under this account. The capital account includes the following things:

1. Equity investment in the form of Foreign Direct Investment (FDI), portfolio investment by non-residents in the equity of domestic companies, including Foreign Institutional Investors (FIIs) and individuals, and investment by non-resident entities in depository receipts.
2. The purchase of debt securities from domestic governments and businesses by non-residents.
3. Domestic companies borrow from foreign commercial banks.
4. Borrowing from external sources, such as the World Bank and the IMF, which may include loans with favourable terms.
5. Capital flows through the financial system.
6. Trade credits.

Some of these sorts of capital flows might not be allowed depending on the exchange control and other laws of the investors' home country and the country where the investment is intend.

B. Capital Account (1 to 5)	**Credit**	**Debit**	**Net**
1. Foreign Investment (a+b)			
(a) In India			
i. Direct			
ii. Portfolio			
(b) Abroad			
2. Loans (a+b–c)			
(a) External Assistance			
i. By India			
ii. To India			
(b) Commercial Borrowings (MT and LT)			
i. By India			
ii. To India			
(c) Short Term			
i. To India			
3. Banking Capital (a+b)			
(a) Commercial Banks			
i. Assets			
ii. Liabilities			
iii. Non-resident Deposits			
(b) Others			
4. Rupee Debt Service			
5. Other capital			
Total Capital Account (1 to 5)			

FIGURE 5.2 Structure of the Capital Account.

5.2.3 The Reserve Account

The other remaining account in India's balance of payment are:

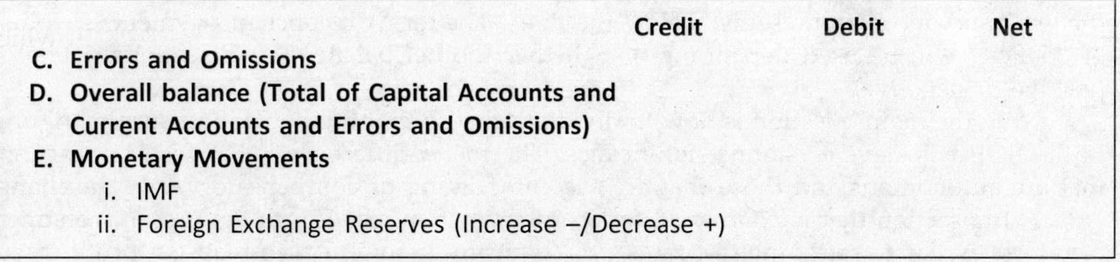

	Credit	**Debit**	**Net**
C. Errors and Omissions			
D. Overall balance (Total of Capital Accounts and Current Accounts and Errors and Omissions)			
E. Monetary Movements			
i. IMF			
ii. Foreign Exchange Reserves (Increase –/Decrease +)			

FIGURE 5.3 Structure of the Reserve Account.

The Foreign Exchange Reserves account keeps track of both credits and debits for reserve assets. The RBI's holdings of SDRs, gold, foreign exchange (in the form of balances with foreign central banks and investments in foreign government securities), and foreign currency are referred to as reserve assets. Special Drawing Rights, or SDRs, are a reserve asset that the IMF created and occasionally distributes to member nations. It can be used to settle foreign payments between monetary authorities of member nations, subject to some restrictions. Retirement is a debit, whereas an allocation is a credit.

5.3 EQUILIBRIUM, DISEQUILIBRIUM AND ADJUSTMENT

In the balance of payments, a "equilibrium position" exists when the demand and supply of any foreign currency in a nation are equal within a specific time period. While a disequilibrium denotes either a shortage or a surplus in the condition. In a perfect scenario when all the components are correctly incorporated in the BOP it should be zero. This indicates that BOP is at equilibrium when the inflows and outflows of money is equal (credit = debit). In most situations, nevertheless, this does not exactly take place.

$$BCA + BKA + BRA = 0$$

where

BCA = balance on the current account
BKA = balance on the capital account
BRA = balance on the reserve account

When a country's exports exceed its imports, its BOP is said to be in surplus. A country's BOP statement shows whether the country has a surplus or a deficit of cash. However, the deficit in BOP shows that the country's imports exceed its exports and these imbalance in inflow and outflow of money causes disequilibrium.

The BOP must always balance if it is a double-entry accounting record, barring errors and omissions. Naturally, "deficit" or "surplus" cannot be used to describe the BOP as a whole but must instead describe an imbalance on a subset of accounts that make up the BOP. It is necessary to consider the "imbalance" in terms of **economic disequilibrium**. The best manner to organise the various accounts within the BOP must be chosen so that an imbalance in one set of account sends the right signal to policy makers, as the concept of disequilibrium is typically connected with a scenario that necessitates some type of policy intervention. Entire BOP is categorised into two sets of accounts: one set is "above the line" and another one set is "below the line". The term "balance of payments surplus" or "deficit" will be used depending on whether the net balance (credits minus debits) is positive or negative.

Now the main question is how to divide things so that the deficit and surplus figures in the BOP will have economic significance. The major difference is between transactions that are autonomous and those that are accommodating or compensatory.

A transaction that is conducted for its own sake, in reaction to the present condition of prices, exchange rates, interest rates, etc., typically in an effort to realise a profit or cut costs, is referred to as an autonomous transaction. On the other hand, an accommodating transaction is one that is made with the intention of balancing the imbalance created by other transactions, such as financing the deficits caused by autonomous transactions. So, all autonomous transactions should be grouped as "above the line" and all accommodating transactions should be grouped as "below the line."

TABLE 5.1 Major items of India's Balance of Payments

	2021–22		
	Credit	*Debit*	*Net*
A. Current Account	798.7	837.4	−38.7
Goods	429.2	618.6	−189.5
Services	254.5	147.0	107.5
Primary Income	25.8	63.0	−37.3
Secondary Income	89.3	8.8	80.5
B. Capital Account and Financial Account	777.4	739.2	38.2
of which:			
Change in Reserve [Increase (–)/Decrease(+)]	16.0	63.5	−47.5
C. Errors & Omissions (–) (A+B)	0.5		0.5

Note: Total of sub-components may not tally with aggregate due to rounding off.

Source: Reserve Bank of India

The trade deficit increased to US$ 189.5 billion from US$ 102.2 billion a year ago, recording a deficit of 1.2% of GDP in 2021–22 as opposed to a surplus of 0.9% in 2020–21.

5.4 DIFFERENT APPROACHES TO ADJUSTMENT

The top three approaches of balance of payments are:

5.4.1 Elasticities Approach

Marshall-Lerner Condition: The elasticity approach to BOP is linked to the Marshall-Lerner condition, which was independently developed by these two economists. It investigates the circumstances under which exchange rate changes restore BOP equilibrium by devaluing a country's currency. This approach is linked to the devaluation price effect.

This approach is based on the following assumptions:

1. Export supplies are perfectly elastic.
2. Product prices are fixed in domestic currency.
3. Income levels are fixed in devaluing country.
4. There is a large supply of imports.
5. The price elasticities of demand for exports and imports are arc elasticities.
6. Price elasticities are expressed in absolute values.
7. The current account balance of the country equals the trade balance.

Given these assumptions, when a country devalues its currency, domestic prices of imports rise while foreign prices of exports fall. Thus, devaluation helps a country's BOP deficit by increasing exports and decreasing imports. However, its success depends on the country's price elasticities of domestic demand for imports and foreign demand for exports.

The Marshall-Lerner condition states that devaluation will improve the country's balance of payments when the sum of price elasticities of demand for exports and imports in absolute terms is greater than unity,

i.e., $$ex + em > 1$$

where, ex = demand elasticity of exports and em = demand elasticity of imports.

Devaluation, on the other hand, will worsen (increase the deficit) the BOP if the sum of the price elasticities of demand for exports and imports is less than unity. If the sum of these elasticities in absolute terms equals unity, devaluation has no effect on the BOP situation, which remains unchanged.

The following is the procedure for removing a devaluing country's BOP deficit using the Marshall-Lerner condition.

Devaluation lowers domestic export prices in terms of foreign currency. Exports increase when prices are low. The extent to which they rise is determined by the demand elasticity of exports. It is also affected by the nature of the goods exported as well as market conditions. If a country is the sole supplier and exports raw materials or perishable goods, its exports will have low demand elasticity. If it competes with other countries by exporting machinery, tools, and industrial products, the elasticity of demand for its products will be high, and devaluation will be effective in correcting a deficit and vice-versa.

5.4.2 Absorption Approach

The absorption approach to balance of payments is based on Keynesian national income linkages and is characterised by general equilibrium. As a result, it is frequently referred to as the Keynesian method. It compares the income effect of devaluation to the elasticity approach's price effect.

According to the argument, a country's balance of payments imbalance indicates that people are 'consuming' more than they are producing. The domestic budget for investment and consumption exceeds the GDP. They are absorbing less if their balance of payments is in surplus. Consumption and investment costs are lower than national income. The BOP is defined as the difference between domestic spending and national revenue in this instance.

5.4.3 Monetary Approach

The entire balance of payment is explained by the monetary approach to the balance of payments. Changes in the balance of payments are explained in terms of the supply and demand for money. A balance of payments deficit, in accordance with this approach is, "always and everywhere a monetary phenomenon." Therefore, the only way to fix it is with monetary measures.

This approach is based on the following assumptions:

1. After deducting the cost of transportation, the "law of one price" applies to similar items sold in different nations.
2. The perfect substitution in consumption assures that there is only one price for each good and a single interest rate applied to all nations, both in the product and capital markets.
3. An external assumption is made regarding a country's level of output.
4. Where wage price flexibility fixes production at full employment, all countries are assumed to have full employment.
5. Due to the concept of one price everywhere, it is presumable that fixed exchange rates make it impossible to sterilise currency flows.
6. The need for money is a stock demand and a constant function of wealth, interest rates, prices, and income.
7. The amount of money in circulation is a multiple of the country's foreign exchange reserves and domestic credit, which together make up the monetary basis.

5.5 CAPITAL ACCOUNT CONVERTIBILITY

The current account includes factor income, unilateral transfers, and the exports and imports of goods and services. The capital account tracks a country's net change in its overseas holdings of assets and liabilities. In order to make payments for balance of payments operations, domestic currency must be convertible into foreign currencies and vice versa. The ability or freedom to convert domestic currency for current account operations is known as current account convertibility, although the same concept applies to capital account convertibility. Capital account convertibility, for instance, was described as the "flexibility to convert local financial assets into foreign financial assets and vice versa" by the Tarapore Committee in 2006.

The level of a nation's economic development and the maturity of its financial markets typically determine the degree of BOP convertibility of that nation. As a result, while emerging market economies (EMEs) are convertible to varying degrees, advanced economies (AEs) are nearly totally convertible.

5.5.1 Importance of Capital Account Convertibility

Free capital movement or globalisation of capital markets, is frequently cited as a crucial driver of global growth. Particularly, the advantages of internationalising capital markets are widely acknowledged, particularly with regard to expanding the investor base for financial assets in receiving countries, enhancing market liquidity, and applying constructive pressure to market practises and infrastructure. International capital markets may lower borrowing costs, promote better risk allocation, and increase global liquidity by providing access to a global savings pool and to diverse currencies (OECD, 2017).

5.5.2 Challenges of Capital Account Convertibility

The various currency and banking crises that have occurred over the past few decades have simultaneously brought to light the benefits and drawbacks of internationalisation, including exposure to global shocks, asset and credit bubbles, exchange rate volatility linked to capital exit on the spur of the moment, and increased refinancing risk. Growing globalisation has highlighted the sensitivity to contagious impacts. There is now a greater understanding that the benefits of internationalisation are not a pure boon and that there is a complex trade-off between growth and crisis risk, despite the argument that such risks are the short-term discomforts necessary to reap long-term profits (Kaminsky and others, 2008). Such knowledge has led to policy attention on three fronts:

First, having strong macroeconomic fundamentals, a developed financial system, and a good market infrastructure—including effective channels for funding and risk transfer—are prerequisites for achieving the benefits of internationalisation.

Second, that nations must create suitable mechanisms to address the hazards of globalisation, particularly macroprudential tools and measures to control the volume and composition of capital inflows.

Third, that dangers associated with various types of capital flows are different; some are riskier than others. According to the generally accepted hierarchy of capital flows, foreign direct investment, followed by equity investment, followed by debt capital is the least risky. While portfolio equity boosts GDP in the short term, FDI is thought to contribute to growth over the long term. Although important, debt flows can be unpredictable. It makes sense that debt flows have been the focus of capital flow and macro-prudential regulations.

5.6 BALANCE OF PAYMENTS TRENDS IN MAJOR COUNTRIES

It is helpful to carefully study balance of payments trends in some of the major countries given the considerable attention that balance-of-payments figures receive in the news media. Figure 5.4 provides the balance on the current account (BCA) for each of the six key countries, India, China, Japan, Germany, the United Kingdom, and the United States, during the period 2001–2021.

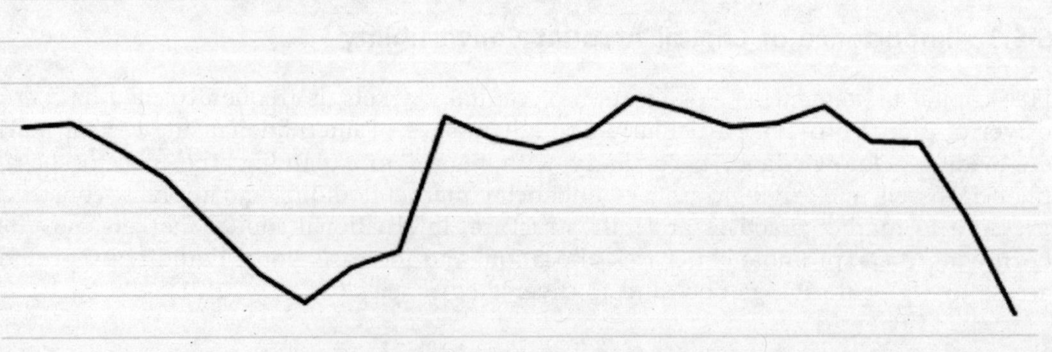

(Contd.)

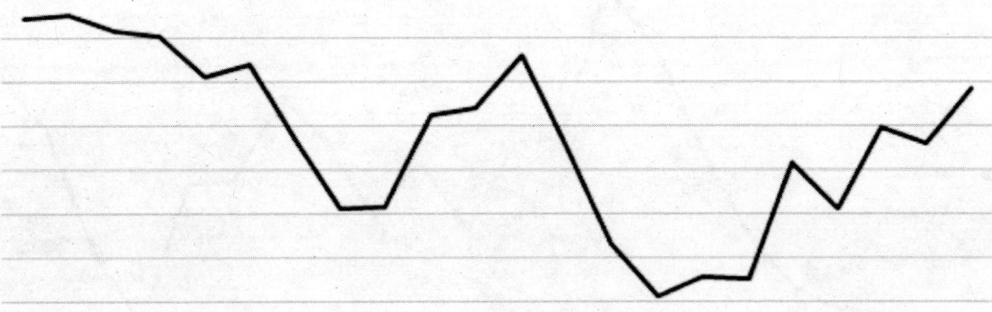
UK
2000 2001 2002 2003 2004 2005 2006 2007 2008 2009 2010 2011 2012 2013 2014 2015 2016 2017 2018 2019 2020 2021

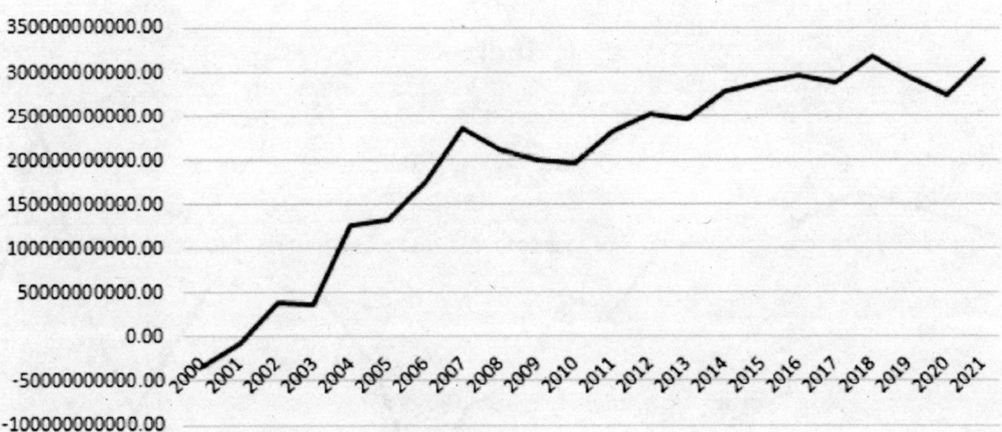
350000000000.00
300000000000.00
250000000000.00
200000000000.00
150000000000.00
100000000000.00
50000000000.00
0.00
-50000000000.00
-100000000000.00
2000 2001 2002 2003 2004 2005 2006 2007 2008 2009 2010 2011 2012 2013 2014 2015 2016 2017 2018 2019 2020 2021

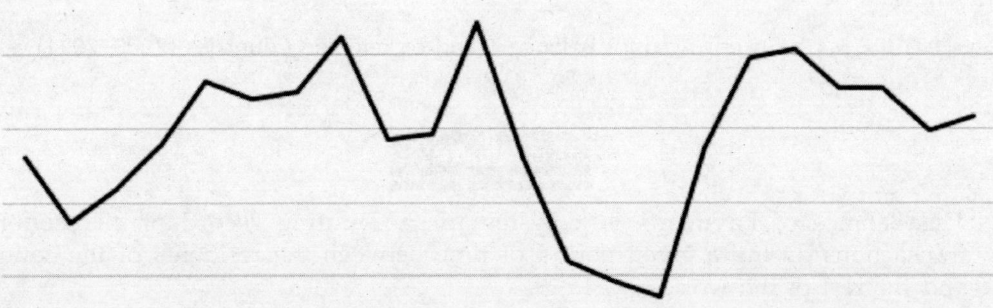
Japan
2000 2001 2002 2003 2004 2005 2006 2007 2008 2009 2010 2011 2012 2013 2014 2015 2016 2017 2018 2019 2020 2021

(*Contd.*)

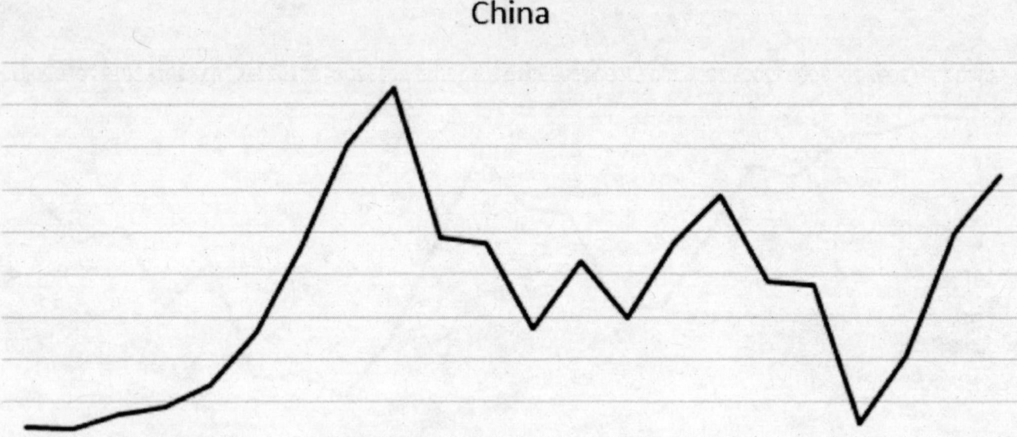

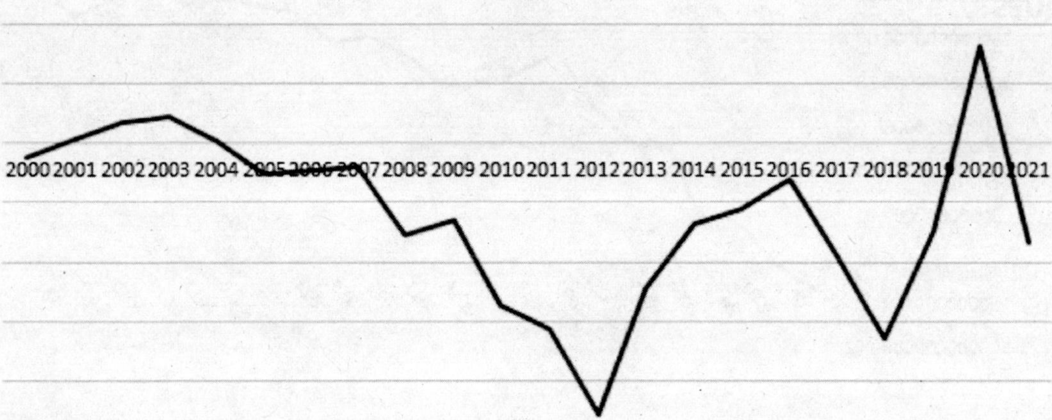

Source: IMF

FIGURE 5.4 Current Account Balance Trend of Selected Countries (2000–2021)

SUMMARY

1. The Balance of Payments is a systematic accounting record of all economic transactions during a given period of time between the residents of the country and the rest of the world.
2. BOP is a collection of accounts that are traditionally divided into three main categories: Current Account, Capital Account and Reserve Account.

3. In the balance of payments, "equilibrium position" exists when the demand and supply of any foreign currency in a nation are equal within a specific time period. While a disequilibrium denotes either a shortage or a surplus in the condition.
4. Capital account convertibility is described as the "flexibility to convert local financial assets into foreign financial assets and vice versa" by the Tarapore Committee in 2006.

KEY WORDS

- Balance of Payments
- Current Account Balance
- Capital Account Balance
- Economic Disequilibrium
- Capital Account Convertibility

QUESTIONS

1. Define Balance of Payments. What are the various components of Balance of Payments Account in India?
2. What are the various approaches to adjust Balance of Payments?
3. Explain how a country can run an overall balance of payments deficit or surplus.
4. Explain Capital Account Convertibility. How is it beneficial for the MNCs?

REFERENCES AND SUGGESTED READINGS

1. Dell, S. and R. Lawrence (1980). *The Balance of Payments Adjustment Process in Developing Countries*, Pergamon Press, New York.
2. Gandolfo, G. (1986), *International Economics*, Springer-Verlag, Berlin.
3. Jones, R.W. and P.B. Kennen (1984), *Handbook of International Economics*, 2 Vols., Elsevier Science Publishers, Amsterdam.
4. Krugman, P. and M. Obstfeld (2000), *International Economics—Theory and Policy*, 5th Edition, Addison, Wesley Longman.

CHAPTER 6

Foreign Exchange Market

LEARNING OUTCOMES

After reading this chapter, the reader will be able to:

- Give an Overview of Foreign Exchange Market
- Discuss Structure of Foreign Exchange Market
- Explain the Meaning of the Spot Market
- Describe Forward Contracts and its Market
- Explain briefly Futures Contract and Options Contract
- Interpret Theories of Exchange Rate Determination
- Discuss Forecasting Exchange Rates

6.1 FOREIGN EXCHANGE MARKET: AN OVERVIEW

The term Forex or Foreign Exchange refers to the conversion of currency of one country into currency of another country. As already discussed in the previous chapter, the value of one currency in the international market is determined by the forces of demand and supply as well as by the exchange rate regime followed by the particular country.

TABLE 6.1 OTC Foreign Exchange Turnover Daily Averages in April (Figures in Billions of US Dollars)

Instrument	2007	2010	2013	2016	2019	2022
Foreign exchange instruments	3,324	3,973	5,357	5,066	6,581	7,508
Spot transactions	1,005	1,489	2,047	1,652	1,979	2,107
Outright forwards	362	475	679	700	998	1,163
Foreign exchange swaps	1,714	1,759	2,240	2,378	3,198	3,810
Currency swaps	31	43	54	82	108	124
Options and other products	212	207	337	254	298	304

Source: 2022 Triennial Survey, Bank of International Settlement.

As per the triennial survey report (2022) by the Bank for International Settlements, the daily averages of over-the-counter (OTC) turnover of foreign exchange market in April, 2022 was $ 7,508 billion. It can be seen from the Table 6.1 that the trading volume increased by about 14% between 2019 and 2022.

TABLE 6.2 Major Geographical Centres of OTC Foreign Exchange Turnover

Country	*Daily averages in April 2022 in Billion Dollars*
UK	3755
US	1912
Singapore	929
Hong Kong SAR	694
Japan	433

TABLE 6.3 Major Currency Traded in Global Forex Market

Currency	*Daily averages in April 2022 in Billion Dollars*
USD	6,641
EUR	2,293
JPY	1,253
GBP	969
CNY	526

TABLE 6.4 Global Foreign Exchange Turnover by Currency Pair

Currency pair	*Daily averages in April 2022, in billions of US dollars*	
	Amount	*Percentage*
USD/EUR	1,706	22.7
USD/JPY	1,014	13.5
USD/GBP	714	9.5
USD/CNY	495	6.6
USD/CAD	410	5.5

TABLE 6.5 OTC Foreign Exchange Turnover of Indian Rupee (INR)

Year	*INR (OTC turnover in Billion Dollar)*
2010	38
2013	53
2016	58
2019	114
2022	122

The major currency trading centres geographically are UK, US, Singapore, Hong Kong and Japan and the major currencies traded are US Dollar, Euro, Japanese Yen, Pound Sterling and Chines Yuan. The Tables above provide in detail the forex trading volume geographically as well as currency wise.

6.2 STRUCTURE OF FOREIGN EXCHANGE MARKET

Foreign Exchange Market (Forex, FX or currency market) refers to the market where currencies are traded. It eases the flow of trade and investments around the globe by facilitating smooth currency conversion. For example, it allows an Indian corporate to import items from US and pay in dollars even though its revenue is in Indian rupees. The Foreign Exchange market, unlike stock market, is decentralized where the trading of currency is carried on by major international banks.

The forex market is formed by Foreign Exchange Dealers Association and the Foreign Exchange Brokers Association. One can participate in the foreign exchange market through a broker only unless one is the member of the foreign exchange dealers association. Foreign exchange market, are generally located in major financial centres such as Frankfurt, Hong Kong, Mumbai, New York, Paris, Tokyo, Singapore, Zurich, etc. For foreign exchange there are no specific trading locations like those for securities or commodities. It is non-localized market. The participants arrange transactions over telephone, telex or use other modern means of communications. The size of the market depends on the size of international transactions, i.e., the trade flows and investments. Since foreign exchange markets are spread over the whole globe, therefore the market for foreign exchange never closes on the globe. In India, Foreign Exchange Dealers Association of India (FEDAI) sets the rules of the game in the Indian forex market. FEDAI fixes the exchange margins, interest rates on various types of payment orders.

The market where currencies of other countries are purchased or sold is termed as foreign exchange market. Individuals, businesses, brokers of foreign exchange, commercial banks, and the central bank are among the buyers and sellers. The foreign exchange market is a system where transactions are not limited to just one or a small number of foreign currencies, like any other market. In the foreign exchange market, a sizable variety of foreign currencies are bought, sold, and exchanged.

The Foreign Exchange market is a two-tier market. One tier is retail market and the other is wholesale market.

6.2.1 Retail Market

The retail market of foreign exchange comprises of individual clients (who need foreign exchange for transaction purpose) as well as forex dealers which are generally the commercial banks. Now-a-days, the retail traders can also speculate or hedge in currency markets with the help of online forex trading platforms.

As per BIS Triennial Survey 2019, the retail market transactions account for approximately 7.18 percent of the Foreign Exchange trading volumes whereas the other 92.82 percent of trading volume is from wholesale market (between international banks and non-bank dealers).

6.2.2 Wholesale Markets

Investment banks and commercial banks make up the wholesale market. This falls under the categories of the interbank market and the central bank market.

Typically, wholesale banking constitutes of fewer very large clients, such as large businesses and governments. The majority of interbank lending in wholesale banking occurs when banks borrow from or lend to other banks, take part in significant bond issuances, or participate in syndicated lending.

Inter-bank

A global network of financial institutions known as the "interbank network" exchanges currencies with one another to control interest rate and exchange rate risk. Private banks make up the majority of the network's participants. The majority of interbank transactions last anywhere from an overnight to a six-month period. There is no regulation of the interbank market.

Central Bank

In the foreign exchange markets, central banks are significant players. They try to maintain the value of their currencies so that they can control the inflation and interest rates. To do so, they can make use of their often-sizable foreign exchange reserves. They serve as the nation's last-resort lender and custodian of its foreign exchange. The foreign exchange market is subject to regulation and oversight by the central bank, which ensures that it operates smoothly. The central bank can directly intervene in the foreign exchange market in case of wild fluctuations in the currency exchange rate (by selling the domestic currency when it is overvalued and purchasing it when it is undervalued) as one of the its primary function is to maintain stable currency exchange rates.

The Commercial Banks

The second-most significant component of the foreign currency market is the commercial banks. Insofar as they offer daily exchange rates for purchasing and selling foreign currencies, banks that deal in foreign exchange fulfil the role of "market makers." Additionally, they serve as clearing houses, aiding in the elimination of the discrepancy between currency supply and demand. These banks purchase foreign exchange from brokers and resell it to customers. Large commercial banks that operate in the foreign currency market include Barclays, Citigroup, JP Morgan Chase, etc. among others.

The Foreign Exchange Brokers

The central bank and the commercial banks, as well as the commercial banks and actual buyers, are connected by the foreign exchange brokers. They are the main repository for market information. These are the people who, in exchange for a commission, negotiate a deal between the buyer and seller rather than purchasing the foreign currency themselves. Thomson Reuters and ICAP are two significant brokerage firms.

6.3 SPOT MARKET

In the spot market, the currencies are bought and sold immediately and the rate at which the transaction takes place is termed as the spot rate. The average spot market trading of foreign exchange around the globe per day $ 2.10 trillion (as per the triennial survey report by BIS, April 2022).

6.3.1 Spot Rate Quotations

The foreign exchange quotation is represented in two ways—the direct and indirect quote. Direct quote, also referred as European quote, is a value of domestic currency per unit of foreign currency, for example, 83.0 INR per USD for buyers in India. On the other hand, the indirect quote, also referred as American quote, is a value of foreign currency per unit of domestic currency, for example, 0.92 USD per Euro is indirect quote for buyers in Europe.

A lower exchange rate in a direct quote means that the value of the home currency is increasing. In contrast, a lower exchange rate in an indirect quote suggests that the value of the home currency is declining since less foreign currency is equivalent to the domestic currency.

In other words, a direct quote in forex tells you how many units of another currency you could buy with one unit of your own. For those who want to quickly convert international exchange rates into their local currency, this is both straightforward and helpful.

The opposite of a direct quote is an indirect quote. When the first placed currency is different from your home currency, the quote is indirect even though a direct quote typically represents the currency that is set initially and is the local currency.

A pip for any currency pair is the smallest unit of price movement. It stands for point in percentage. For example, in the currency quote, the movement from 83.4325 INR/USD to 83.4326 is one pip. In general, the value of one pip is 0.0001 but for currency pair USD/JPY, one pip denotes 0.01. Currency quotation up to four decimal points is considered standard but nowadays, some brokers provide currency quotes up to 5 decimal points as well. The 1/10th of standard pip is called a fractional pip or pipette. For all the currency pairs (without JPY), one pipette represents the value at 5th decimal place whereas for JPY currency pairs, one pipette represents the value at 3rd decimal place.

6.3.2 Bid Ask Spread

The dealer in the foreign exchange market quotes a two-way price representing the bid (purchase) and ask (sell) price. The difference between bid and ask price is termed as spread which is the margin of dealer. Though in the retail market, the spread—the distinction between the ask and bid prices for a currency—may be substantial and can vary from one dealer to the other.

The rate at which a trader will purchase a currency is known as the bid price, whereas the ask price is the price at which the same dealer will sell it.

Let's imagine an Indian citizen who needs Japanese Yen to travel to Japan. On the currency market, the exchange rates are roughly 1 INR = 0.0120 USD and 1 JPY = 0.0082 USD. Accordingly, the estimated JPY/INR spot exchange rate would be JPY 1 = INR 0.6833 (0.0082/0.012). An Indian currency dealer can give you a rate like JPY 1 = INR 0.6400/0.7200, which translates to 0.72 INR to buy single JPY and 0.64 INR for a single JPY sold.

6.3.3 Cross Exchange Rate

Since the US dollar (USD) is the most widely used currency, it is typically against which exchange rates are presented. However, exchange rates can also be quoted in relation to the money of other nations, a practice known as cross currency.

A cross rate is an exchange rate used when two currencies are being exchanged that are both being valued against a different currency. The cross rate is the exchange rate between currencies A and C that results from the exchange rates between A and B and B and C.

The US dollar is the currency that is typically used to determine the values of the pair being exchanged in foreign exchange markets. The value of the US dollar is always 1, since it is the base currency.

A cross-currency pair trade actually involves two transactions. The trader starts by exchanging one currency for its value in dollars. After that, the US dollars are converted into another currency. The US dollar is utilised to determine the value of each of the two currencies being traded in the aforementioned transaction.

Only the currencies with high liquidity, like the US dollar, euro, pound sterling, etc., are quoted by the currency vendor. The cross rates are typically used to determine exchange rates between different currencies using quotes for the major currencies.

Cross Rate with Mid-point Exchange Rate

Let's say the pound is now trading at £ 0.80 per euro. The pound exchange rate for the Swiss franc is 1.20 Swiss francs per pound. Swiss Franc conversion rate in euros:

Swiss franc per Euro = Swiss franc per pound/Euro per pound

= 1.20/0.80 francs per euro = 1.5 francs per euro

Taking the reciprocal of the conversion rate determined above would result in the same exchange rate in Euro per swiss franc. The euro per swiss francs exchange rate would be 0.67 (=1 (€ 1.M5 per Swiss franc)).

Cross Rate with Bid-ask Quote

Suppose we were in the UK, the $/£ exchange rate would be 1.860–1.870 and ¥/£ would be 136.06–136.50.

We first require the cross exchange rate in the form of $/¥, which has $ in the numerator and ¥ in the denominator, in order to calculate the $/¥ exchange rate.

We already have currency rates in the form of $/£ and ¥/£. To ensure that the British pound cancels out when we multiply, we must take the reciprocal of any one of the conversion rates. The bid and ask legs of the reciprocal exchange rate for ¥/£ are taken, and their positions are then switched, to produce the value of £/¥, which is equal to 0.007326 – 0.007349(1/136.50 – 1/136.06). Due to the fact that the bid must always be lower than the ask, we have changed the positions.

The bid leg of the $/¥ cross rate is 0.0136 (= 1.860 × 0.007326) and the ask leg is 0.0137 (= 1.870 × 0.007349). The cross-rate quote is 0.0136–0.0137.

6.3.4 Triangular Arbitrage

When the direct exchange rate between two currencies differs from the cross-exchange rate, the triangular arbitrage opportunity occurs.

In the actual world, triangular arbitrage possibilities are rare. The structure of currency exchange markets can account for this. Numerous participants, including both individual and institutional traders, participate in the fiercely competitive forex markets. Arbitrage opportunities are short-lived because market inefficiencies are continually being corrected by market competition.

Nowadays, high-frequency traders frequently take advantage of triangular arbitrage chances. The traders can instantly identify mispricing using high-speed algorithms and carry out the required transactions right away. However, the markets are considerably more effective because of the significant presence of high-frequency traders. As a result, there are less prospects for arbitrage. The triangular arbitrage approach also has applications in the trading of cryptocurrencies. As the markets and exchanges in cryptocurrency are still at a nascent stage, there exists relatively more arbitrage opportunities than the traditional currency markets.

Due to the nature of currency exchange markets, price differences between different currencies are typically only a few cents or perhaps a tenth of a cent. As a result, a triangular arbitrage opportunity involves exchanging large sums of money.

Margin trading is frequently used in the trades to increase the rewards. A dealer must also be conscious of transaction expenses. High transaction costs could make any gains from price disparities insignificant.

Traders would often use three currency pairs to identify triangular arbitrage opportunities. A base currency and two additional counter currencies are involved in such a chance. The equation used is as follows:

1. The equation is $A/B \times B/C \times C/A = 1$, Where A is the base currency and B and C are the counter currencies.
2. When the aforementioned equation does not equal 1, it suggests that one market is undervalued while the other is overvalued, creating a triangular arbitrage opportunity.

Let's first gain an understanding of what it means to purchase or sell a certain currency pair before looking at an arbitrage example.

1. Purchase INR/USD, which entails exchanging dollars for rupees (purchasing currency B with currency A).
2. Sell INR/GBP; this indicates you are buying the pound and selling rupees (purchasing currency C using currency B).
3. Sell GBP/USD, which entails purchasing dollars and exchanging pounds for dollars (purchasing currency A using currency C).

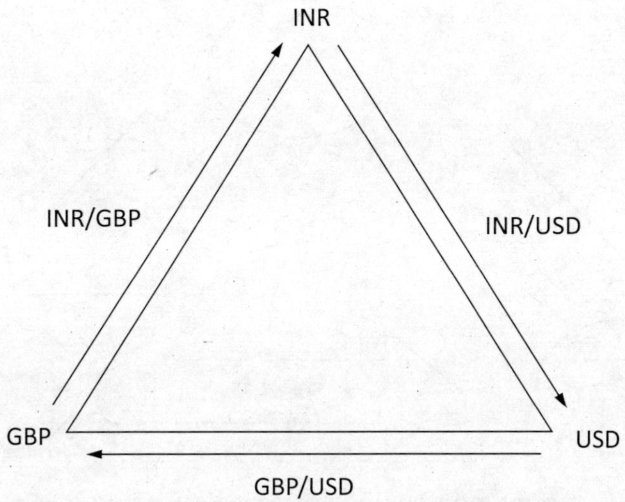

FIGURE 6.1 Triangular Arbitrage.

In the above transactions:

1. The dollar purchase in transaction three offsets the dollar sale in transaction one. The selling of rupees in transaction two offsets the purchase of rupees in transaction one.
2. The selling of pounds in transaction three offsets the purchasing of pounds in transaction two.

Illustration

'*A*' is a currency trader who has \$1 million available. He discovers the subsequent exchange rates:

'A' decides that the euro/pound exchange rate is valued less than the calculated cross rate involving the dollar. The pair's cross rate is:

$$€/£ = 1.05 \times 1.10 = 1.155$$

The three currencies—the US dollar, the euro, and the pound—can all be subject to triangular arbitrage. 'A' should carry out the following measures in order to take advantage of the triangular arbitrage opportunity:

1. Purchase euros in exchange of dollars: \$1,000,000 × 1.05 = € 1,050,000
2. Sell euros for pounds: € 1,050,000/1.15 = £ 913,043.48
3. Convert pounds for dollars: £913,043.48 × 1.10 = \$1,004,347.83

'A' was able to turn his initial investment of $1,000,000 into $1,004,347.83 with a profit of $ 4,347.83 by taking advantage of the differences in the price quotations of the three currencies. Note that even the utilization of a sizably large capital produced only modest gains due to the negligible price discrepancy (only 0.005). We didn't take transaction costs into account in our example. As a result, the profit would be significantly lower in real life.

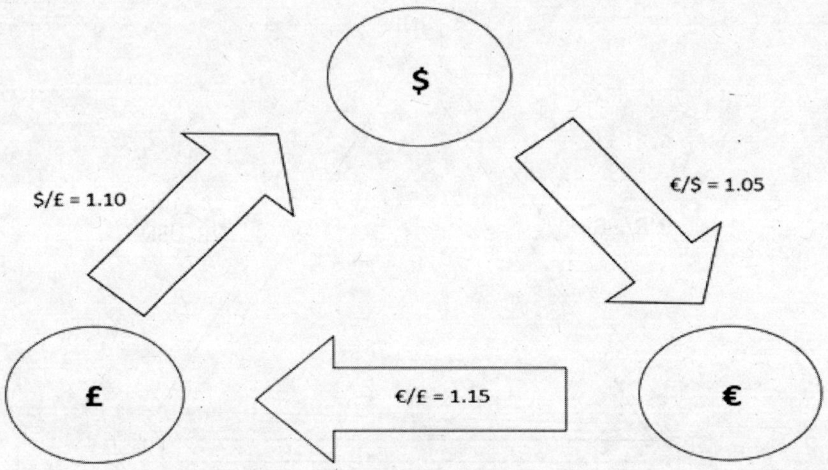

FIGURE 6.2 Illustration of Triangular Arbitrage.

6.4 FORWARD CONTRACT AND ITS MARKET

In a Forward contract, the purchaser and seller contract today to purchase and sell a currency at a fixed exchange rate on a specific future date. A forward exchange rate (forward rate) is the price at which currency is contracted to be exchanged and forward market is the place where transactions are performed for the sale and purchase of currencies at specific future dates.

The forward price can be same as the spot price, but frequently it is higher or lower than the spot price. For a range of maturities, forward exchange rates are quoted for the majority of the major currencies. There are widely available quotations from international banks for maturities of 1, 3, 6, 9, and 12 months. There are additional quotes available for nonstandard or broken-term maturities. A maturity extending out to 5, 10, or even 30 years is achievable for good bank customers. Maturities extending beyond one year are becoming more common.

6.4.1 Settlement

For the delivery of foreign currency at a future date that may be selected, forward exchange rates apply. In forward exchange transactions, there are two alternatives. Suppose Air India is buying aircrafts from Airbus, a Dutch corporate. It will have to pay Airbus in Euros, for instance in 6 months. Now, Air India can either pay Airbus the due amount in euros by converting rupees into euros at the spot exchange rate at the due time (after 6 months). In this case, the settlement date will follow the spot exchange transaction. Or, it can buy euros 6 months forward, today at a forward price (fixed today). In the second alternative, Air India avoids foreign exchange risk and the settlement takes place at the maturity date of forward contract.

6.4.2 Forward Rate Quotation

In this book, we have used Fn(A/B) to denote the forward price, which refers to the price of one unit of currency A in terms of currency B for delivery in n months.

6.4.3 Long and Short Forward Positions

When one purchases a currency in forward market, it is termed as long position whereas when one sells a currency in forward market, it is termed as short position.

If one uses the forward contract, he has "locked in" the forward price for forward purchase or sale of foreign exchange. He will have to purchase (in case of long position) or sell (in case of short position) regardless of the spot exchange rate at the time of maturity. Traders use forward contracts for speculative purposes as well.

6.4.4 Forward Cross Exchange Rate

Forward cross-exchange rate quotations are calculated in a similar manner to spot cross-rates. In simple terms, the forward cross exchange rate for currency A in terms of Currency B will be:

$$F_N(A/B) = F_N(\$/B)/F_N(\$/A)$$

where, Dollar is the base currency.

or $$F_N(A/B) = F_N(A/\$)/F_N(B/\$)$$

6.4.5 Forward Premium/Discount

When the forward price of a currency is higher (lower) than the spot price, it is said to be trading at a premium (discount) in the forward market.

The premium or discount of a forward rate is frequently expressed as an annualised percentage difference from the spot rate. When comparing the forward premium (or discount) to the difference in interest rates between two nations, this information is helpful. Term quotations from the United States or Europe can be used to compute the forward premium or discount.

The formula for calculating the forward premium or discount for currency A in American terms is:

$$f_{N,A} = \{F_{N(\$/A)} - S_{(\$/A)})\}/S_{(\$/A)} \times 360/\text{days}$$

6.5 FUTURE CONTRACTS

Both Forward and Future contracts come under derivatives as their value is derived from the underlying item (commodity or currency). They are very similar in nature but the future contracts are standardized and traded on exchange whereas the forward contracts are customized by international banks as per the requirement of their clients.

An agreement between two parties to buy or sell a specific item of standardised quantity at a price fixed today (the strike price or future's price), with delivery and payment at a specified future date, is known as a futures contract (more often, futures).

6.6 OPTION CONTRACTS

An investor who purchases a currency option has the opportunity, but not the duty, to buy or sell a certain amount of currency at a certain price on or before the option's expiration date. A "call option" is a right to sell a currency, and a "put option" is a right to purchase a currency.

Options can be viewed as a form of insurance that allows buyers or sellers to benefit from lower or higher prices should market circumstances change after the option is purchased.

6.7 THEORIES OF EXCHANGE RATE

The exchange rate theories provide insights into the determination and forecasting of currency exchange rates. These theories follow the law of one price that must hold in equilibrium conditions.

When the markets are perfect, the price of products will be same across all markets. However, imperfections in markets do exist, which causes arbitrage opportunities. Arbitrage is the purchase and sale of the same product at the same time in different markets in order to make profit from the price difference arising out of imperfect market conditions. Equilibrium exists when there is absence of such arbitrage profit opportunities. The theories of exchange rates are based on this arbitrage equilibrium condition.

6.7.1 Purchasing Power Parity Theory

The Purchasing Power Parity (PPP) theory links the buying power of the currencies, i.e., the basket of products or services that could be bought with one unit of the currencies to their respective exchange rates. PPP theory has two versions:

1. Absolute purchasing power parity, and
2. Relative purchasing power parity.

Absolute PPP Theory

As per absolute version of Purchasing power parity, the prices of same basket of products/items should be same in different countries. This means that the price of a product in nation A and the price of similar product in Nation B should be proportionate to their respective exchange rates. The law of one price should be operational between the two countries.

The theory lies on three assumptions:

1. The transportation cost of commodities is nil;
2. The currency conversion cost is nil; and
3. No trade barriers exist between the nations.

When P_A is the price of an item in Nation A, P_B is the price of an identical item in nation B, A is the currency of Nation A; and B is the currency of Nation B, then:

Price of an item in Nation A/Price of an item in Nation B = Currency of Nation X/ Currency of Nation B

or $$P_A/P_B = A/B$$

where, A/B is the direct exchange rate for Nation A.

Arbitrage opportunities arise when the absolute version of PPP is violated between the two nations. Arbitragers will start buying from Nation A where the prices are lower and sell at higher price in Nation B until the equilibrium between two nations is achieved. Absolute PPP doesn't apply to non-tradable items (such as real estate, health care services, water supply, etc.) that cannot be exported to another nation and hence, are not traded in international markets.

Relative PPP Theory

The price of goods will rise more in Nation A than in Nation B when the inflation rates are higher in the former. The value of A's currency will decrease in relation to B's currency since the Law of One Price dictates that an identical commodity should cost the same amount in both nations. The rate of depreciation in currency of nation A will be same as the inflation differential between the two currencies. Hence, the expected exchange rate $E(S_n)$ and expected inflation rates (I) in two nations are linked, according to the relative form of PPP.

Relative PPP states that the price differences arising out of variation in inflation, effects the currency exchange rates. However, if it works the other way around and an undervalued (overvalued) currency drives up (down) the prices in a nation, the magnitude of the price increase (decrease) is known as the "pass through" impact. Commodity prices in Nations A and B are impacted by the expected inflation rates in those two nations because expected inflation rates have an impact on a commodity's future price.

When P is the present price of the product and I is the expected rate of inflation, the price of the product after one year (P_1) is

$$P_1 = P_0\ (1 + I)$$

In Nation A: $P_{A1} = P_{A0}\ (1 + I_A)$

In Nation B: $P_{B1} = P_{B0}\ (1 + I_B)$

The ratio of the prices after one year is:

$$[P_{A0}\ (1 + I_A)]/[P_{B0}\ (1 + I_B)]$$

This can be written as $S_{A/B}\ [(1 + I_A)/(1 + I_B)]$ as (P_{A0}/P_{B0}) is the current spot rate, $S_{A/B}$.

Since the expected exchange rate after one year, $E(S_{A/B})$, is a ratio of the prices after one year, it is:

$$E(S_{A/B}) = S_{A/B} [(1+ I_A)/(1 + I_B)] \qquad \dots (1)$$

The above equation can be rearranged as $E(S_{A/B})/S_{A/B} = [(1 + I_A)/(1 + I_B)]$

The left hand side of this equation can be written as:

$$1 + [\{E(S_{A/B}) - S_{A/B}\}/S_{A/B}]$$

where $[\{E(S_{A/B}) - S_{A/B}\}/S_{A/B}]$ is the rate of change in the spot rate.

Denoting $[\{E(S_{A/B}) - S_{A/B}\}/S_{A/B}]$ by '**e**':

$$(1 + e) = [(1 + I_A)/(1 + I_B)]$$

On simplification $e = (I_A - I_B)/(1 + I_B)$

The denominator on the right hand side, $(1 + I_B)$ can be ignored for small values of I_B. Then,

$$e \approx (I_A - I_B) \qquad \dots (2)$$

According to this equation, e is roughly equivalent to $(I_A - I_B)$. The relative PPP theory asserts that the rate of change in the spot rate is roughly equal to the inflation differential since e is nothing more than the rate of change in the spot rate $[\{E(S_{A/B}) - S_{A/B}\}/S_{A/B}]$. The market is in equilibrium when this circumstance is true. As it includes non-tradable commodities as well, relative PPP is more accurate than absolute PPP in terms of price fluctuations (As the price index that captures inflation accounts for both tradeable and non-tradeable items).

6.7.2 Interest Rate Parity Theory

Interest rate parity theory governs the relationship between interest rates and currency exchange rates. Following are the assumptions of the theory:

1. There are no charges associated with exchanging one currency for another or purchasing or selling financial securities. Hence, there are no transaction costs.
2. There is complete capital mobility and free flow of money between the two nations.
3. An investor has the option of purchasing financial securities that are denominated in his own Nation's currency (domestic currency–denominated financial securities) or purchasing financial securities that are denominated in a different nation's currency (foreign currency–denominated financial securities). If he chooses to invest in foreign currency–denominated financial securities, he is exposed to foreign exchange risk (due to volatility of currency exchange rates) and hence to hedge such risk, the investor will use forward market operations.

The theory holds that the forward exchange rate $(F_{A/B})$ for two currencies is determined by the current spot rate $(S_{A/B})$, and the nominal interest rates (i_A and i_B) in the two nations.

The forward rate is:

$$F_{A/B} = S_{A/B}\{[1 + i_A]/[1 + i_B]\} \quad \text{... (3)}$$

where,

$F_{A/B}$ is Forward rate for currency A/B
$S_{A/B}$ is Spot rate for currency A/B
i_A is interest rate in Nation A
i_B is interest rate in Nation B

This is Covered interest parity theory. It asserts that covered investments in both the countries results in same returns when markets are efficient.

Subtracting one from both side and rearranging the above equation (S, which resembles the relative PPP theory's equation for the expected spot rate $E(S_{A/B})$, results in:

$$(F_{A/B} - S_{A/B})/S_{A/B} = (i_A - i_B)/(1 + i_B)$$

Keep in mind that when $F_{A/B}$ is less than $S_{A/B}$, the term $(F_{A/B} - S_{A/B})$ on the left side of the equation is negative (the forward rate is at a discount to the spot rate). When $F_{A/B}$ exceeds $S_{A/B}$, the forward rate is at a premium to the spot rate.

The denominator $(1 + i_B)$ on the right hand side of equation can be ignored for small values of i_B, in such case the equilibrium is said to exist when,

$$(F_{A/B} - S_{A/B})/S_{A/B} \approx (i_A - i_B) \quad \text{... (4)}$$

Profitable chances for covered interest arbitrage emerge when the left hand side of the above equation is bigger than the interest rate difference $(i_A - i_B)$.

The IRP states that an investor will not care whether they invest in assets denominated in domestic or foreign currency if the return is same and the quoted forward rate is same as the forward rate determined using equation 3. Equilibrium exists when he is unconcerned about the financial securities' currency denomination.

An investor can gain by borrowing money in one currency, converting it into another, investing the proceeds, and protecting himself against exchange rate risk if, on the other hand, the stated forward rate differs from the forward rate determined using equation 3. This process is called covered interest arbitrage (CIA).

Covered Interest Arbitrage

Let's take an example to understand covered interest arbitrage process.

Suppose, in the US the annual rate of interest is 6% and, in the Canada, it is 8%, the spot exchange rate is USD 0.80/CAD and 1 year forward rate is USD 0.75/CAD. The arbitrager can borrow USD 1,000,000 or CAD 1,250,000 currently.

Here, $i_A = 6\%$, $i_B = 8\%$, $S_{A/B} = 0.80$ and $F_{A/B} = 0.75$

First, we will check if the IRP is holding or not.

Substituting the data in right hand side of the equation, $F_{A/B} = S_{A/B}[\{1 + i_A\}/\{1 + i_B\}]$

$$0.80(1.06/1.08) = 0.785$$

which is not equal to left hand side of the equation, 0.75.

In the above example,

$$F_{A/B} < S_{A/B} [\{1 + i_A\}/\{1 + i_B\}]$$

As we can see, IRP is not holding, which means the arbitrager can make profit here. Since, the real USD/CAD forward rate is lower than the forward rate calculated by the equation, the arbitrager must borrow in the Canada and invest in US.

Transactions for CIA

1. Borrow CAD 1,250,000 in Canada. The payment in 1 year will be CAD 1,350,000 (1,250,000*1.08)
2. Purchase USD 1,080,000 spot using CAD 1,350,000
3. Invest USD 1,080,000 in the US. The return after 1 year will be USD 1,144,800 (1,080,000*1.06)
4. Sell USD 1,144,800 forward for CAD 1,930,667 (1,144,800/0.75)

After one year, the arbitrager will get USD 1,144,800 on his US investments, which will be used to settle the forward contract in return for CAD 1,930,667. Out of this amount, CAD 1,350,000 will be used to repay the loan in Canada. The arbitrager is left with CAD 580,667, which is the arbitrage profit. The above transaction involved no risk as the arbitrager carried out covered interest arbitrage. He simultaneously borrowed at one interest rate and invested at another rate while hedging the exchange risk with forward contract.

In real life, the arbitrage profit is much lower for small transactions. Also, the opportunity exists for a short period only. As soon as the traders detect deviations from IRP, they will instantly carry out arbitrage transactions, and as a result, IRP will be restored.

Let's understand this with the above example. As every trader will borrow in Canada and invest in US as well as purchase USD spot and sell it forward; it will result in the rise in rate of interest in Canada and decline in rate of interest in US as well as the appreciation of USD in spot market and depreciation of USD in the forward market.

Equilibrium Condition under IRP

The rate of change in the forward rate and the spot rate, $(F_{A/B} - S_{A/B})/S_{A/B}$ and the rate of change in the nominal interest rates $[(i_A - i_B)/(1 + i_B)]$ are identical, the equilibrium exists, and hence there would not be any scope for CIA.

6.7.3 International Fisher Effect (IFE) Theory

According to this theory, even without taking exchange rate risk into account in the forward market, market participants' actions will still cause the forward rate ($F_{A/B}$) and the expected spot rate $[E(S_{A/B})]$ to be equal. Hence, it is also called the uncovered interest parity theory.

When the Forward Rate ($F_{A/B}$) Exceeds the Expected Spot Rate [$E(S_{A/B})$]

On the day the forward contract must be honoured, all market participants will sell the currency B forward in the hopes of purchasing it in the spot market at the expected spot rate. The forward rate will decrease until it is equal to the expected spot rate as everyone is selling the currency B forward. As the theory predicts, at this time, profit-making chances vanish and the forward rate ($F_{A/B}$) and the expected spot rate E($S_{A/B}$) will be identical.

When the Forward Rate ($F_{A/B}$) is Lower than the Expected Spot Rate [E($S_{A/B}$)]

Participants in the market will purchase the currency B forward with the intention of selling it at a profit at the expected spot rate on the day the forward contract comes due. The forward rate will increase as more people acquire dollars in advance until it reaches at par with the expected spot rate. Profitable opportunities end at this time, and according to theory, the forward rate ($F_{A/B}$) and the anticipated spot rate E($S_{A/B}$) will be equal. As a result, market movements will cause the forward rate to increase until it reaches the expected spot rate.

6.8 FORECASTING EXCHANGE RATES

The flexible exchange rate system was introduced in 1973, and since then, exchange rates have been a lot more unstable and volatile. The range of corporate activities has expanded significantly internationally at the same time. As a result, many company choices are now based on predictions of future exchange rates, whether they be implicit or explicit. For currency traders who actively engage in speculating, hedging, and arbitrage in the foreign exchange markets, precisely anticipating exchange prices is a matter of utmost importance. Also, multinational firms who are developing their global sourcing, production, finance, and marketing strategies should seriously consider this issue. The accuracy of exchange rate estimates will be a key factor in determining how well these corporate decisions turn out.

While some businesses create their own projections, others take services from outside. Although forecasters employ a wide range of forecasting methods, the most fall into one of three categories.

6.8.1 Efficient Market Approach

If the current asset values accurately represent all the significant and available information, then financial markets are said to be efficient. The University of Chicago's Professor Eugene Fama is substantially responsible for the efficient market hypothesis (EMH), which has significant forecasting implications.

Assume that the currency exchange markets are efficient. This means that all important information, including money supply, inflation rates, trade balances, and production growth, has already been factored into the current exchange rate. After that, the exchange rate won't move until the market is informed of fresh information.

As news can not be predicted, so the exchange rate will fluctuate erratically over time. In other words, small changes in the exchange rate will not be influenced by its prior performance. Future exchange rates are anticipated to be equal to current exchange rates if the exchange rate does truly follow a random walk, that is,

$$S_t = E(S_{t+1})$$

In a sense, the random walk hypothesis contends that the exchange rate of today is the most accurate predictor of the exchange rate of tomorrow.

There is no theoretical reason why exchange rates should follow a pure random walk, despite the fact that scholars find it challenging to disprove the random walk hypothesis for exchange rates on the basis of empirical evidence.

If the foreign exchange markets are efficient, then $F_t = E(S_{t+1} \mid I_t)$, then the parity connections we previously mentioned suggest that the present forward exchange rate can be considered as the market's projection of the future exchange rate based on the existing information (It).

The forward exchange rate will differ from the present spot exchange rate to the degree that interest rates are different between two nations. This indicates that a change from the current spot exchange rate should be anticipated in the exchange rate in the future. Individuals who accept the efficient market hypothesis may be able to make future predictions on exchange rates based on the current foreign exchange rates or forward exchange rates.

The two benefits of predicting exchange rates using the efficient market theory are—First, creating projections is free since the efficient market technique is based on prices that are set by the market. The current spot and forward exchange rates are both available to the general public. As a result, anyone can use it without charge. Second, considering how well-functioning foreign currency markets are, it is challenging to beat estimates based on such markets unless the forecaster has access to proprietary data that hasn't yet been reflected in the current exchange rate.

6.8.2 Fundamental Approach

Several models are used to forecast exchange rates. For instance, the monetary approach to exchange rate determination contends that three independent (explanatory) variables—relative money supply, relative money velocity, and relative national outputs—are responsible for determining the exchange rate.

So, the monetary method can be expressed empirically as follows:

$$s = \alpha + \beta_1(m - m^*) + \beta_2(v - v^*) + \beta_3(y^* - y) + u$$

where,

s = natural log of the spot exchange rate.
$m - m^*$ = natural log of domestic/foreign money supply.
$v - v^*$ = natural log of domestic/foreign velocity of money.
$y^* - y$ = natural log of foreign/domestic output.
u = random error term, with mean zero.
α, β's = model parameters.

With the basic approach, forecasting would include the following three steps:

Step 1: Calculation of the numerical values for the parameters, such as α and β's, using a structural model estimation method, as mentioned in the above equation.

Step 2: Forecasting the values of the independent variables $(m - m^*)$, $(v - v^*)$, and $(y^* - y)$ in the future.

Step 3: To produce the exchange rate projections, substitute the estimated values of the independent variables into the calculated structural model.

For instance, the forecaster must estimate the values that the independent variables will have in one year if he has to accurately anticipate the exchange rate one year from now. The structural model that was fitted to historical data will then substitute these values.

There are three key issues with the fundamental method for projecting exchange rates. To forecast the exchange rates, a set of independent factors must first be predicted. The former will undoubtedly be vulnerable to inaccuracy and may not always be simpler to foresee than the latter. Second, as government policies and/or the underlying structure of the system change over time, the parameter values—that is, α and β's — that are estimated using historical data may do so as well. Even if the model is accurate, either challenge can reduce forecast accuracy. Lastly, even the model itself can be flawed. For instance, the equation's description of the model can be inaccurate. A flawed model cannot produce a forecast that is particularly accurate. Unsurprisingly, researchers discovered that the fundamental models were less effective at predicting exchange rates than the forward rate model and the random walk model.

6.8.3 Technical Approach

In order to uncover "patterns", the technical approach first examines the historical behaviour of exchange rates. These "patterns" are then projected into the future to produce projections. It is obvious that the technical strategy is built on the idea that history repeats itself (or at least rhymes with itself). Hence, the technical method and the efficient market approach are at odds. It also differs from the fundamental approach in that it does not foresee using important economic factors like money supplies or trade balances. However, technical analysts occasionally use different transaction data to support their analyses, including trading volume, open positions, and bid-ask spreads. Following, we will go through two most commonly used tools of technical analysis: the head-and-shoulders pattern and the moving average crossover rule.

Head and Shoulder Pattern

The head-and-shoulders (HAS) pattern indicates that an upward going market is about to reverse. A head, two shoulders (left and right), and the neckline make up the HAS design (support level). This pattern is frequently seen as indicating that the currency (for which the pattern is studied) has peaked and a significant reversal is about to occur. The left shoulder happens as the currency achieves a regional high point in a rising market and subsequently declines back to the neckline. The currency then increases to the head, an even higher level, before declining once again to the neckline. When the currency gains again, but only to a local high point below the head, the right shoulder appears. When the support level or neckline are broken, the HAS pattern is finished. When the currency loses value over the neckline, this happens. The completion of the HAS pattern predicts a big decline in the value of the currency.

Although academic research frequently questions the veracity of technical analysis, many traders rely on it for their trading techniques. It may make sense for a trader to use technical analysis if he or she is aware that other traders do it. The forecasts made by technical analysis can, at least temporarily, become self-fulfilling if enough traders employ it.

Moving Average Crossover

Moving averages are frequently computed by technical analysts or chartists as a technique of isolating short- and long-term trends from the fluctuations of daily exchange rates. As recent changes in the exchange rate weigh more heavily on the short-term moving average (SMA) (such as 50-day) than the long-term moving average (LMA) (such as 200-day), the SMA will be lower (higher) than the LMA when the currency (for which the pattern is studied) is depreciating (appreciating) against the base currency. This suggests that based on the crossover of the moving averages, one could predict changes in the exchange rate. This rule states that the currency may continue to strengthen if the SMA crosses over the LMA at a point when the SMA is rising and LMA declining. On the other hand, a crossover of the SMA below the LMA at point when SMA is declining and LMA is rising indicates the possibility of a temporary decline in the value of the currency. The former crossover, also known as the "golden cross", is a buy indication for traders while the latter crossover is often known as the "death cross", is a sell signal.

SUMMARY

1. The term Forex or Foreign Exchange refers to the conversion of currency of one Nation into currency of another Nation.
2. In the spot market, the currencies are bought and sold immediately and the rate at which the transaction takes place is termed as the spot rate.
3. The market in which the deals for the sale and purchase of currency at some future dates are made is called a Forward Market and the rate at which the transaction will be executed is the forward rate.
4. The Purchasing Power Parity theory links the buying power of the currencies, i.e., the basket of goods or services that could be purchased with one unit of the respective currencies to their exchange rates. There are two versions of PPP theory: One is absolute purchasing power parity and second is relative purchasing power parity.
5. The IRP theory holds that the forward exchange rate ($F_{A/B}$) for two currencies is determined by the current spot rate ($S_{A/B}$), and the nominal interest rates (i_A and i_B) in the two nations.
6. International Fisher Effect suggests that the forward rate ($F_{X/Y}$) and the expected spot rate [$E(S_{X/Y})$] will be identical because, even without covering exchange rate risk in the forward market, actions of market participants will make them equal.

KEY WORDS

- Foreign Exchange
- Spot Market
- Forward Market
- Triangular Arbitrage

- Purchasing Power Parity
- Interest Rate Parity
- International Fisher Effect

QUESTIONS

1. Who are the market participants in the foreign exchange market?
2. What are the differences between direct and indirect quote in foreign exchange market?
3. Calculate the cross exchange rate between Chinese yuan and Indian rupee if yuan-dollar and rupee-dollar exchange rates are 6.84 yuan/dollar and 82.85 rupee/dollar respectively.
4. Discuss in detail the absolute and relative purchasing power parity theory.
5. What does Random Walk theory suggest about forecasting exchange rates?

REFERENCES AND SUGGESTED READINGS

1. Triennial Survey Report, 2022, Bank for International Settlements
2. Fisher, Irving. *The Theory of Interest*, rpt. ed. New York, Macmillan, 1980.
3. Abuaf, N., and P. Jorion. "Purchasing Power Parity in the Long Run", *Journal of Finance* 45 (1990), pp. 157–74.
4. Adler, Michael, and Bruce Lehman. "Deviations from Purchasing Power Parity in the Long Run", *Journal of Finance* 38 (1983), pp. 1471–87.
5. Aliber, R. "The Interest Rate Parity: A Reinterpretation", *Journal of Political Economy* (1973), pp. 1451–59.

CHAPTER 7

Foreign Exchange Exposure and Risk Management

LEARNING OUTCOMES

After reading this chapter, the reader will be able to:

- Explain Foreign Exchange Exposure
- Describe Risk Management Process
- Discuss and Differentiate between Transaction Exposure and Translation Exposure
- Describe Determinants and Management of Economic/Operating Exposure
- Explain Interest Rate and Currency Swaps with Examples

7.1 INTRODUCTION

In this era of globalisation, each and every business is connected to the global economy in one way or the other. The cross-border movement of goods, services and capital, results in the movement of currencies. This movement of currencies with several other factors causes variation in currency exchange rates. The fluctuation in exchange rate impacts the operations of a business. Thus, it has become a considerable source of risk for a firm. Under such environment, the firm has an interest in estimating its exchange rate exposure, the risk it causes and then the way to manage that risk.

Exposure in foreign exchange transactions refers to the possibility of financial loss brought on by an unfavourable change in the exchange rate. To put it another way, exposure describes the aspects of a company's operations that might be impacted by changes in the exchange rate. Exposure to foreign exchange might result from a variety of different activities.

An exporter who sells his goods invoiced in foreign currency runs the risk of having reduced income in his own currency if the value of that foreign currency decreases. Similarly, when an importer purchases items invoiced in foreign currency, there is a chance that the value of that foreign currency will appreciate and drive up the cost in local currency more than anticipated.

Foreign Exchange Exposure refers to the sensitivity of a firm's cash flows, operating profit or the value of assets and liabilities due to the volatility of currency exchange rates. Whereas the foreign exchange risk is defined as the variability of the firm's cash flow, operating profit or the value of assets and liabilities due to its exposure to the movement of currency exchange rates. For example, an exporting firm is exposed to foreign exchange movements because of the nature of its business, but the risk only arises when the exchange rates are volatile.

Foreign exchange exposure, if left unmanaged, can affect the firm's competitiveness and performance. Foreign Exchange Risk Management is the way to minimize the risk (Cash flow variability) arising out of the fluctuations in currency exchange rates.

7.2 RISK MANAGEMENT PROCESS

Risk management process consists of four major steps:

1. Choosing suitable target performance variable.
2. Identifying the factors that can have significant impact on the selected performance variable.
3. Quantifying the impact of risk factors on performance variable. In case of transaction exposure, the measurement is fairly easy. Measurement of operating exposure requires in depth analysis of parameters like competitive response, demand elasticity, etc.
4. Selecting appropriate hedging technique to reduce or eliminate the risk.

Non-financial companies, commonly use operating cash flows as their target performance variable. Nowadays, financial companies are adopting Value at Risk (VAR) to measure the risk. VAR is a single, concise statistical estimate of the potential decline in portfolio value caused by typical market fluctuations in the underlying risk variables over a specified time horizon. More specifically, it is a cap on value loss that will only be surpassed with a very low likelihood that has been pre-determined. In other words, if the VAR for a certain portfolio of assets and liabilities is "X" (dollars, rupees, or whatever) with a 95% confidence level, it means there is a 5% chance that the portfolio's value will decrease by more than that amount.

Foreign Exchange Risk Management involves using both internal and external hedging techniques. Internal techniques include leading and lagging, netting, selection of invoicing currency, product differentiation, methods of costing, etc. External techniques consist of using currency derivatives such as forwards, futures, options and swaps. The techniques of hedging used depends upon the type of exposure the firm is exposed to.

Foreign Exchange Exposure can be classified into three categories:

1. Transaction Exposure
2. Translation Exposure
3. Economic Exposure

7.3 TRANSACTION EXPOSURE

When a firm enters into a contract that requires payment or receipt of foreign currency at a future date, it exposes itself to transaction exposure. As the currency exchange rates are volatile/uncertain, the appreciation or depreciation of the foreign currency impacts the value the firm will have to pay or receive in its domestic currency, thus causing the uncertainty in future cash flows.

Transaction exposure are often termed as contractual exposure as they arise due to contractual obligations. They are short term in nature.

Suppose an Indian firm has entered into a contract to buy inventory from US costing $100000. The inventory will be delivered after a month and the payment has to be made at that time only in US dollars. The current exchange rate is INR 75/USD. After a month, if the INR depreciates to INR 80/USD, the firm will have to pay INR 8,000,000 rather than INR 7,500,000, thus incurring a loss of INR 500,000 only because of the variability in exchange rates.

The amount of foreign currency that a firm has to pay or receive, is the magnitude of transaction exposure.

7.3.1 Techniques to Hedge Transaction Exposure

Various financial and non-financial techniques are used to hedge such kind of exposure. Some of the commonly used techniques are:

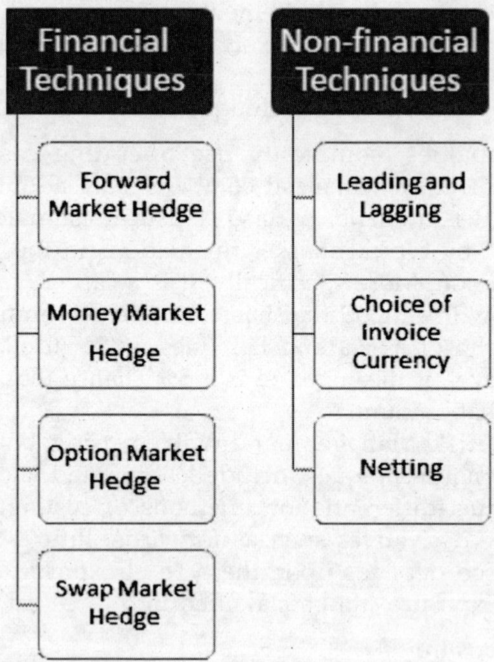

FIGURE 7.1 Hedging Techniques.

Let's take an example to understand the hedging techniques better. Suppose Tata Motors has imported auto components from a supplier in UK for GBP 100,000, which is payable in a year. The currency exchange rates as well as money market rates are as follows:

- Spot exchange rate: 80 INR/GBP
- 1 year forward exchange rate: 82 INR/GBP
- Interest rate in UK: 6%
- Interest rate in India: 8%

1. *Forward Market Hedge*

Transaction exposure is most commonly hedged using forward contracts. Under this method, the firm enters into a forward contract to either purchase foreign currency (in case of payables) or sell foreign currency (in case of receivables) forward.

Let's understand this with the example we have states above. Tata Motors has to pay GBP 100,000 in a year, so it can enter into a 1 year forward contract to buy GBP 100,000 at the rate of 82 INR/GBP. On the maturity of the contract, Tata Motors will have to buy GBP 100,000 for INR 8200,000 irrespective of the then spot rate. It will obviously use the proceeds from contract to payback the due amount. As the receipt of GBP from forward contract is offset by the payment of GBP to its supplier, the net exposure becomes nil.

2. *Money Market Hedge*

Under this technique, the firm invests beforehand in the currency it has payables denominated whereas borrows in the currency it has receivables denominated. In our example, the firm has pound payables. In such case, it would invest pounds in UK today, for a year and will use the proceeds of the investment to fulfil its liability at maturity.

The following steps must be followed in this case:

(a) Borrow INR 7547200.
(b) Convert INR 7547200 into GBP 94340 at the current spot rate of 82 INR/GBP.
(c) Invest GBP 94340 in the UK.
(d) Receive GBP 100000 (94340*1.06) at maturity and use it to pay the liability.
(e) Pay INR 8150976 (7547200*1.08) to service the loan.

Transaction	*Current Cash Flow*	*Cash Flow at Maturity*
Borrow INR	7547200 INR	–8150976 INR
Buy GBP spot with INR	GBP 94340 (–7,547,200 INR)	—
Invest in UK	–94340 GBP	100,000 GBP
Use GBP proceeds from investment to settle the payable amount	—	–100,000 GBP
Net Cash Flow	0	–8,150,976 INR

Thus, in this case the firm has to pay INR 8150976 to settle the payable. Since, the amount is fix and known beforehand, the firm will be able to avoid uncertainty if it hedges its positions.

3. *Option Market Hedge*

The major drawback of using forward and money market hedging technique is that they completely eliminate the foreign exchange exposure. There are chances of exchange rates moving in favourable direction and hence benefitting the firm.

Hedging through options contract is better as it lets the firm retain the profit opportunities while providing an insurance against the loss. In case of foreign exchange payables, call option is purchased and in case of foreign exchange receivables put option is purchased.

4. *Swap Market Hedge*

If there is exposure arising out of a recurring foreign currency receivable or payable, it is better to hedge it with a currency swap contract. Under currency swap contract, the counterparties agree to exchange one currency for another at pre-determined rate on series of future dates. The rate of each transaction varies as per their respective maturities.

5. *Leading and Lagging*

Leading means to prepone the payment or receipt and lagging means to delay the payment or receipt. Under the strategy of leading and lagging, the firm delays the payment denominated in foreign currency, if it expects the currency to depreciate whereas it makes the payment early, if the given currency is expected to appreciate. Similarly, in case of receivables, leading strategy is used when the invoiced foreign currency is expected to depreciate and lagging strategy is used when it is expected to appreciate.

6. *Choice of Invoice Currency*

Transaction exposure risk can be avoided if the firm uses its domestic currency as invoicing currency as the whole risk will be shifted to the counterparty. However, only the importer or exporter that has substantial market power can do so. For example, due to the high demand of Russian natural gas, importers from countries like Germany are buying the same in Russian currency roubles. Other way is to share the risk by invoicing the equal portion of bill in both currencies. Sometimes, the currency of both parties are not suitable for international settlement, in such case, currency like USD or basket of currencies like SDR can be used as invoicing currency to diversify the risk.

7. *Netting*

Often the firm has many receivables and payables denominated in foreign currency. Instead of hedging the exposure arising out of each and every receivable and payable in a given currency, the firm must adjust them and hedge only the net exposure.

A lot of multinational firms have centralized the function of exposure netting by setting up a reinvoice centre. All the intrafirm invoices (receivables or payables) involving foreign currency are netted there and only the residual exposure is considered for hedging.

7.4 TRANSLATION EXPOSURE

Translation exposure, as the name suggests, is the variability in the reporting values of firms assets and liabilities that are denominated in foreign currency. If a firm has subsidiaries in countries other than the home country, those subsidiaries must be maintaining their respective financial statements in the functional currency of the country where they are operating. At the end of financial year, the parent firm has to present consolidated financial statements to its shareholders, investors as well as other stakeholders to present its position. As the consolidated financial statements are denominated in functional currency of the parent firm, it has to translate all the assets and liabilities of subsidiaries (denominated in other currency) into its own functional currency. Thus, exposing itself to foreign exchange exposure.

Translation exposure is also a short-term exposure. It is also known as accounting exposure as it only effects the accounting values and there is no real impact on the firm's cash flows or operating profitability. However, translation exposure may impact the image of firm among its stakeholders and hence, it is important to consider this exposure as well.

7.5 ECONOMIC/OPERATING EXPOSURE

Economic exposure (sometimes referred as operating exposure) affects the long-term cash flows and operating profits of the firm by affecting its overall competitiveness in the market. For instance, the US dollar is very strong compared to currencies of developing countries like India. For this reason, a lot of times INR depreciates vis-a-vis USD. This makes the firms from India who are exporting to US more competitive in the US markets as their product will costless to the US consumers. On the other hand, this also makes the imports from US costlier for Indian firms. Thus, impacting the overall operating profits of the firms and compelling them to develop some long-term strategy to tackle this kind of exposure.

7.5.1 Determinants of Operating Exposure

The operating exposure of the firm depends on two factors:

1. *The Market Structure:* The market in which the firm operates influence the extent of operating exposure to a great degree. For instance, if a US firm exporting to India, faces no competition from domestic firms or firms from other nations, the appreciation of USD won't impact its business but on the other hand the US firm is competing with Chinese firm in Indian markets and the USD appreciates while CNY is stable, it will have an adverse impact on business of the US firm.
2. *The Ability of Firm to Adjust:* If the firm is able to modify its sources of inputs, product mix or the market in case it will be able to avoid the operating exposure.

7.5.2 Management of Operating Exposure

As the impact of movements in currency exchange rates impacts the operating performance of the firm to a great degree, it becomes necessary for firms to manage the resultant operating measure with long-term strategic tools. Some of the effective measures to do so are:

1. *Product Differentiation*

Effects of exchange rate risk on firm's operating profits can be minimized substantially through continuously developing differentiated products. As differentiated products are price insensitive, the market of such product wouldn't be impacted much by the change in price due to the fluctuations in exchange rate.

2. *Market Diversification*

Operating in multiple markets reduces the exposure of firm. Appreciation in currency of one market can be compensated by the depreciation in currency of another market. Until the value of currencies doesn't move in same direction, by diversifying the export destination, the firm can have stable operating cashflows to some extent.

3. *Cost Effective Production Sites*

The firm can set production sites in those countries whose currencies are undervalued (developing countries are the best options as the cost of production is low plus they have conducive business environment), when its domestic currency is strong and hence effecting its competitive position negatively.

4. *Flexible Sourcing*

Setting production facilities in other countries require huge capital investment. If the firm has not that much of resources, alternatively, it can source its inputs of production including human resources from countries where the inputs are cheap. A lot of US MNCs employ Indians who work for them remotely with much less salaries and benefits compared to employees from developed countries.

7.6 INTEREST RATE AND CURRENCY SWAPS

For hedging foreign exchange risks as well as interest rate risks, interest rate swaps and currency swaps are often used. In the next section, we are going to examine them.

A financial organisation that helps counterparties execute swap transactions is referred to as a swap bank. An independent operator, a merchant bank, an investment bank, or an international commercial bank can all be swap banks. The swap bank might act as a swap dealer or broker. The swap bank acts as a broker, matching counterparties but not taking any of the swap's risks. For this service, the swap broker is compensated with a commission. The majority of swap banks nowadays act as market makers or dealers. The swap bank is a market maker and is prepared to take either side of a currency swap, lay it off later, or match it with a counterparty. In this role, the swap bank takes on a position in the swap and as a result, some risks. Since the dealer capacity carries a higher level of risk, the swap bank would be compensated for taking on this risk by receiving a share of the cash flows that flowed through it.

Swaps are not a funding or investment instrument; they are a tool for obtaining the desired asset or form of financing indirectly that could otherwise be unavailable or expensive. Swaps are a contract under which two parties agree to exchange a series of cash flows. The present values of the two series of cash flows are identical at the beginning. The value of a swap is therefore initially zero, just like a forward contract.

Single currency swap (commonly referred as interest rate swap or plain vanilla swap) and cross currency swap (commonly referred as currency swap) are the two kinds of interest rate swaps.

7.6.1 Interest Rate Swaps

These are the basic fixed to floating interest rate swaps (plain vanilla swaps), under which two parties exchange their respective interest rates (fixed or floating) on debt obligation for the other on regular intervals in the future till a particular termination date. The debt obligations of both parties are denominated in the same currency. The party that pays at fixed rate (fixed rate payer), makes fixed payments at regular intervals that are pre-determined. The floating rate payer, makes payments that are decided on the basis of the specified floating rate index (such as LIBOR).

Take an example to understand the fixed for floating interest rate swap. There is an international bank, Globex, that is rated AAA. It needs to finance floating rate term loans to its clients. For that, it is planning to raise $ 1,000,000 floating rate notes indexed to LIBOR. As the bank is AAA rated, it can also issue fixed rate five-year bonds at 8%. On the other hand, there is a manufacturing firm, Infitech corporation, that needs funds ($ 1,000,000) in US dollar for 5 years to finance an upcoming project. The firm is not highly rated (say its rating is BBB), hence, the cost of issuing 5-year bond would be 10% for it. Or, it can go for 5-year floating rate notes, whose cost would be LIBOR + 0.75%.

Globex and Infitech Corporation, both will approach a swap bank for their requirements, which will set a fixed-for-floating interest rate swap that will be advantageous to both counterparties. Now, for setting up the transaction the swap bank will charge some commission. Suppose, the rate quoted by swap bank for US dollar interest rate swaps is 8.50–8.75 against LIBOR flat. A quality spread differential (QSD) is a prerequisite for the swap to exist. Default-risk premium differentials on fixed-rate and floating-rate debt are different from one another, and this difference is known as a QSD. The former is typically greater than the latter. This is due to the fact that the yield curve for debt with lower ratings has a tendency to be steeper than the yield curve for debt with better ratings. Financial theorists have provided numerous explanations for this occurrence, but none of them are entirely convincing. The QSD calculation is shown in Table 7.1. Given the existence of a QSD, each counterparty may issue the debt option that is least favourable to them (given their financing requirements), then swap interest payments to ensure that each counterparty receives the desired type of interest payment at a lower all-in cost than it could arrange independently.

TABLE 7.1 Quality Spread Differential

	Globex	*Infitech Corporation*	*Differential*
Fixed Rate	8%	10%	2%
Floating Rate	LIBOR	LIBOR + 0.75%	0.75%
			1.25%

The situation that the swap bank might set up for the two counterparties is shown in Figure 7.2.

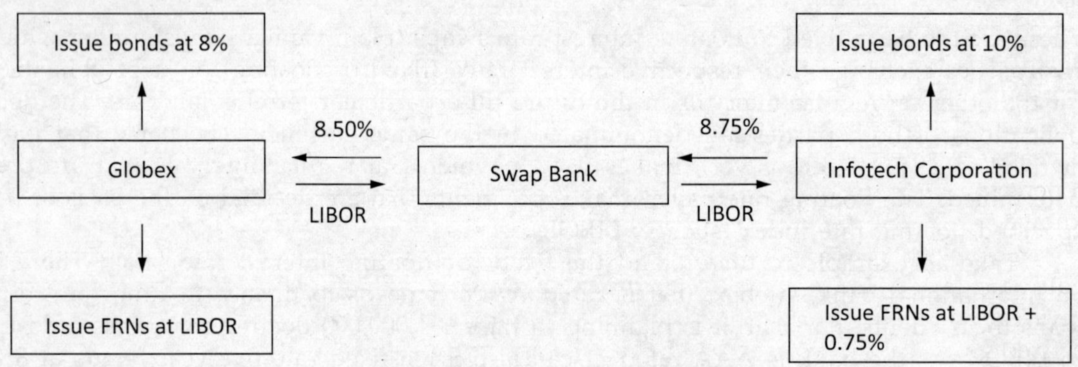

FIGURE 7.2 Interest Rate Swap.

The Globex has absolute advantage in the debt market because of its higher ratings than the Infitech corporation and it has comparative advantage in case of fixed rate debts. Hence, Globex will issue 5-year fixed rate bonds at the rate of 8% from the market on the other hand the Infitech corporation will issue FRNs at LIBOR plus 0.75%. Now, Globex through swap bank gets 8.50% of the notional principal in return as interest while it has to only pay 8% of the notional principal to service the debt obligation. On the other hand, it has to pay at the rate of LIBOR to the swap bank. Similarly, Infitech corporation through swap bank gets LIBOR, whereas it has to pay LIBOR + 0.75% to service the debt obligation on FRNs, while paying 8.75% on the notional principal to the swap bank. In the whole transaction, the swap bank earns its commission of 0.25% whereas both the counterparties benefited because of the low cost of debt. The whole transaction is explained in the Figure 7.2 and Table 7.2 as well.

TABLE 7.2 Net Cash Flows

	Globex	*Swap Bank*	*Infitech Corporation*
Pays	LIBOR	8.50%	8.75%
	8%	LIBOR	LIBOR + 0.75%
Receives	– 8.50%	– 8.75%	– LIBOR
		– LIBOR	
Net	LIBOR – .50%	0.25%	9.5%

7.6.2 Currency Swaps

Under currency swaps, the two parties exchange the interest rate on debt raised in their respective currencies. The two currencies must be different in the cross-currency swaps.

Take following example to understand the currency swap:

A US Corporation has to invest in France in order to expand its operations there. It has decided to set up another plant for its French subsidiary there with an economic life of 5 years. The cost of plant is estimated to be €50,000,000. The current currency exchange rate is $1.10/€1.00. The Corporation has the option to raise $55,000,000 via bonds for five years at the rate of 7 percent in the US capital market, and then convert the raised amount in euros for the project. The plant is estimated to be profitable and hence able to service the liabilities arising out of the loan. But, in this case, long-term transaction exposure will be created as the repayment has to be made in dollars. The US corporation can also raise the required amount (€50,000,000) by issuing euro-denominated bonds for 5 years in international market. Let's say the cost for issuing 5 years Eurobonds will be 6 percent for the corporation because it is not well known (the rate is 5 percent for a well-known firm).

Suppose, there is a French corporation with similar financing requirement and equivalent credit rating. Its US subsidiary requires $55,000,000 to finance a capital investment with a five-year economic life. The French parent may raise €50,000,000 at a fixed rate of 5% on the French bond market and convert the money to dollars to pay for the expense. Yet, if the euro significantly strengthens versus the dollar, transaction exposure is produced. In this situation, it might be difficult for the American subsidiary to make enough money in dollars to pay the obligation. The French parent can also issue Eurodollar bonds in the US capital market, but as its not well known there, the cost of borrowing would be a fixed rate of 8.5 percent.

The difficulty that each MNC has, namely, being exposed to long-term transaction risk or having to borrow money at a disadvantageous rate, could be resolved by a currency swap arranged by a swap bank that is acquainted with the financing requirements of the two Companies. The swap bank would suggest each parent company to raise capital in its domestic capital market, where it enjoys a competitive advantage due to brand recognition.

The principal amounts would then be traded via the swap bank. The French subsidiary would send €2,500,000 in interest (5 percent of €50,000,000) to its American parent each year, to be transferred through the swap bank to the French Corporation to pay the euro debt payment. In order to pay the US Corporation's dollar debt service, the French Corporation's US subsidiary would send $3,850,000 in interest (7 percent of $55,000,000) on a yearly basis. The subsidiaries would send the principal amounts to their respective parents at the debt retirement date so that they could be exchanged through the swap bank to pay off the bond issuance on the national capital markets.

The image depicts the structure of this currency swap. It proves that each counterparty saves money owing to their relative competitive advantage in their respective national capital markets. Instead of paying 6.5 percent on the Eurobond market, the US Company borrows euros through a currency swap at an all-in cost (AIC) of 5 percent. Instead of paying an interest of 8.5 percent on the Eurobond market, the French Business can borrow dollars at a 7 percent rate through the swap. The purpose of the currency swap is also to contractually lock in a range of future foreign exchange rates for each counterparty's debt payment obligations (Figure 7.3).

At the time of the transaction, the principal amounts are converted into euros at the rate of $1.10 to the euro, or $55,000,000 to € 50,000,000. The swap agreement requires the counterparties to exchange $3,850,000 in interest on the dollar debt for € 2,500,000 in interest on the euro debt each year prior to debt retirement; this corresponds to a contractual rate of $1.54/ € 1.00. A final exchange, consisting of the last interest payments and a re-exchange of the principal amounts, would happen on the maturity date: $58,850,000 for € 52,500,000. Hence, at year five, the contractual exchange rate is $1.3245 to € 1.00. In order for each counterparty to fulfil its debt service commitments during the swap's tenure, foreign currency rates are obviously locked in by the swap.

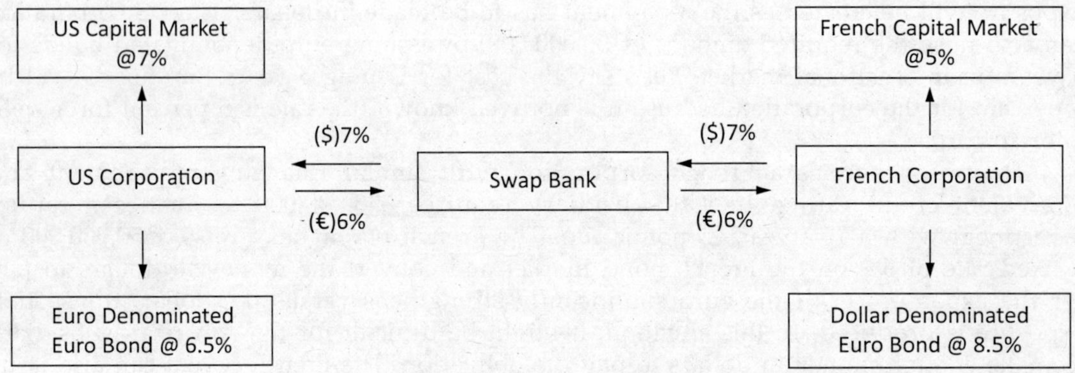

FIGURE 7.3 Currency Swap.

7.6.3 Risks of Interest Rate and Currency Swaps

Interest-rate risk refers to the risk of interest rates changing unfavourably before the swap bank can lay off on an opposing counterparty the other side of an interest rate swap entered into with a counterparty.

Basis risk refers to a situation in which the floating rates of the two counterparties are not pegged to the same index. Any difference in the indexes is known as the basis. For example, one counterparty could have its FRNs pegged to LIBOR, while the other counterparty has its FRNs pegged to the US Treasury bill rate. In this event, the indexes are not perfectly positively correlated and the swap may periodically be unprofitable for the swap bank. In our example, this would occur if the Treasury bill rate was substantially larger than LIBOR and the swap bank receives LIBOR from one counterparty and pays the Treasury bill rate to the other.

Exchange-rate risk refers to the risk the swap bank faces from fluctuating exchange rates during the time it takes for the bank to lay off a swap it undertakes with one counterparty with an opposing counterparty.

Credit risk refers to the probability that a counterparty, or even the swap bank, will default. These days a central clearing party stands between the swap dealer and each counterparty, guaranteeing fulfilment of both sides of an interest rate swap but not a currency swap.

Mismatch risk refers to the difficulty of finding an exact opposite match for a swap the bank has agreed to take. The mismatch may be with respect to the size of the principal sums the counterparties need, the maturity dates of the individual debt issues, or the debt service dates. Textbook illustrations typically ignore these real-life problems.

Sovereign risk refers to the probability that a country will impose exchange restrictions on a currency involved in a swap. This may make it very costly, or perhaps impossible, for a counterparty to fulfil its obligation to the dealer. In this event, provisions exist for terminating the swap, which results in a loss of revenue for the swap bank.

SUMMARY

1. Foreign Exchange Exposure refers to the sensitivity of a firm's cash flows, operating profit or the value of assets and liabilities due to the volatility of currency exchange rates. Whereas the foreign exchange risk is defined as the variability of the firm's cash flow, operating profit or the value of assets and liabilities due to its exposure to the movement of currency exchange rates.
2. It is conventional to classify foreign currency exposure into three categories: transaction exposure, translation exposure and economic exposure.
3. When a firm enters into a contract that requires payment or receipt of foreign currency at a future date, it exposes itself to transaction exposure. Transaction exposure can be hedged through financial techniques like money market hedge, forward market hedge, options and swaps and non-financial techniques like leading and lagging, netting and use of invoice currency.
4. Translation exposure, as the name suggests, is the variability in the reporting values of firms assets and liabilities that are denominated in foreign currency. It is not considered as real exposure but it surely effects the perception of firms for its stakeholders.
5. Economic exposure (sometimes referred as operating exposure) effects the long-term cash flows and operating profits of the firm by affecting its overall competitiveness in the market. The market structure in which the firm is operating as well as its ability to adjust its strategies as per the risk it faces, determines the extent of economic exposure. A firm can manage such exposure through long-term strategic measures like product differentiation. Market diversification, relocation of production sites, etc.

KEY WORDS

- Foreign Exchange Exposure
- Transaction Exposure
- Translation Exposure
- Economic Exposure
- Foreign Exchange Hedging

- Leading and Lagging
- Interest Rate Swap
- Cross Currency Swap

QUESTIONS

1. Define Transaction Exposure. How is it different from Translation Exposure?
2. Explain the various financial and non-financial techniques to hedge transaction exposure.
3. What is Economic Exposure? Why Economic Exposure has long-term effects on the performance of a firm?
4. Discuss the determinants of economic exposure.
5. Explain how cross currency swap helps in hedging transaction exposure.

REFERENCES AND SUGGESTED READINGS

1. Adler, Michael, and Bernard Dumas. "Exposure to Currency Risk: Definition and Measurement", *Financial Management*, Spring (1984), pp. 41–50.
2. Allayannis, George, and Eli Ofek. "Exchange Rate Exposure, Hedging, and the Use of Foreign Currency Derivatives", *Journal of International Money and Finance* 20(2001), pp. 273–96.
3. Pringle, John, and Robert Connolly. "The Nature and Causes of Foreign Currency Exposure", *Journal of Applied Corporate Finance,* Fall (1993), pp. 61–72.

CHAPTER 8

International Banking System

LEARNING OUTCOMES

After reading this chapter, the reader will be able to:

- Discuss Growth of International Banking
- Interpret Theories and Expansion of International Banking
- Draw Framework of International Banking
- Explain Benefits of International Banking
- List Major Central Banking System
- Discuss Objective and Functions of the Federal Reserve Bank of United States
- Explain Organisational Structure and Functioning of the European Central Banking System
- Explain Organisational Structure and Functioning of Reserve Bank of India

8.1 GROWTH OF INTERNATIONAL BANKING

The global economy is so interconnected that international banking is an inevitable consequence of this reality. The development of international banking, as well as the transnational extension of banks via branches and subsidiaries, were both "pull" and "push" forces which helps in expanding financial and economic globalisation in the twentieth century as well as during the period preceding 1931 (Lessambo, 2016). The difference between international banking and other types of banking services is that international banking is conducted across many countries or globally. In other words, international banking is an agreement made by a residential bank in one nation to provide financial services to residents of another country in the same or a different country. This banking facility is used for transactions by the majority of global organisations as well as individuals. The worldwide financial market is significantly influenced by international banking activities (Brier & lia dwi jayanti, 2020). While studying the international banking there involves two set of problems, first industrial organisation concerns, which focus on the growth aspects of banks subsidiary outside the boundaries of domestic country and also for the banks based in the foreign industrial nations and the competitive advantage are the two sets of questions engaged in the examination of international banking. Second, international finance problems, concerns the part that banks play in international and cross-currency financial flows emanating from their headquarters and overseas operations (Hsing, et al., 2016). Overseas banks are a subgroup of local banks that have a considerable number of foreign branches and subsidiaries, therefore despite the focus on international banking, there are few truly international organisations. Additionally, although foreign cross-currency financial flows emanating from their headquarters and overseas operations (Hsing, et al., 2016). Overseas banks are a subgroup of local banks that have a considerable number of foreign branches and subsidiaries, therefore despite the focus on international banking, there are few truly international organisations. Additionally, although foreign currency trading may seem to be a distinctively international banking activity, in many countries, the majority or all of that trading is conducted by local banks with no or very few overseas offices. The expansion of major banks' overseas offices and affiliates happened in two distinct phases (Birindelli, et al., 2022). The first happened in the decades leading up to World War I; British banks with headquarters in the UK had 2,000 overseas branches, while their French and German counterparts had 500. US and Canada based banks have a less overseas offices. Since 1960, a second wave of foreign operations, subsidiaries, and other companies has emerged, bringing the total to 45,000. The fact that there aren't many influential banking system, global banks shouldn't detract from the reality that there are plenty (Hernandez, 2019). In 1975, there were 84 "deposit-taking bank with branches or majority-owned,". For more than a century, local and regional bank mergers have become national bank mergers. Some may view this trend as a natural progression that would eventually lead to the establishment of domestic banks' foreign branches and subsidiaries. A small number of banks control at least 80% of the deposit and loan markets in most countries. This is true for both major and small nations. Only in the United States, the top 100 banks account for less than 50% of market transactions. Analogies from other areas of international economics aid the understanding of the growth of banks into other nations. Thus, the standard questions presented in international commerce theory may be extended to international banking activity. The core issue of the theory of direct foreign investment may be extended to the international banking sector to assess whether the ownership structure of international banks is random or systematic in terms of the size or number of banks based in various countries. If the pattern of international banking is not random, then identifying the elements that determine ownership structures in international banking is one of the greatest obstacles (I. Settlements, 2009). One aspect of industrial organisation is that a company's ability to develop is contingent on its capacity to obtain money on more favourable terms than its rivals. Even though banks are so highly leveraged, the terms under which they can attract capital may play a central role in elucidating the trends in international banking, as small differences in the efficiency of individual banks or their operating, their profit rates significantly impacted by the environmental factor. Therefore, the pattern of growth of international banks must be linked with the issue of whether banks located in certain nations find it easier to recruit capital than those headquartered in others.

8.2 THEORY AND EXPANSION OF INTERNATIONAL BANKING

According to current banking theories, banking institutions undertake two separate activities: portfolio transformation and brokerage. In order to connect borrowers and lenders, brokers must gather, process, and provide information without changing the nature of the claims being exchanged. As brokers, banks benefit from reduced search, information, and transaction costs that help them overcome the information asymmetries and lessen market inefficiencies. By offering assessment, advice, and monitoring services, they generate revenue. Banks fulfil a role of portfolio transformation when they also provide solutions that qualitatively change the type of claims exchanged. Portfolio formation differs depending on the particular method used and the risk-reduction assurances provided (BATTILOSSI, 2000). When banks buy big assets as well as give borrowers debts that reflect a fraction of those assets without altering their liquidity features, this is known as a "liquidity distribution". Banks offer "liquidity services" and act as "liquidity creation agents" when they engage in "quality intermediation" and issue contracts to lenders and borrowers that are qualitatively distinct. By taking part in "maturity transformation," banks offer "liquidity insurance" to depositors and lenders (Bertay & Bruhn, 2017)." Since that they are taking on greater interest, credit, and default risks, their management may have a greater incentive to assess, regulate, and control borrowers in order to reduce the risks for negative selection and ethical hazard. Finally, banks provide off-balance sheet services, such as intermediate-level guarantees and commitments, which might obfuscate the distinction among brokerage and portfolio transformation.

The gravitational pull effect occurs when banks go overseas to service their domestic clients who have relocated abroad. The lack of capacity of domestic banks in the host nations to service the local branches of source-country companies is used to explain the nineteenth-century expansion of colonial banks' abroad subsidiaries (Casella & Berger, 1994). However, throughout the last several decades, many of the multinational banks' overseas branches have been opened in industrialised nations that have strong host-country banking systems. The revised justification is that banks follow their domestic clients overseas to lessen the possibility that they would lose their business to banks in the host nation. These international branches are likely to provide credit and offer other services to the same companies' overseas affiliates as they do at home (Finel-Honigman & Sotelino, 2015).

According to a casual observation theory, the overseas development of industrial companies with headquarters in a given country reflects the foreign expansion of banks with that country's headquarters in numerous foreign markets. As a result, American corporations and banks both saw tremendous international growth in the early periods (Altamura & Zendejas, 2020). In contrast, banks with headquarters in several Western European nations and Japan grew in the United States in the late 1970s and early 1980s.

According to one interpretation of the pattern of expansion, banks with headquarters in nations with relatively small spreads between the interest rates they charge for deposits and the interest rates they receive for loans would be more likely to open branches oversea due to having developed low-cost intermediation technologies (McPhilemy & Moschella, 2019). Instead of being a firm-specific advantage held by a collection of businesses that operate in a certain area, the low spreads might represent a location-specific advantage that reflects the factor endowments of that country.

Expansion of global banks may be attributed to the eclectic theory of production, which incorporates benefits associated with ownership and geographical location. This theory of multinational banking seems to have had little capacity to foresee the explosive increase of investment in US banks till late 1970s (McCauley, et al., 2002).

Perhaps the most obvious manifestation of financial globalisation was the growth of banks' international activity outside of the "core" industrialised nations. Most nations allowed foreign banks to operate freely, subject only to certain political and economic circumstances. Agencies, branches, subsidiaries, or joint ventures were involved. Two major patterns of transnationalization emerged from a variety of motivations, strategies, organisational structures, and operating standards that varied between banks and nations. The benefits of economic and financial infiltration into the host countries were the motivation for one, while direct access to global financial markets was the motivation for the other. There is a long history of resilience among the foreign banks at the time of facing the external and internal shocks like mergers and acquisitions, reorganisations, crises, and financial turmoil. Banks like Deutsche Bank, United Bank of Switzerland, HSBC, UniCredit, and Citibank transformed from global powerhouses to multinational conglomerates in the latter decades of the 20th century, with profits increasingly coming from their overseas investment and corporate arms rather than their domestic retail operations (Claessens, 2017; B. for I. Settlements, 2022). As transactions have grown to rely on the political and economic circumstances of more than one country, as well as the stability and efficacy of more than one set of regulations and financial mores, the interconnectedness of international banks has expanded (Jervis, 2016).

8.2.1 Framework of International Banking

In international banking system, banks are responsible for number of activities including interbank lending, allocation of resources, risk diversification, assisting the savers regarding mobilization of their saving, equity investment, paying dividend and issue intragroup loans as shown in Figure 8.1.

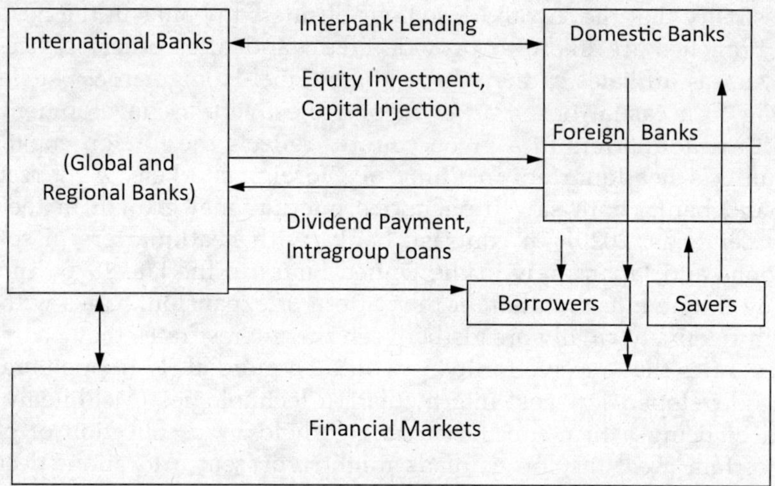

FIGURE 8.1 Framework of International Banking.

8.2.2 Benefits of International Banking

Flexibility

The ability to transact in several currencies is made possible by this banking service for global corporations. The euro, dollar, British pound, Indian rupee, and sterling pound are the principal currencies that transnational corporations and people may work with. Through this banking, businesses having headquarters in other nations may effectively control existing bank accounts and use financial services elsewhere.

Accessibility

Accessibility and simplicity of doing business are provided by international banking to businesses from several nations. Anywhere in the globe, a person or MNC may utilise their money. They now have the flexibility to do business and utilise their money to fulfil any financial need anywhere in the globe.

International Bank Transfers

Due to global banking, the corporation are able to pay bills abroad. The firms can send and receive money easily because of the smooth currency conversion mechanism. Moreover, benefits for overseas transactions are always available, including overdraft facilities for the larger institutions, providing loans, and giving access to deposit globally, etc. Correspondent banking is quite helpful in these kinds of transactions.

Accounts Maintenance

International banking can assist multinational corporations in fairly maintaining the records of their worldwide finances. The books of every bank in the world include a record of every transaction made by the organisation. The company's accounting may be kept up with by assembling the data and numbers.

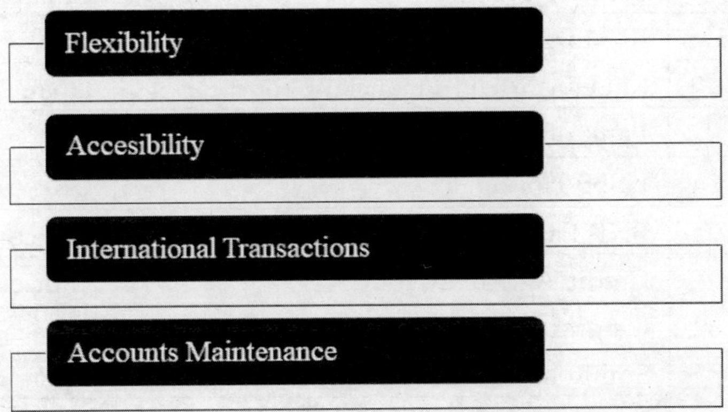

FIGURE 8.2 Benefits of International Banking.

In 2021, major Chinese bankers continued to hold the top spot as the largest financial institutions in the world, but European banks' dominance in the rankings of global asset size diminished somewhat. According to S&P Global Market Intelligence, 27 among 37 European banks on the list of the 100 biggest banks in the world had their positions drop from one to nine spots as of the end of 2021 from the previous year as shown in Table 8.1. The combined assets of all the listed European banks decreased by 2.16% to $36.890 trillion in 2021 from $37.707 trillion the previous year. Due to competition from large US lenders, several European lenders witnessed a decline in their balance sheets after reducing their operations there. For instance, Spain's Banco Bilbao Vizcaya Argentaria SA dropped one spot to No. 47 after selling a US operation with 639 branches and around $103 billion in total assets. However, by shifting its focus to Asia's wealth management market, HSBC Holdings PLC was able to somewhat offset the effects of selling its retail banking businesses in the United States and France to preserve its position and asset size. The effect of the Russia-Ukraine war and a rebound of Covid-19 infections in numerous regions of the globe are projected to weigh on the international economy this year. As production began to recover from the epidemic in the majority of the nations in 2021, growth was already anticipated to decline. These two elements are anticipated to make the normalisation of monetary policy more challenging as global central banks become wary about preventing economic recovery from being harmed by premature tightening in the face of excessive inflation.

TABLE 8.1 World's 20 Largest Banks, 2022

Current Rank	*Previous Rank*	*Bank*	*Country*	*Total Assets (US$ billion)*
1	1	Industrial and Commercial Bank of China	China	5,536.53
2	2	China Construction Bank	China	4,762.46
3	3	Agricultural Bank of China	China	4575.95
4	4	Bank of China	China	4206.53
5	6	JP Morgan Chase		3743.57
6	5	Mitsubishi UFJ Financial Group	Japan	3176.84
7	9	Bank of America	US	3169.50
8	8	HSBS Holdings	UK	2953.64
9	7	BNP Paribas SA	France	2905.83
10	10	Credit Agricole Group	France	2674.35
11	11	Citigroup Inc.	US	2291.41
12	12	Sumitomo Mitsui Financial Group	Japan	2176.94
13	13	Japan Post Bank	Japan	1998.98
14	20	Postal Saving Bank of China	China	1981.53
15	14	Mizuho Financial Group	Japan	1897.87
16	15	Wells Fargo	US	1948.07
17	17	Barclays PLC	UK	1874.40
18	21	Bank of Communications	China	1836.38
19	16	Banco Santander SA	Spain	1814.90
20	19	Groupe BPCE	France	1724.12

Source: S&P Capital IQ (World, et al., 2016)

Major Chinese banks maintained its four largest positions while expanding their balance sheets, increasing their advantage over the majority of other banks worldwide as shown in Table 8.2. In 2021, the combined assets of these banks increased 10.2% from $17.321 trillion to $19.081 trillion. China has reportedly been encouraging banks to increase lending to infrastructure development projects and small businesses while cutting interest rates to free up more money for lending, according to Nathan Stovall, chief analyst at Market Intelligence. The program's goal was to speed up the economic recovery, which started to slow down once more during the latter half of the year 2021 as a result of an increase in real estate developers' bond payment defaults.

TABLE 8.2 Top 100 World Largest Bank by Country

Number of Banks in Top 100	*Country*
27	European Union
19	China
11	United States
8	Japan
6	France
6	United Kingdom
6	South Korea
5	Canada
5	Germany
4	Spain
4	Australia
4	Brazil
3	Sweden
3	Netherland
3	Switzerland
3	Singapore
2	Italy
1	Austria
1	Belgium
1	Denmark
1	Finland
1	India
1	Norway
1	Russia
1	Qatar

Source: S&P Capital IQ

8.3 MAJOR CENTRAL BANKS ACROSS THE WORLD

8.3.1 The Federal Reserve Bank (US)

The Federal Reserve Bank has been the country's central bank. Instead of carrying out commercial banking operations, the Federal Reserve's objective is to sustain steady economic expansion. The Federal Reserve was initially founded by the Owen-Glass bill, which was proposed to both chambers of Congress and enacted on December 1913. Since its creation, the Federal Reserve has been tasked with three core duties:

1. to provide a flexible money supply;
2. to offer a systematic procedure for commercial debt discounting; and
3. to oversee and control the country's banks.

Later, the Federal Reserve was also given the task of ensuring employment as well due to changes in the contemporary economy and demands. It is essential to throw light on the historical events that served as the foundation for the Federal Bank of the United States in order to better comprehend the Banking system. Throughout the 19th and 20th century, there were several crises in the US financial sector. During the economic crisis, many corporations and banks risked insolvency. One of the main causes of the economy's vulnerability to financial panic was the nation's banking system's failure to effectively finance struggling depository institutions. After the financial crisis of 1907, Congress created National Monetary Commission, that put out suggestions for creating a body to help avoid and manage future financial crises. Payments were interrupted nationwide at this period due to the refusal of several institutions at the time of clearing cheques made on the behalf of specific companies; this practise led to the demise of some otherwise viable banks. Since, none of these actions has been approved by the President or by the government, it is typically viewed as an autonomous central bank. However, the US Congress has oversight over it. The broad goals of the government's policies must be followed by the Federal Reserve in its operations and the central banking system failed to adopt the same. As a consequence, there was tension between the need to hire a government agency and the desire to establish a strong private central bank. Finally, in the progressive Era, the Federal Reserve Act of 1913, which merged private banks with governmental control, was proposed by President Woodrow Wilson and passed by Congress. The organisation structure of Federal Reserve has been shown in Figure 8.3.

FIGURE 8.3 Organisational Structure of Federal Reserve.

Functions of Federal Reserve System

Determining the Level of Reserve Rates: The amount that member banks are required to reserve against deposits is determined by the federal reserve bank. Banks may raise the percentage of cash they can lend to clients by decreasing the necessary reserve-level rate. The reserve-level rates are one of the measures the Federal Reserve may consider when the economy is stagnant or weak in order to stimulate it.

Deciding Discount Rates: A rise in the discount rate during an inflationary period tends to slow down economic activity since banks then charge borrowers higher interest rates. A reduction in the discount rate aims to increase commercial activity. A "discount window" is another name for a Fed Reserve facility that lends money to a member bank.

Federal Fund Rates: It is a significant instrument that has an impact on typical bank operations. This is the price for an overnight loan of cash from a depository institution to another. Whenever a bank is cash-strapped and another is full of cash, this situation arises. The rate is flexible and might vary between bank to bank and day to day.

Open Market Operations: The FOMC carries out these actions, which are often known as "quantitative easing." Several times every week, the Federal banks buys and sells Treasury bills and other US government assets from financial organisations. The sums that banks possess and available for lending. For instance, when the Fed purchases securities, banks have more money, which leads to a decrease in interest rates. When the Fed sells its securities, the reverse happens. In general, open market operations are the Fed's most effective weapon for influencing monetary policy.

8.3.2 The European Central Banking System

EU leaders take the historic move towards the integration of Europe by signing the Rome Treaty (1957) on May 3, 1998. Substantially, they agreed that the Economic and Monetary Union (EMU) of the EU would take over the sole responsibility for monetary policy inside the Union from the central banks of EU member states. The majority of EMU countries had decided that national currencies will not be used, which became the foundation of the union. Virtually all national currencies have been replaced by the euro (€). To be eligible for membership in the European System of Central Banks (ESCB), a member country must fulfil the following criteria:

1. strong price stability,
2. good public finances,
3. a stable exchange rate, and
4. structure of interest rates.

The ESCBs and the central banks of the 16 European Union countries that use the euro form the Eurosystem.

The ESCB and the European Central Bank were both established in June 1998. In spite of the fact that no founding members envisioned a unified currency, the groundwork for what would eventually become the ECB and the EMU was laid in January 1958, in accordance with the Rome Treaty. The ECB officially adopted the euro as its single currency in January 1999. The previous national currencies of the participating member states have their exchange rates frozen indefinitely, and an unified monetary policy for the Euro area has been established. So, the European Union's member states have effectively abandoned its autonomy in the area of monetary policy by declaring euro the sole currency in use in the Eurozone. Because to the creation of the euro currency, that was intended to bring EU states closer together economically, the EU's weaker members can draw strength from the more productive ones and narrow the growth and productivity gap.

Organisation Structure of European Central Bank

The organisational structure of European Central Bank consists of Executive board, governing council and general council as shown in Figure 8.4.

Executive Board: The President and Vice President of the ECB sit on the Executive Board, together with four others chosen by the heads of state or government in the Eurozone. All of the aforementioned individuals, plus the heads of the central banks of the 16 countries that make up the Eurozone, make up the Executive Board. Non-renewable eight-year periods are assigned to Executive Board members.

It is the duty of the Executive Board to execute monetary policy as set out by the Governing Council and to provide directives to national central banks in this regard. It is also in charge of managing the ECB on a day-to-day basis and preparing for Governing Council meetings.

Governing Council: The Governing Council of the ECB is the institution inside the ECB that is tasked with making the most important decisions. The governors of the 15 central banks that make up the Eurozone are included in its membership along with 6 executive board members. It is presided over by President of the ECB. Its principal responsibility is to establish monetary policy and particular in determining the interest rates of commercial banks' lending from Central Bank. In addition, it is responsible for determining the composition of policy for the European Union.

General Council: ECBs general council is composed of the President and Vice President of the European Central Bank, as well as the Governors of the National Central Banks of each of the 27 EU Member States. The General Council is responsible for approving rules and making decisions that will guarantee the Eurosystem will continue to execute the duties that have been assigned to it.

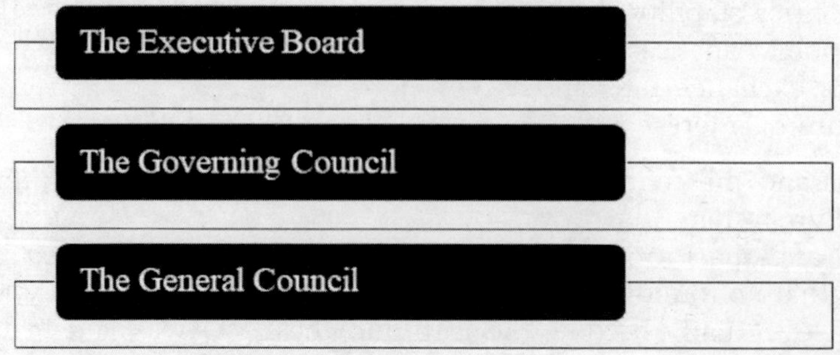

FIGURE 8.4 Organisational Structure of European Central Bank.

8.3.3 Reserve Bank of India

Improving the banking services throughout the country and to divide monetary policy from fiscal policy, Hilton Young Commission proposed the creation of a central bank in 1926. RBI, the country's central bank, is in charge of overseeing the banking and payment systems, maintaining monetary stability, and managing currency. The RBI bank is crucial to the Indian economy since it manages both the currency and the credit systems. But as the nation's economic climate has changed and the economy has become more worldwide, so have its functions. Prior to being becoming a government entity by The Banking Regulation Act of 1940, the RBI was once a private enterprise. Once located in Kolkata, the RBI's current headquarters have been in Mumbai, since 1937. The Reserve Bank of India is comprised of a central office and 26 regional and branch locations around India.

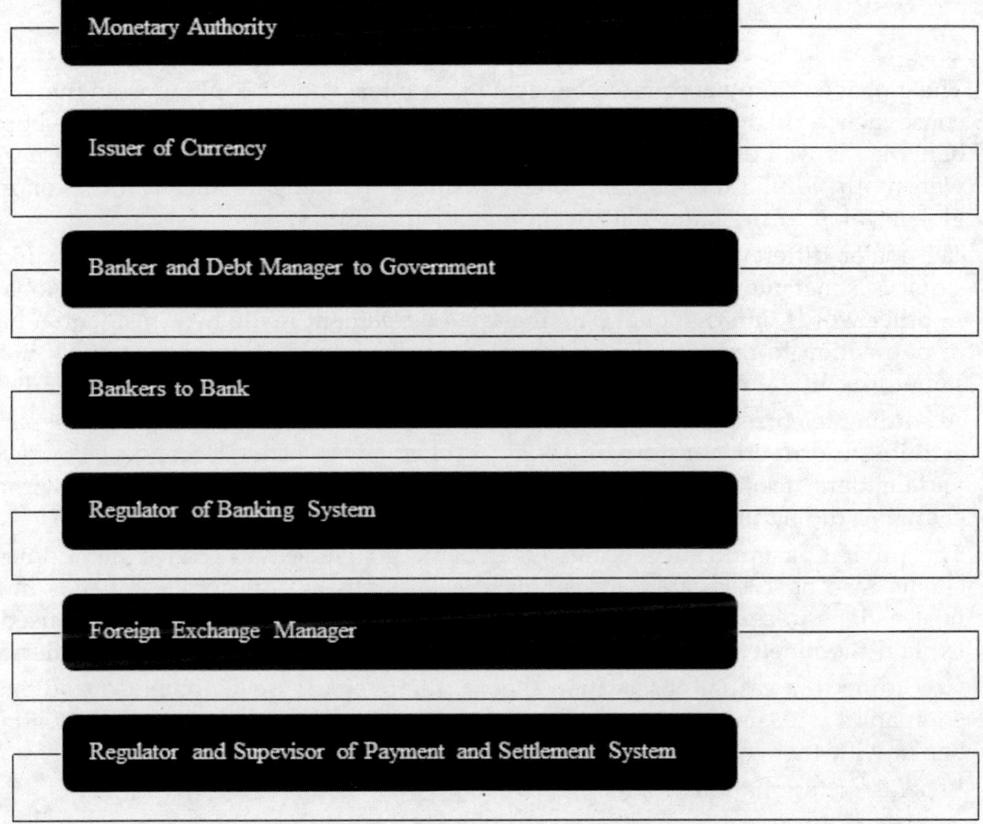

FIGURE 8.5 Functions of RBI.

Organisational Structure of RBI

Central Board of Directors: The RBI is run by the Central Board. There are 20 people constitutes the board.

- The head of the Reserve Bank of India (RBI) is appointed by the national government for a five-year term and may be reappointment for a second term. The Governor serves as the head and board chairman.

- Deputy Governor, consist of four members appointed by government as well for the period of five-year.
- Fifteen Directors are appointed by central government for the period of four years.

The Local Board: The local board consists of five members and are chosen by the government for a 4-year term that may be extended. The Chairman is chosen by each Local Board among its members. The Local Boards' authority is constrained.

Structure of RBI: The RBI is divided into 26 departments, each of which focuses on local policy concerns. In addition to these divisions, there are twenty-six regional offices and branches that serve as the RBI's public face, as well as research institutions, subsidiaries, and training facilities that provide formation, training, and updates.

SUMMARY

1. The global economy is so interconnected that international banking is an inevitable consequence of this reality. The development of international and cross-border banking, as well as banks' transnational expansion via branches and subsidiaries, were both "pull" and "push" forces within expanding financial and economic globalisation in the latter half of the twentieth century.
2. The major difference between international banking and other types of banking services is that international banking is conducted across many countries or globally. In other words, international banking is an agreement made by a residential bank in one nation to provide financial services to residents of another country in the same or a different country.
3. According to current banking theories, banking institutions undertake two separate activities: portfolio transformation and brokerage. In order to connect borrowers and lenders, brokers must gather, process, and provide information without changing the nature of the claims being exchanged.
4. The gravitational pull effect occurs when banks go overseas to service their domestic clients who have relocated abroad. The lack of capacity of domestic banks in the host nations to service the local branches of source-country companies is used to explain the nineteenth-century expansion of colonial banks' abroad subsidiaries.
5. According to a casual observation theory, the overseas development of industrial companies with headquarters in a given country reflects the foreign expansion of banks with that country's headquarters in numerous foreign markets.
6. Benefits of International Banking:
   - Accessibility
   - Flexibility
   - International Transactions
   - Account Maintenance
7. Major Central Banks across the World:
   - Federal Reserve Bank of United States
   - The European Central Bank
   - Reserve Bank of India

KEY WORDS

- International Banking
- Gravitational Pull Effect
- Casual Observation Theory
- Open Market Operations
- Inter-Bank Lending
- International Transactions

QUESTIONS

1. Explain the growth of international banking in phases.
2. What are various theories involved in international banking?
3. Explain the expansion and structure of international banking.
4. What are the benefits of international banking?
5. Write a brief note about the following:
    - Federal Reserve Bank of United States
    - The European Central Bank
    - Reserve Bank of India

REFERENCES AND SUGGESTED READINGS

1. Altamura, C.E., & Zendejas, J.F. (2020). Politics. International Banking, and the Debt Crisis of 1982, *Business History Review*, 94(4), 753–778. https://doi.org/10.1017/S0007680520000653
2. BATTILOSSI, S. (2000). Financial innovation and the golden ages of international banking: 1890–1931 and 1958–81, *Financial History Review*, 7(2), 141–175. https://doi.org/10.1017/s0968565000000093
3. Bertay, A., & Bruhn, M. (2017). *International Banking, A conceptual framework for understanding international banking*. http://www.worldbank.org/financial-development
4. Birindelli, G., Bonanno, G., Dell'Atti, S., & Iannuzzi, A. P. (2022). Climate change commitment, credit risk and the country's environmental performance: Empirical evidence from a sample of international banks, *Business Strategy and the Environment*, 31(4), 1641–1655. https://doi.org/10.1002/bse.2974
5. Brier, J., & lia dwi jayanti. (2020). *A Theory of Domestic and International Trade Finance* (Vol. 21, Issue 1). http://journal.um-surabaya.ac.id/index.php/JKM/article/view/2203
6. Casella, G., & Berger, R. L. (1994). *A Theory of International Organization*, Oxford University Press, 3025(1), 3025.
7. Claessens, S. (2017). Global banking: Recent developments and insights from research, *Review of Finance*, 21(4), 1513–1555. https://doi.org/10.1093/rof/rfw045

8. Finel-Honigman, I., & Sotelino, F.B. (2015). International banking for a new century, In *International Banking for a New Century*. https://doi.org/10.4324/9781315723174
9. Hernandez, C. (2019). *Globalisation, the IMF, and International Banks in Argentina* (Issue September).
10. Hsing, Y., Stability, R., Reforms, S., Debrun, X., Library, L.S.E., Pamphlets, L.S. E.S., Buckberg, E., Economics, D., Studies, E., Journal, B., Studies, E., Economics, J., & Shambaugh, J.C. (2016). International Banking : A Survey Author, *Journal of Money Credit and Banking, 16*(1), 301–352.
11. Jervis, R. (2016). Theories of international relations, In *Explaining the History of American Foreign Relations*. https://doi.org/10.1017/CBO9781107286207.002
12. Lessambo, F. (2016). *The International Banking System*.
13. McCauley, R. N., Ruud, J. S., & Wooldridge, P. D. (2002). Globalising international banking, *BIS Quarterly Review, March*(March), 41–51. http://www.bis.org/publ/qtrpdf/r_qt0203e.pdf
14. McPhilemy, S., & Moschella, M. (2019). Central banks under stress: Reputation, accountability and regulatory coherence, *Public Administration*, 97(3), 489–498. https://doi.org/10.1111/padm.12606
15. Settlements, B. for I. (2022). *Statistical release*: BIS international banking statistics and global liquidity indicators at end-December 2020. *April*, 1–20.
16. Settlements, I. (2009). International banking and financial market developments. *Policy, December* (June), 1–72. www.bis.org
17. World, T., Corporations, L., July, F. M., & Magazine, F. (2016). *The World's 100 Largest Corporations*, *47*, 1–3.

CHAPTER 9

International Money Market

LEARNING OUTCOMES

After reading this chapter, the reader will be able to:

- Give the Overview of Money Market
- Compare Domestic Financial Market vs. International Financial Centers
- Elucidate Globalisation of the Money Market
  - ♦ Discuss US, European, and Asian Money Markets
- Elucidate History and Function of the International Monetary Market
- Discuss Major Currency Crisis of the World

9.1 MONEY MARKET: AN OVERVIEW

The money market is essential to the growth of economies because it offers borrowing power and lends money for short periods, often with maturities of one year or less. The developed economies have fairly structured money markets where short-term loans are made, and the local currency is utilised in exchange. Regarding the regularity authority of the national and central banks, the UK, the US, Japan, and Germany have fully matured markets. Even though these are domestic markets, the emphasis will be on the so-called Eurocurrency market, which serves as a hub for international markets accepting deposits in local domestic currencies outside their home nations.

The trading of foreign currencies in the international money market takes place among central banks of the countries. Gold or US dollars are the important foundation for these trades. Money borrowed or loaned by governments or major financial organisations is fundamental activity of the international money market. The trans-border financial transfer policies of different countries' currencies control the international money market (Chismolm, 2009). Managing currency exchange between nations is one of the primary responsibilities of the international money market. Forex trading is the term used to describe the exchange of one currency for another. The foreign money market has relatively substantial financial transfers, unlike share markets. Large financial institutions comprise most of the market's participants rather than individuals (Accominotti, et al., 2021). Investments made in the foreign money market are less hazardous, and as a result, they also provide lower profits. The rates at which the international money market constantly monitors different currency pairings trade hands refer as mid-market exchange rate where each currency pair have their mid-market rate which is influenced by national and international macroeconomic forces. Popular indexes that subtly influence the international money market include currency trades and exchange rate frameworks.

9.2 DOMESTIC FINANCIAL MARKET VS. INTERNATIONAL FINANCIAL CENTERS

Mobilizing money and allocating it to different consumers based on predicted risk-adjusted returns seem to be the primary roles of a money market and its intermediaries. The financial system allows for the smooth passing of risk and the mitigation of uncertainty. The financial markets play a role in the oversight and control of corporations and their management once investors have put their money to work. The liquidity provided by financial markets allows investors to sell their holdings before they mature, encouraging them to put their money into productive long-term endeavours. An increased number of innovative projects are funded, managers are pushed to operate enterprises in line with client objectives, the pace of creativity increases, and people are empowered to choose their desired spending patterns and risk-reward trade-off (Glasner, 2009; Hachey, 1983; Journals & Studies, 1983). When property rights are protected, contracts are simple to uphold, meaningful accounting information is readily available, and both borrowers and investors are held accountable for the decisions they make and the economic repercussions of their actions, financial markets can function at their highest level of efficiency (Klopstock, 1965). The inability of markets to allocate capital, which negatively impacts economic growth effectively, results from the lack of specific criteria. The economic debacle in Asia demonstrates the perils of distributing money via nepotism and bureaucratic dictates instead of using a reasonable method and is controlled by accurate evaluations of the potential risks and rewards involved. Such control capitalism led to the development of inefficient financial markets, which spent hundreds of billions of dollars' worth of hard-earned resources on worthless investments and extravagant projects, and also gave rise to corruption that has no end in sight. The disaster that has befallen Japan's banking industry is a continual demonstration of the difficulties that might occur in a financial system when the core components of transparency and accountability are not only lacking in the system but also run counter to the official policy (Altavilla, et al., 2021). Similarly, the global financial crisis that emerged due to the subprime mortgage fiasco is an example of how fast and broadly wealth may be lost when financial incentives are distorted, and financial contracts are not transparent.

9.3 THE GLOBALISATION OF THE MONEY MARKET

The advancement in technologies and interconnection among the economies have reduced the cost of capital and provided better access to multinational firms for financing. Combining it with deregulation and regulatory support inhibits the competitive environment that protects the domestic market and provides better opportunities. So, the globalisation of money markets brings out unprecedented competition among the key international money market centres and assists multinationals in raising funds at a decreased cost. The increase in competition among the financial centres led to increased deregulation for the money markets worldwide, which fasten the process of **"Arbitraging"** where money market regulators issue and trade instruments in financial centres and with lower regulations from financial institutions and government and hence decrease the cost as well.

9.3.1 Origin and Development

Large multinational corporations, pension funds, insurance companies, government states, regulatory authorities, financial institutions like banks and corporations, and the government and its agencies are the participants on both the borrower and investor sides of the international money markets. The US, European and the Asian money market are three significant components of the established international money market.

US Money Market

The period after the great depression saw a sudden change in the shifting laws of banks, and gold was withdrawn from internal circulation in 1933. The US government restricted their gold payment only to settle their international payment requirement. Thus, the price was raised, and the US dollar became the key currency for the international gold bullion standard. The Federal Reserve system takes charge and issues commercial bank deposits to lower reserve ratios.

The Federal Reserve system, consisting of the twelve federal reserve banks as well as a board of governors chosen by the president and confirmed by the senate, was established in 1913. As a result, the Federal Open Market Committee, which is made up of governors, the president of the New York Bank, and 11 district banks, makes all the regulatory decisions with regards to the supply and circulation of the money market. Currently, the US money market is one of the largest in transactions compared to any other market around the world. The market participants are pretty heterogeneous, including financials and non-financials firms (Jurnal & Saham, 2021; Li, et al., 2021). Also, the market consists of a wide variety of substitutes.

European Money Market

The decades following the World War II, particularly during the period of 1960s and 1970s, can be identify as the origins of the European market. This was when the MNCs were expanding their businesses across the border and needed international funds to monitor their operations as the foreign nations widely accepted the US dollar for international trade (Eagly & Smith, 2022; Li, et al., 2021). Companies placed dollars in European banks for this reason as well as to do commercial activity in European nations. Banks took the deposits in dollars to lend to the European corporate customer base. The dollars that were placed in the bank were called as **Eurodollars**, as well as the marketplace where they are traded is called the **Eurocurrency Market.** Still, the exciting thing here is that people often mistake these Eurodollars with the "Euro," which is the common currency of European nations. There were many reasons for the rapid rise of Eurocurrency market including the policy measure taken in US which restricted US banks' ability to lend abroad in 1968, due to which multinational corporations faced the problem obtaining US dollars, so these foreign subsidies moved towards the Eurocurrency market for obtaining the US dollars from the banks in Europe (Baghai, et al., 2022; Rime et al., 2022). Another important reason for the growing importance of the Eurocurrency market is the dominant position of OPEC. OPEC needs the payment of oil in the form of dollars, and they started depositing their portion of oil revenues in banks. These types of deposits are known as petrodollars. At the time of cash sorting, these petrodollars are used to pay oil-importing countries. This process helps many countries in the smooth flow of funds.

There are many other developed international money markets today, but the European money market still plays a crucial role. London had been and still is the primary hub for euro currency transactions. The LIBOR's popularity has increased significantly (Rao, et al., 1983). Table 9.1 shows the LIBOR interest rates by the currencies USD, GBP, and JPY for overnight, one month, three months, six months, and for a year, and Table 9.2 shows the alternative interest rates of Sterling Overnight Interest Rates (SONIA) and European Interbank Interest Rates (EURIBOR). Several banks will lend money to one another in the London money market, and that rate is known as the London Interbank Offered Rate (LIBOR). Starting in 2022, LIBOR will be available in five different maturities (ranging from overnight to 12 months) and three different currencies. Every business day at 11:45 am, the official LIBOR interest rates are released.

TABLE 9.1 LIBOR Rate Quotations: December 16, 2022

	Overnight	*One Month*	*Three Month*	*Six Month*	*One Year*
USD LIBOR	3.81586%	4.32629%	4.73629%	5.12529%	5.40686%
GBP LIBOR	3.38790%	3.48780%	3.79420%	4.29550	4.25590%
JPY LIBOR	−0.06005%	0.03758&	−0.004836%	0.03713%	0.04836%

Source: globalrates.com

TABLE 9.2 First Interest Rate Per Month for Year 2022

First Rate Per Month (SONIA)	*EURIBOR Rates 2022*		*First Rate Per Month*
December	2.9279%	December	1.398%
November	2.1856%	November	1.159%
October	2.1880%	October	0.659%
September	1.6902%	September	−0.073%
August	1.1910%	August	−0.071%
July	1.1907%	July	−0.565%
June	0.9389%	June	−0.577%
May	0.6906%	May	−0.568%
April	0.6906%	April	−0.564%
March	0.4451%	March	−0.565%
February	0.1957%	February	−0.567%
January	0.1947%	January	−0.587%

Source: globalrates.com

Implications of Euro-Currency Markets

First, the prevalence of Euro-currency funds has made liabilities of commercial banks denominated in a currency different from their own, its principal medium for international money market activities for participants apart from central banks. Such commitments are non-negotiable, require no collateral, and are supported only by the document, verifying either to telephone or through telex message as contractual proof. Nonetheless, these worldwide markets span the boundaries of several nations, often demand maturities far further out than local markets, and trade in currencies other than the depositor and acceptor (Jackson & Sim, 2013; Metinsoy, 2022). According to reports, short-term borrowing and long-term lending were prevalent in the eurocurrency markets. Such findings aren't meant to doubt the robustness of the global deposits market but rather to highlight that the value of loans in these markets is of an entirely different order than that of markets in which the largest obligors are governments, governmental businesses, or prominent financial institutions. Even though the Euro-currency market has incurred only minor losses and has consistently shown its durability, it remains to be seen how resilient it will be at times of extreme stress and pressure.

The strong connection between anonymity term deposit operations and lending to corporate entities is yet another facet of this market's structure and size that cannot be overlooked when evaluating its design and importance. As non-bank lenders have joined the market through their initiative, these connections have lately gotten closer. Large multinational firms want and achieve rates comparable to those offered for interbank market transactions (Ansidei, et al., 2021; Bhatt & Virmani, 2005; Black, 1973; Rime, et al., 2018). Significant trade borrowers have developed the practice of searching for sums among overseas banks to augment or replace domestic sources of loan supply. In several nations where companies borrowing money through international banks is prohibited or complicated, overseas associates are sometimes directed to seek the necessary cash from local or international banks. Less well-known businesses that require European funds negotiate through its local banking links a security of repayment of funds received from the global money market, at reasonable interest rates. Without a question, the marketplace has served many important purposes. Particularly for funding of commercial transactions, but in certain countries it has accessed and diverse types and sources. The market has become the conduit via which momentarily idle monies in several regions of the globe are swiftly and effectively transferred. As a consequence, interest rates on international trade loans are under pressure in a number of nations (Allen & Winters, 2021). It is hard to state with certainty where marketplace balances would have been deposited if the market had not evolved. The market has greatly aided the capacity of banks to finance current clients and to attract new clients by allowing companies to provide lending facilities at favourable rates. This, in turn, has benefited the worldwide economy. It has helped commercial borrowers in Europe and abroad get access to cheaper borrowing by contributing to the development of an international loan market in which certain banks infringe on the domain of banks in other nations.

Eurocredits

Eurocredits are eurocurrency loans made by Eurobanks to companies, national countries, subprime banks, or multilateral agencies for terms ranging from short-term to medium-term. These loans are monetary obligations issued in denominations different from the Eurobank's base currency (Omarova, 2021). Since these loans are typical of a size that a single bank cannot manage, Eurobanks often come together to create a banks' lending consortium to divide the risk associated with the loans.

These loans have a greater extent of credit risk than money market loans provided to other financial institutions. Because of this, the interest rate on Eurocredits has to be high enough to pay the bank or banking consortium for the increased credit risk. LIBOR is the primary lending rate for Eurocredits that originated in London. The interest rate applied to these credits is expressed as LIBOR plus X percent, where X is the loan margin that is applied and is determined by the lender's reputation. Furthermore, a rolling price was implemented for Eurocredits to ensure that European financial institutions do not lose money on Eurocurrency time deposits relative to the interest they get on Eurocredit loans. A Eurocredit is therefore a collection of loans with shorter periods. The loan is renewed at the end of each time period, and the source interest rate is adjusted to the current LIBOR for the subsequent time period. This process occurs at the end of each period.

Asian Money Market

Similar to the European money market, the Asian money market has historically dealt mostly with deposits denominated in dollars. Thus, at first it was also referred to by the Asian dollar market. At that time, the market served the multinational corporations for the need for the U.S. dollar, which was the need for international trade. Due to the difference in countries' time zone, these businesses cannot entirely depend on European or the US money markets for their operations (Shavshukov, 2018). The international money market, which is mainly concentrated in Hong Kong and Singapore, received huge amounts of funds and makes loans available to corporations in various foreign currencies. With their excess cash, the government and the giant multinational corporations deposit their funds in this market, which are a significant source of deposits, and lend them to the manufacturer and other borrowers. Also, interbank borrowing and lending is another yet important function of the international money market. Instead of borrowing US dollar deposits from European banks, Asian governments, banks, and enterprises connected with the IMM to promote trade and commerce more rapidly (Choudhry, 2001; Davidson, 2009).

Similar to European banks, Asian banks were burdened with dollar-denominated deposits as a consequence of the US dollar's hegemony, which caused all dealings to be in dollars. Therefore, more deals were required to enable the trading of other currencies, especially the euro. Asia and the EU would later see a boom in commerce and the IMM trading of two of the most popular international currencies. To make sure that bid prices are lower than ask prices, the three-month LIBOR is removed from the IMM Index base of 100. Table 9.3 and Table 9.4 depict the Indian money market operations for the year 2022 and 2021 which shows the volume and weighted average rate of different securities like call money, notice money, term money, triparty repo, market repo and repo in corporate bond traded within the country (published as per the RBI reports).

Figure 9.1–9.4 shows the money market indices by the United Kingdom, China, Japan, and the US for the last five years. Apart from Japan Government Bill Index, all the indices are showing upward trends which shows that investors from Japan are becoming less interested in Government Bills due to less lucrative returns. The US treasury bill Index shows an upward trend showing the attraction towards the US treasury bill.

TABLE 9.3 Indian Money Market Operations as on December 15, 2022 (Amount in crore, the rate in percent)

	Volume	*Weighted Average rate*	*Range*
A. Overnight Segment (l+ll+lll+IV)	5,15,156.89	6.19	0.01–6.50
I. Call Money	10,625.65	6.20	4.30–6.40
II. Triparty Repo	369,411.15	6.17	5.00–6.40
III. Market Repo	1,35,020.09	6.23	0.01–6.50
IV. Repo in Corporate Bond	100.00	6.15	6.15–6.15
B. Term Segment			
I. Notice Money	130.04	5.85	5.50–6.21
II. Term Money	560.00	—	6.00–6.70
III. Triparty Repo	1,250.00	5.99	5.95–6.20
IV. Market Repo	1,615.00	6.39	6.00–6.50
V. Repo in Corporate Bond	0.00		

Source: (RBI)

TABLE 9.4 Indian Money Market Operations as on December 15, 2021 (Amount in crore, the rate in percent)

	Volume	*Weighted Average rate*	*Range*
A. Overnight Segment (l+ll+lll+IV)	464,934.02	3.33	1.00–5.15
I. Call Money	9,162.07	3.29	2.00–3.45
II. Triparty Repo	355,864.75	3.33	3.28–3.40
III. Market Repo	99,857.20	3.34	1.00–3.45
IV. Repo in Corporate Bond	50.00	5.15	5.15–5.15
B. Term Segment			
I. Notice Money	179.05	3.26	2.75–3.45
II. Term Money	436.50	—	3.30–4.02
III. Triparty Repo	855.85	3.40	3.30–3.45
IV. Market Repo	2,475.00	3.70	3.65–3.73
V. Repo in Corporate Bond	244.30	5.50	5.50–5.50

Source: (RBI)

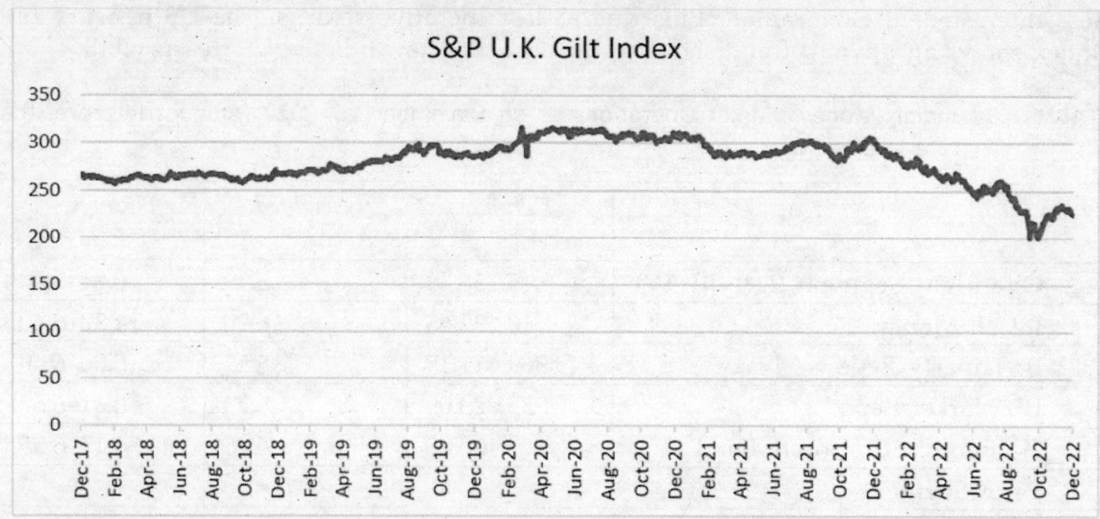

Source: S&P Global

FIGURE 9.1 United Kingdom Gilt Index from December 2017 to December 2022

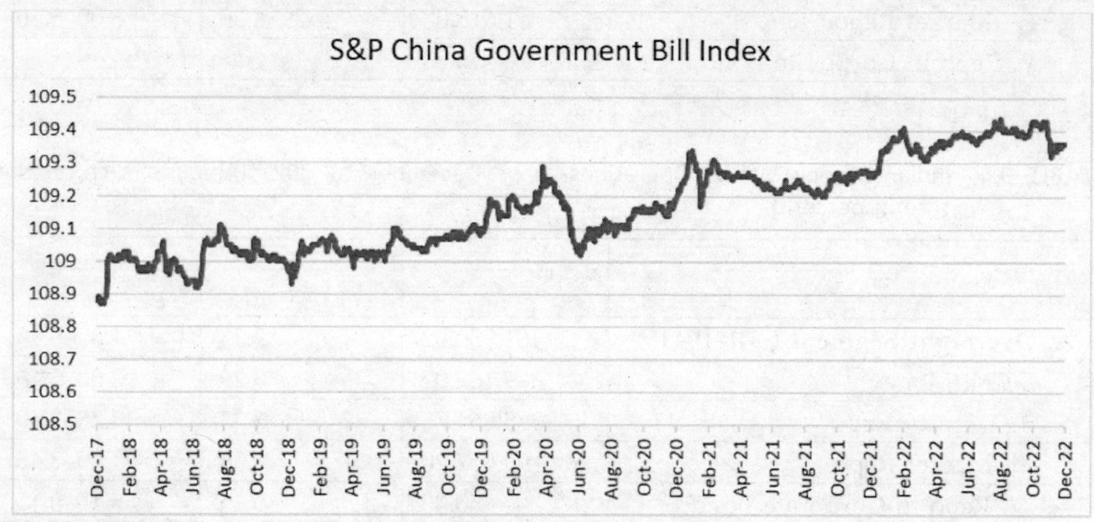

Source: S&P Global

FIGURE 9.2 China Government Bill Index from December 2017 to December 2022

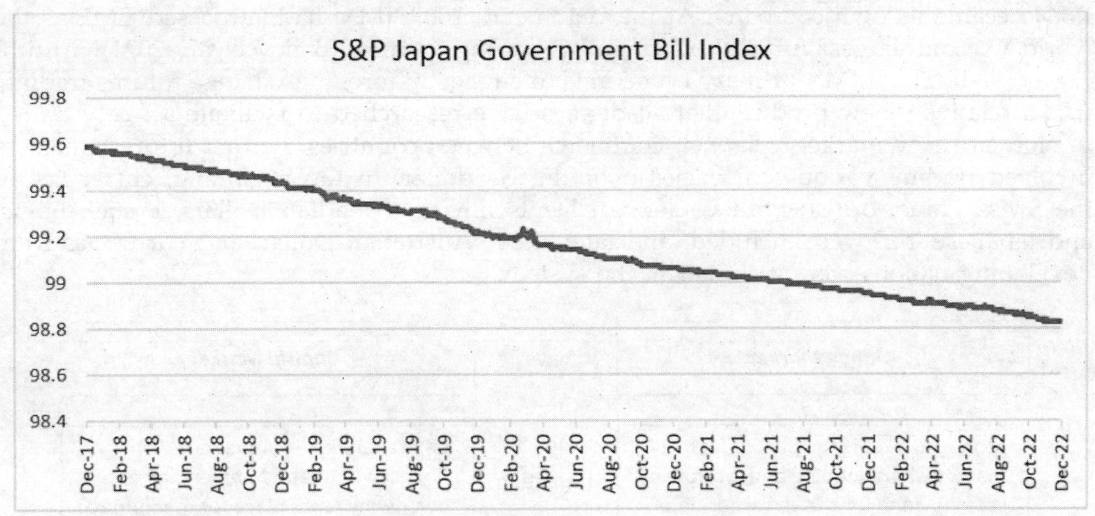

Source: S&P Global

FIGURE 9.3 Japan Government Bill Index from December 2017 to December 2022.

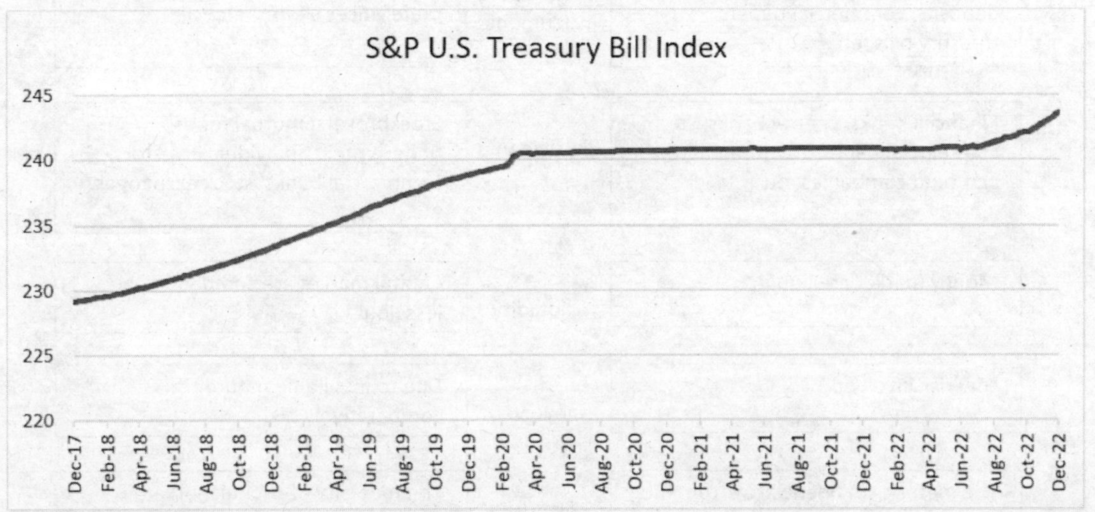

Source: S&P Global

FIGURE 9.4 US Treasury Government Bill Index from December 2017 to December 2022.

9.4 THE INTERNATIONAL MONETARY MARKET

After being proposed in December 1971, the International Monetary Market was officially formed in May 1972. The end of Bretton Woods, the Smithsonian Agreement of 1971, and Nixon's decision to remove the dollar's convertibility to gold are all related events that gave rise to IMM. When the Chicago Mercantile Exchange (CME) and the IMM split, the

IMM became its own company. At the year's end, 2009, IMM had surpassed CME as the world's second-largest futures exchange by trading volume (Bailey et al., 2021; Griffith-Jones, 1980). The IMM's primary function is to engage in foreign exchange futures trading. It is a relatively new product that academics have researched to facilitate a freely traded foreign currency market to launch commerce between countries. Its first futures transfers involved trading various currencies over the Us dollar. In the beginning, currencies of the Swiss Franc, British Pound, German Deutschmark, Canadian Dollars, French Franc, and Japanese Yen were included, and later Euro, Australian Dollar, and currencies from developing nations were included in the system.

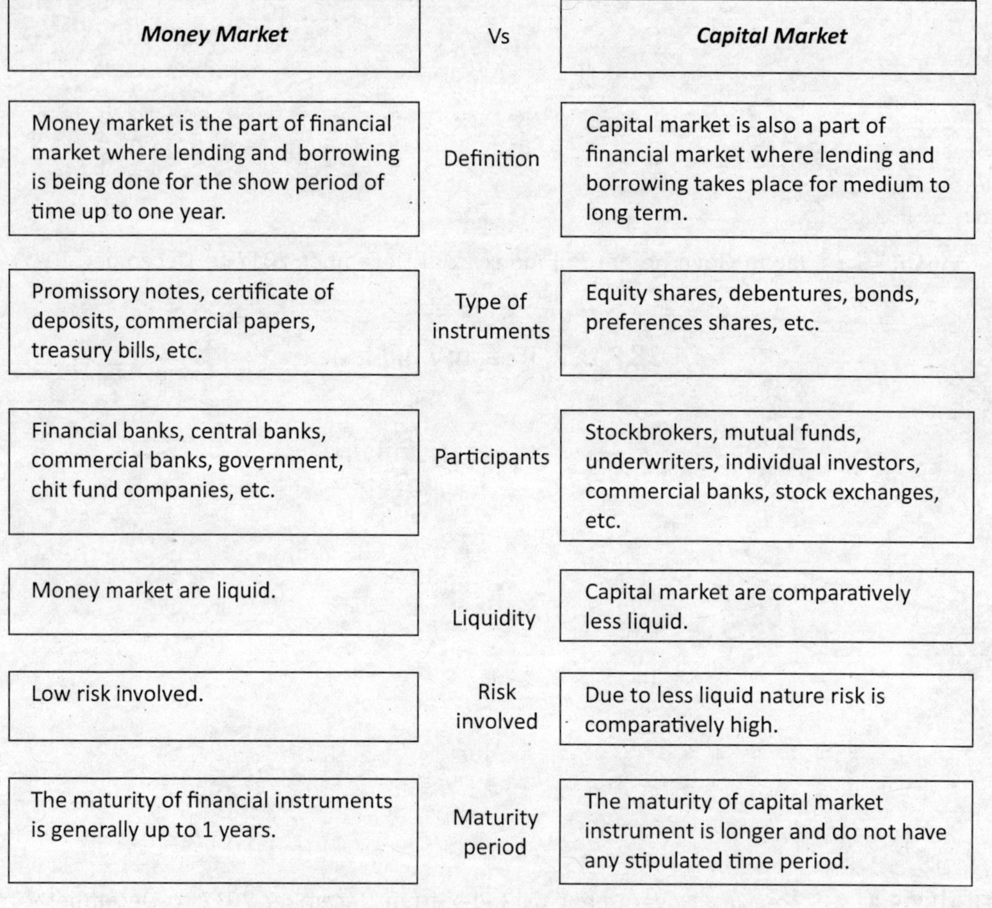

FIGURE 9.5 Money Market vs. Capital Market.

9.5 MAJOR CURRENCY CRISIS ACROSS THE WORLD

In recent times, there have been various events of currency crises across the world. A currency crisis is a sharp decline in a nation's currency, accompanied by market fluctuations and a decline in investor confidence in the economy. Currency crises can occasionally be predicted by countries, although they typically happen all at once with no warning. However, the outcomes are often the same resulting in a loss of money, harming the economy, and damaging a nation's reputation worldwide.

9.5.1 The Mexican Peso Crisis (1994)

Mexican Peso, which is the legal currency of Mexico after the country gained its independence in 1821. The crisis began when Mexico announced the devaluation of their currency by 15% on 20th December 1994. The IMF and investors were both shocked because of the sudden devaluation of the currency, and investors quickly took out their money from the market after being taken off guard. On 22nd December 1994, the peso was compelled to be circulated, and in less than a week, it lost 40% of its total value. Figure 9.6 also exhibits the devaluation of the Mexican Peso in terms of US dollars (Ortiz Martinez, 1998). After that, IMF came into action and determined that the government securities, which would mature within three months, would deplete the foreign currency reserves more than it is depleted now. South American countries saw a severe dip in their currencies and a decrease in reserves as soon as the Mexican peso was devalued. Mexico lost foreign investment, but the crisis caused financial instability in emerging countries. Although the experts recognised the peso's overvaluation, little was understood about Mexico's economy's vulnerability (Morales, 1997).

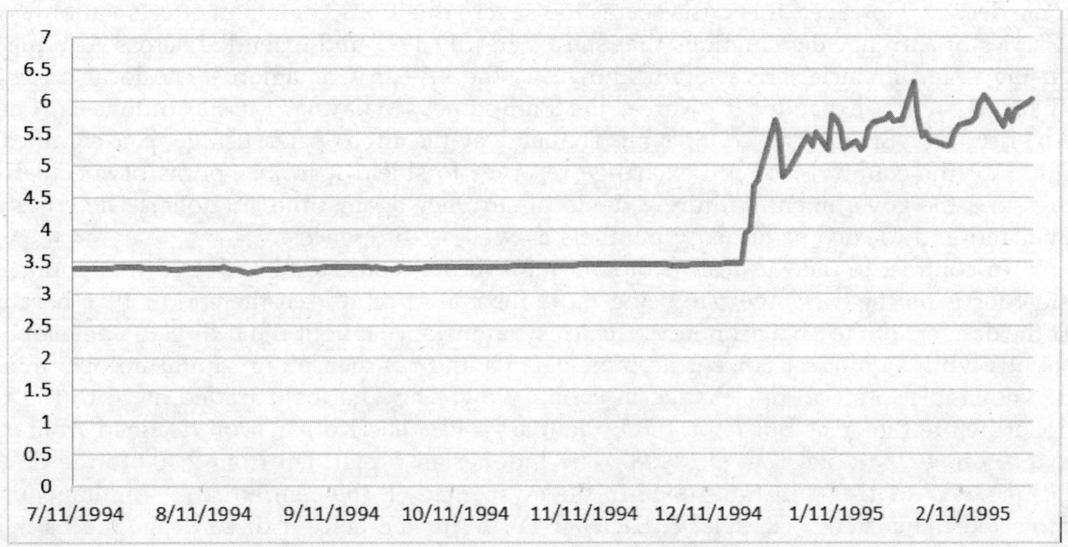

Source: (www.exchangerates.org)

FIGURE 9.6 Mexican Peso vs US dollar Exchange Rate (November 1994–February 1995).

Mexico did not find itself in a catastrophe overnight. When there were indications that the macroeconomic situation was worsening, the government failed to react appropriately. A focal element in crisis was the dollar's volatility in current account deficits. The total balance was favorable from 1991 to 1993 as a result of the huge deficits in current accounts and more than offsetting capital inflows. Although the capital inflows surpassed an 8% current account deficit, foreign reserves climbed from US$10 billion in 1991 to US$30 billion in 1994 (Eichengreen, 1999). Investors would not see any signs of weakening only by looking at the rising foreign reserves. The first quarter of 1994 saw a change in the direction of capital flows, as may be seen with the benefit of hindsight. In fact, between March 1994 and December 1994, foreign reserves fell precipitously (Edwards, 1997; Eichengreen, 1999; Sachns, et al., 1996). For many months prior to the devaluing, the Mexican central bank had not provided data upon that level of foreign reserves; as a result, the loss was not made public.

The crisis is noteworthy since it could be the earliest significant global currency crisis caused by a cross-border movement of foreign money. Before the crisis, it was reported that international mutual funds diversified in Mexican equities approx.—$ 45 billion in recent three years. Fund managers swiftly sold off the holdings of assets from Mexico and other developing markets as the peso dropped. The result was a highly infectious destabilisation of the global financial system. This type of contagion effect, in which the impact of one country is readily seen on the other, will likely occur shortly as the global market continues to integrate more.

9.5.2 The Asian Currency Crisis (1997)

After the Mexican, the Asian currency crisis was another major global currency crisis in the same decade. However, this crisis seems too severe due to its contagion effects nationwide. A series of currency devaluations that started in July 1997 and extended across Asia made up the Asian financial crisis, often known as the "Asian Contagion." The local crisis in Thailand swiftly expanded to Korea, the Philippines, Malaysia, Russia, Indonesia, Latin America, and Brazil. The conflict hit Thailand at the time. After using up a significant chunk of the country's foreign exchange reserves to shield it from months of speculative pressure, the government withdrew the local currency against the US dollar. The crises in Thailand and Mexico have many parallels as well as differences.

In contrast to the Mexican situation, the IMF has consistently advised that countries must focus on the exchange rate being more flexible since at least the end of 1996 because of the dangers of the Thai economy. The Mexican instance taught the IMF that a developing country with significant current account deficits and compensating capital inflows might be vulnerable to an abrupt change in capital flow. The Thai baht traded at 26 to the US dollar before the crisis but fell to 53 by January 1998. The Korean won declined from 900 to 1,695 in 1997 (Radelet, et al., 1998). The Indonesian rupiah fell from 2,400 to the dollar in June 1997 to 14,900 in June 1998. In the swap market, the central bank simultaneously protected the currency (Radelet & Sachs, 1999). With the help of these deals, the Bank of Thailand could keep its interest rate, reported foreign reserve balance, and currency rate all reasonably steady while also committing to sell more dollars in the future.

The conventionally defined foreign reserves were periodically reported, but the net amount of reserves were kept hidden. From December 1996 through May 1997, the central bank and speculators engaged in conflict. During one week in May 1997, there was a lot of speculating. When all was said and done, Despite having an undeclared forward position of more over $20 billion to sell, the Bank of Thailand's foreign reserves barely surpassed the amount of forward contracts (Benson, et al., 2000; Wang, 1999). On May 14, the Bank of Thailand instituted capital restrictions, prohibiting local financial institutions from lending baht to foreigners. This delayed further speculative action.

Reasons for Asian Currency Crisis

- Current account deficit
- Increased level of foreign debts
- Government budget deficit
- A high amount of bank lending
- Poor debt service ration
- Imparity between capital inflows and capital outflows

9.5.3 The Argentine Peso Crisis

Beginning in the 1980s, Argentina had a prolonged era of economic turmoil, along with the Latin American debt dilemma and high inflation. This is when the Argentine Peso issue first surfaced. More specifically, in 1989, when the government in Argentina transformed, Carlos Menem was selected as President of the country and appointed Domingo Cavallo as the Economic minister. They bring many economic reforms, including trade liberalization, privatization, tax reforms, and deregulation. In 1995, the contagion effect of the Mexican crisis-hit Argentina, and its GDP declined by 2.8% (Hornbeck, 2002).

Further, in 1996–1997, the country tried to boost its economic growth, but its current account deficit and debt situation worsened. In July 1997, the East Asian crisis reached Russia and Brazil in 1998, and then Argentina, where the employment crisis began. The IMF accepted Argentina's request for a three-year, $7.2 billion stand-by agreement, subject to severe budgetary restraints and the assumption of 3.5% GDP growth in 2000. In contrast, the actual growth rate was only 0.5% (Kehoe, 2003). The IMF decides to add $7.0 billion to the March 10, 2000 deal in response to Argentina's ongoing poor economic performance. According to the agreement, GDP would increase by 2.5% in 2001. To increase Argentina's competitiveness abroad, the currency exchange rate of goods trade is set at a 50/50 dollar-euro peg, thus permitting a 7% depreciation for overseas commerce. Several experts express concerns about the consequences of the exchange rate regime's reliability (Hornbeck, 2002). Argentina completes a second debt exchange in which it trades $60 billion in bonds with an 11–12% rate for notes with longer maturities with an interest rate of about 7%. Global bond rating agencies see it as an actual default. A bank run starts with central bank resources dropping by $2 billion in a single day. Therefore, the government limits personal bank withdrawals to $1,000 monthly (Nechio, 2010). After the imposition of withdrawal limits, the protest began in the country, and the unemployment rate reached to record 18%. The government of Argentina intends to devalue the peso by 29% for significant international business transactions. The economic plan also includes restrictions on bank accounts and converting all debts to $100,000 into pesos (Setser & Gelpern, 2006). After this restriction, the Argentine Peso fell immediately to 1.7 per dollar and reached as low as 2.05 to the dollar by January 2002. Argentina's request for a one-year extension on a $936 million payment due on January 17 is approved by the IMF, preventing Argentina from falling behind (Ford, 1956). The IMF approached the Argentine government and asked them to adopt the floating exchange rates for the near future.

9.5.4 Remedies to Adopt for Avoiding a Currency Crisis

Improved Fiscal Policy: The government finances the deficits by borrowing from international bodies or countries abroad. So, by tightening the fiscal policy, the government can avoid the deficits which will immediately result in the reduction of debts from the international market.

Capital Outflow Restrictions: The restriction in the domestic currency exchange and impositions on the domestic capital outflows will result in less movement of funds across borders and limit the enormous sales of the domestic currency.

IMF Bailout Funds: The bailout funds by the IMF, as seen in the case of the Mexican and Argentine currency crisis, can also help overcome the situation. However, the countries do not prefer this kind of setup due to their various assumptions and restrictions.

Rising Interest Rates: Increasing the interest rate in the domestic market to encourage investment in countries and attract international investment will reduce the crisis risk.

Adopting a Floating Exchange Rate: Adopting a floating exchange rate regime was the key to overcoming the Argentine and Asian crises. Allowing the exchange rate to float freely during the crisis against the policy regime. If following the fixed exchange rate, currency devaluation is the next best alternative.

SUMMARY

1. The exchange of foreign currencies among several central banks of different nations on the international money market.
2. Popular indexes that subtly influence the international money market include currency bands, fixed exchange rates, exchange rate frameworks, connected exchange rates, and floating exchange rates.
3. The increase in competition among the financial centers led to increased deregulation for the money markets worldwide, which fasten the process of **"Arbitraging,"** where money market regulators issue and trade instruments in financial centers and with lower regulations from financial institutions and government and hence decreases the cost as well.
4. Currently, the US money market is one of the largest in transactions compared to any other worldwide market. The market participants are pretty heterogeneous, including financials and non-financials firms (Jurnal & Saham, 2021; Li, et al., 2021).
5. The dollars deposited in the bank came to be known as **Eurodollars,** and the market of these Eurodollars is known as **Eurocurrency Market.**
6. Eurocredits are eurocurrency loans made by eurobanks to companies, national countries, subprime banks, or multilateral agencies for terms ranging from short-term to medium-term.
7. Interbank borrowing and lending are another essential international money market function. Instead of borrowing US dollar deposits from European banks, Asian governments, banks, and enterprises connected with the IMM to promote trade and commerce more rapidly (Choudhry, 2001; Davidson, 2009).

8. The International Monetary Market was officially formed in May 1972. The end of Bretton Woods, the Smithsonian Agreement of 1971, and Nixon's decision to remove the dollar's convertibility to gold are all related events that gave rise to IMM.
9. The Mexican peso was compelled to be circulated and lost 40% of its total value in less than a week. Mexico did not find itself in a catastrophe overnight. When there were indications that the macroeconomic situation was worsening, the government failed to react appropriately.
10. The consequences of the Asian currency crisis had multifold effects, including the fall of The Thai baht, which traded at 26 to the U.S. dollar before the crisis but fell to 53 by January 1998. The Korean won declined from 900 to 1,695 in 1997. The Indonesian rupiah fell from 2,400 to the dollar in June 1997 to 14,900 in June 1998.
11. The Argentine Peso fell due to the crisis effect to 1.7 per dollar and reached as low as 2.05 to the dollar by January 2002. Argentina's request for a one-year extension on a $936 million payment due on January 17 is approved by the IMF, preventing Argentina from falling behind.

KEY WORDS

- International Money Markets
- Eurocredits
- Euro-currency Markets
- Asian Money Markets
- International Monetary System
- Currency Crisis

QUESTIONS

1. What is the role of the international money market in globalizing the monetary system?
2. The national financial market acts as an international financial center. Explain in brief.
3. Write a brief note about the following:
   - US money market
   - European money market
   - Asian money market
4. What is the role of the international monetary system in assisting the international money market?
5. What is the difference between the capital market and the money market?
6. Explain the role of IMF in the currency crisis.

7. Crisis arises from a single country and affects the multiple countries. Explain the statement with emphasis on Contagion effect.
8. What are the major causes of currency crisis, response and remedies for the crisis?

REFERENCES AND SUGGESTED READINGS

1. Accominotti, O., Lucena-Piquero, D., & Ugolini, S. (2021). The origination and distribution of money market instruments: sterling bills of exchange during the first globalisation, *Economic History Review*, 74(4), 892–921. https://doi.org/10.1111/ehr.13049
2. Allen, K. D., & Winters, D. B. (2021). Auditor response to changing risk: money market funds during the financial crisis, *Review of Quantitative Finance and Accounting*, 56(3), 1057–1086. https://doi.org/10.1007/s11156-020-00918-5
3. Altavilla, C., Lemke, W., Linzert, T., Tapking, J., & von Landesberger, J. (2021). Assessing the Efficacy, Efficiency and Potential Side Effects of the Ecb's Monetary Policy Instruments Since 2014, In *SSRN Electronic Journal*. https://doi.org/10.2139/ssrn.3928300
4. Ansidei, J., Bengtsson, E., Frison, D., & Ward, G. (2021). Money Market Funds in Europe and Financial Stability, *SSRN Electronic Journal, 1*. https://doi.org/10.2139/ssrn.3723331
5. Baghai, R. P., Giannetti, M., & Jäger, I. (2022). Liability Structure and Risk Taking: Evidence from the Money Market Fund Industry, In *Journal of Financial and Quantitative Analysis* (Vol. 57, Issue 5). https://doi.org/10.1017/S0022109021000338
6. Bailey, A., Bakkar, I., Baranova, Y., Barton, C., Brazier, A., Bridges, J., Carr, A., Coppins, G., Denbee, E., Elliot, J., Ferrara, G., Gual-Ricard, B., Hall, J., Hall, S., Jackson, N., Jones, J., Kashyap, A., Mclaren, N., Mehta, A., … Hauser, A. (2021). *From Lender of Last Resort to Market Maker of Last Resort via the dash for cash: why central banks need new tools for dealing with market dysfunction Speech given by*. 1–13. https://www.bankofengland.co.uk/-/media/boe/files/financial-stability-report/2020/august-2020.pdf.
7. Benson, J. N., Goldstein, M., Noland, M., Liu, L.-G., Robinson, S., Wang, Z., & Posen, A. (2000). The Asian Financial Crisis: Causes, Cures, and Systemic Implications, *Canadian Public Policy / Analyse de Politiques, 26*(4), 502. https://doi.org/10.2307/3552620
8. Bhatt, V., & Virmani, A. (2005). Global integration of India's Money Market: Interest rate parity in India, *Indian Council for Research on International Economic Relations, WP No* 164(164). http://hdl.handle.net/10419/176186
9. Black, S. W. (1973). International Money Markets and Flexible Exchange Rates, *Princeton Studies In International Finance*, 32(32), 67. http://web.archive.org/web/20171127102603/https://www.princeton.edu/~ies/IES_Studies/S32.pdf%0Ahttps://www.princeton.edu/~ies/IES_Studies/S32.pdf
10. Chismolm, A. M. (2009). *An Introduction to International Capital Markets* (Second), Wiley. https://www.ptonline.com/articles/how-to-get-better-mfi-results.

11. Choudhry, M. (2001). The Bond and Money Markets : *Butterworth-Heinemann*.
12. Davidson, A. (2009). *How the Global Financial Markets Really Work* (First, Vol. 2018, Issue February).
13. Eagly, R. V., & Smith, V. K. (2022). Domestic and International Integration of the London Money Market, *The Journal of Economic History*, 36(1), 198–212.
14. Edwards, S. (1997). *The Mexican Peso Crisis: How much did we know? When did we know it?*
15. Eichengreen, B. (1999). The baring crisis in a Mexican mirror, *International Political Science Review*, 20(3), 249–270. https://doi.org/10.1177/0192512199203002
16. Ford, A. G. (1956). Argentina and the baring crisis of 1890. *Oxford Economic Papers*, *8*(2), 127–160. https://doi.org/10.1093/oxfordjournals.oep.a042258
17. Glasner, D. (2009). A proposal for monetary reform, *Free Banking and Monetary Reform*, 4(3), 227–248. https://doi.org/10.1017/cbo9780511528408.012
18. Griffith-Jones, S. (1980). The Growth of Multinational Banking, the Euro-currency Market and their Effects on Developing Countries, *The Journal of Development Studies*, *16*(2), 204–223. https://doi.org/10.1080/00220388008421755
19. Hachey, G. A. (1983). *Eurocurrency and National Money Market Interest Rates: An Empirical Investigation of Causality Author (s): Fred R. Kaen and George A. Hachey Source: Journal of Money, Credit and Banking, Aug., 1983, Vol. 15 , No. 3 (Aug., 1983), Published by: Ohio State University Press Stable URL: http://www.jstor.com/stable/1992483 All use subject to https://about.jstor.org/terms Eurocurrency aand National Money Market Interest Rates An Empirical Investigation of Causality*. *15*(3), 327–338.
20. Hornbeck, J. (2002). The Argentine Financial Crisis: A Chronology of Events, *CRS Report for Congress, January 31*, 1–6.
21. ITO, T. (2007). Asian Currency Crisis and the International Monetary Fund, 10 Years Later: Overview, *Asian Economic Policy Review*, 2(1), 16–49. https://doi.org/10.1111/j.1748-3131.2007.00046.x
22. Jackson, C., & Sim, M. (2013). Recent developments in the sterling overnight money market, *Bank of England Quarterly Bulletin*, *1*, 223–232. http://www.bankofengland.co.uk/publications/Documents/quarterlybulletin/2013/qb130304.pdf
23. Journals, P. M., & Studies, I.B. (1983). *Political Sources of Risk in the International Money Markets: Conceptual, Methodological and Interpretive Refinements Author (s): Thomas L. Brewer Source : Journal of International Business Studies , Spring–Summer, 1983, Vol. 14, No. Published by: Published by: Palgrave Macmillan Journals on behalf of Academy of International Business. Stable URL: https://www.jstor.org/stable/154336 POLITICAL SOURCES OF RISK IN THE INTERNATIONAL MONEY MARKETS: CONCEPTUAL, METHODOLOGICAL*, 14(1), 161–164.
24. Jurnal, S. & Saham, E. (2021). *SEKURITAS Analysis of Potential and Risks Investing in Financial Instruments and Digital Cryptocurrency Assets during the Covid-19 Pandemic*. 1, 1–12. http://www.interac.org/en_n2_01_milestones.html.,
25. Kehoe, T.J. (2003). What can we learn from the current crisis in Argentina? *Scottish Journal of Political Economy*, 50(5), 609–633. https://doi.org/10.1111/j.0036-9292.2003.05005002.x

26. Klopstock, F. H. (1965). The International Money Market : Structure , Scope and Instruments, *The Journal of Finance*, 20(2), 182–208.
27. Li, L., Li, Y., Macchiavelli, M., & Zhou, X. (Alex). (2021). Liquidity Restrictions, Runs, and Central Bank Interventions: Evidence from Money Market Funds, *Review of Financial Studies*, 34(11), 5402–5437. https://doi.org/10.1093/rfs/hhab065
28. Metinsoy, S. (2022). "Selective Friendship at the Fund": United States Allies, Labor Conditions, and the International Monetary Fund's Legitimacy, *Politics and Governance*, *10*(3), 143–154. https://doi.org/10.17645/pag.v10i3.5303
29. Morales, I. (1997). The Mexican Crisis and the Weakness of the NAFTA, *The Annals of the American Academy of Political and Social Science*, 550, 130–152.
30. Nechio, F. (2010). The Greek Crisis: Argentina Revisited, *Journal of Modern Greek Studies*, 28(2), 306–309. https://doi.org/10.1353/mgs.2010.0433
31. Omarova, S.T. (2021). The People's Ledger: How to Democratize Money and Finance the Economy, *Vanderbilt Law Review*, 74(5), 1231–1300. https://doi.org/10.2139/ssrn.3715735
32. Ortiz Martinez, G. (1998). What lessons does the Mexican crisis hold for recovery in Asia, *Finance and Development*, 35(2), 6–9.
33. Radelet, S., & Sachs, J. (1999). What have we learned, so far, from the Asian financial crisis? *Enero*, *4*(16), 16. http://www.cid.harvard.edu/archive/hiid/papers/aea122.pdf
34. Radelet, S., Sachs, J.D., Cooper, R.N., & Bosworth, B.P. (1998). Harvard Institute for International Development, The East Asian Financial Crisis: Diagnosis, Remedies, Prospects, *Prospects*, 1(1), 1–90.
35. Rao, R.K.S., Smith, S.D., & Shapiro, A.C. (1983). Multinational Financial Management, In *The Journal of Finance* (Vol. 38, Issue 5). https://doi.org/10.2307/2327599
36. Rime, D., Schrimpf, A., & Syrstad, O. (2018). Segmented Money Markets and Covered Interest Parity Arbitrage, In *SSRN Electronic Journal* (Issue 15). https://doi.org/10.2139/ssrn.3057973
37. Rime, D., Schrimpf, A., & Syrstad, O. (2022). Covered Interest Parity Arbitrage, *The Review of Financial Studies*, 35(11), 5185–5227. https://doi.org/10.1093/rfs/hhac026
38. Sachns, J., Tornell, A., & Velasco, A. (1996). *The Mexican Peso Crisis: Sudden Death pr Death Foretold*.
39. Setser, B., & Gelpern, A. (2006). Pathways through financial crisis: Argentina, *Global Governance*, 12(4), 465–487. https://doi.org/10.1163/19426720-01204009
40. Shavshukov, V. M. (2018). The BRICS in the international money and debt capital markets, *Journal of Business and Retail Management Research*, 12(3), 113–125. https://doi.org/10.24052/jbrmr/v12is03/art-10
41. Wang, H. (1999). The Asian financial crisis and financial reforms in China, *Pacific Review*, 12(4), 537–556. https://doi.org/10.1080/09512749908719305.

CHAPTER 10

International Bond Market

LEARNING OUTCOMES

After reading this chapter, the reader will be able to:

- Provide an overview of Bond Market
- Discuss the need for the Development of International Bond Market
- Explain the Origin of International Bond Market
- Discuss World's Bond Market with Statistical Perspective
- Classify Bonds
- List Advantages and Disadvantages of Investing in International Bond

10.1 BOND MARKET: AN OVERVIEW

International bonds are those issued by a company or country other than the investor's native country. In response to companies' ongoing quest for the cheap method of borrowing money, the global bond market is expanding quickly. A company might increase investor interest by issuing bonds internationally. Moreover, it could help to loosen regulations. The global bond market increased rapidly starting in the 1980s (Albagli, et al., 2019). Particularly, the foreign bond market has drawn private sector lending out of domestic markets. More than two thirds of the global bond market's capitalization come from public sector issuance, yet the government uses the global market relatively less. On the other hand, more than a quarter of the outstanding private sector bond issuance by the end of 1990 were created on the global market (Hale, et al., 2020). It now makes up a significant portion of the overall amount of bonds existing on the international bond market. Most transactions might be carried out on the borrower's local bond market, despite the fact that the bonds are issued and sold internationally. As a result, there is rivalry between the local and foreign bond markets. Additionally, much like most other bond kinds, foreign bonds pay interest at regular intervals and return the capital to the holder when the bond matures (Barr & Priestley, 2004). The movement of money across international borders and the desire of agents to change the conditions, including the currency of issuance, on which they borrow and invest, are the two primary drivers behind the formation of the global bond market. These two variables not only have an impact on international bond markets, most of which now have a significant amount of foreign participation but it also attracts borrowers to use bond markets outside of their home countries (Fidora, et al., 2007).

Some borrowers lack access to highly developed domestic bond markets, in particular the governments of the majority of non-OECD nations (Bredin, et al., 2010). This category of borrower has historically been significant in the international bond markets, but since only a few of them were able to continue to raise money from this source after the debt crisis began in 1982, by the end of 1989 their share of all outstanding international bonds had decreased to less than 3% (Abakah, et al., 2021). The most straightforward way to get around government restrictions on domestic markets is to start a problem in a different market. Another example is the fact that previous to 1986, bullet bonds were not allowed on the domestic Dutch guilder market, which had the effect of diverting issuance to the international market (Piljak, 2013). In some domestic markets, bonds are subject to withholding tax. The best approach to avoid having to pay withholding tax in certain circumstances is to place a bond on the foreign market, with pound bonds being the most significant example. When the German government announced its intention to impose a 10% withholding tax on domestic bonds in the years 1988–1989, withholding tax had a significant role in stimulating issuance by German borrowers in the international bond market (Smaoui, et al., 2017). Despite the fact that the use of international bonds has been promoted for all of the aforementioned reasons, regulatory limitations and central banks often impose limits on the issuing of foreign bonds denominated in the currency under their control.

10.2 NEED FOR THE DEVELOPMENT OF INTERNATIONAL BOND MARKET

The fundamental goal of developing a bond market throughout the majority of nations has been to finance fiscal deficits. Several governments in developing countries were able to meet a substantial percentage of their borrowing demands before 1980s by simply mandating banking institutions to hold government paper. This was done primarily to meet stringent reserve levels. The government deficit was "financed" in several nations in part via inflation. Additionally, borrowing from abroad was an option. In a previous era of fixed exchange rates, the exchange rate risk of such borrowing seemed to be quite low. Progressive global financial market and capital flow liberalization, anti-inflationary policy adoption, and flexible exchange rate adoption have all undercut such financing techniques (Dungey, et al., 2006). Governments were being compelled to borrow money from domestic markets more and more. Several nations have also had to find ways to fund extremely significant unusual expenses. One notable example in many developing nations is the financing needed for bank liberalisation.

The need to control significant capital inflows served as a second explicit justification for creating a local bond market. Several central banks found this to be a particularly challenging task throughout the first half of the 1990s (Adelegan & Radzewicz-Bak, 2016; Pradhan, et al., 2020). The central bank can only undertake open market operations using short-term debt instruments since there are no well-developed bond markets. Short-term interest rates often rise and more investments in such paper are encouraged when liberalisation is solely based on the issuance of short-term paper. This runs the danger of shortening the structure of inflows. Such a danger is decreased by sterilisation via the selling of bonds. Borrowers throughout the private sector also require access to long-term credit, either directly from capital markets or via banks' intermediary services, despite the fact that the public sector provided the majority of the particular impetus for building bond markets (Ilmanen, 1995). Projects for permanent investments that are projected to pay off only in the long run must be financed by corporations. The purchase of homes by households is another instance. Therefore, in certain instances, it was particular individual financial needs that aided in the growth of debt markets.

The development of debt markets is motivated by a number of broad factors. The most important rationale is to create market interest rates that represent the opportunity cost of money at each maturity, which will improve financial markets more comprehensive. For effective investment and finance choices, this is crucial. Additionally, the availability of tradable instruments aids with risk management. Borrowers may be vulnerable to severe discrepancies among both assets and liabilities if they only have a limited selection of instruments at their disposal. For instance, in the absence of bond markets, businesses may be forced to take on short-term debt in order to fund the purchase of long-term assets (Burger & Warnock, 2006; Hardie, 2006). They may thus favour short-term initiatives and discourage entrepreneurial endeavours in their investment strategies. Businesses run the danger of taking on too much foreign currency risk if they borrow money from international bond markets to make up for the absence of a local bond market (Bhattacharyay, 2012). To avoid focusing intermediation just on banks is a second common justification for the growth of bond markets. Due to banks' high levels of leverage, the economy may be more susceptible to crises. In the absence of a properly functioning bond market, the harm inflicted by such crises to the actual economy is often far worse and the restructuring process more challenging (Clare & Lekkos, 2005). However, it is only reasonably envisaged that well-developed capital markets would replace banks. Bank intermediation still rules in many developing economies, if not the majority of them.

The ability of such markets to aid in the implementation of monetary policy is a third broad justification for encouraging debt markets. As monetary policy increasingly depends on indirect tools of control, a healthy money market is crucial for the seamless transmission of policy (Hartmann, et al., 2006). Prices in the long-term bond market can provide useful information on forecasts for anticipated macroeconomic events and market responses to changes in monetary policy.

10.3 ORIGIN OF INTERNATIONAL BOND MARKET

For more than 150 years, the issue of foreign bonds has served as a conduit for cross-border financial movements. Foreign bond issuers, most often governments and railroad firms, have been present in the London financial markets since the 1820s. Up to the start of World War I, London and Paris served as the primary financial hubs for the huge international bond markets that existed throughout the latter part of the nineteenth century. However, in the 1920s, the UK government tried to limit the issuing of foreign sterling notes in London due to issues with liberalisation, a substantial national debt and assuring the restoration of the pound to the gold standard (Pearson, 2015). Exchange restrictions were implemented in the United Kingdom at the start of World War II, and until they were abolished some 40 years later, no foreign sterling bonds were issued. New York had already established itself as the most significant foreign bond market during the interwar era, and the US financial markets solidified this position over the first 15 years after 1945. One estimate states that between 1946 and 1963, the dollar foreign bond market raised around $14 billion in capital (Burger, et al., 2018).

Foreign bond markets for the Swiss franc and the Japanese yen quickly grew in the 1980s. In fact, the Swiss franc foreign bond market had surpassed the Yankee bond market in size by the decade's conclusion. There were other smaller foreign bond markets in addition to these three major ones, the majority of which were controlled by the issuance of supranational borrowers. The Eurobond market has a far shorter history than the foreign bond markets, accounting for more than three-quarter of all outstanding international bonds by 1990 (Plummer & Click, 2005). The market's beginnings may be discovered in the early 1960s, however there is considerable debate over whether issue could be referred to as the first Eurobond. At first, it was largely a market for dollar bonds, and two things made it easier for it to grow. The first of these was the build-up of offshore dollar balances in the late 1950s and early 1960s, which was brought on by regulations, the worry that US dollar accounts might be frozen, significant outward direct investment by US multinational corporations, and, in the 1960s, a string of current-account deficits (Leigland, 2020). Although trading and issuance of these dollars took place in New York, the holders of these dollars grew to be significant investors in international dollar bonds, which meant that both borrowers and investors were often from Europe. This raised the potential that debtors would sell bonds directly to European investors instead of going via the US capital market with its ratings and security requirements. The second element was the gradual deterioration of the Bretton Woods system in the 1960s and the corresponding actions taken by the US government as this issue grew. A number of policies that were designed to stop money from the United States were developed in an effort to stop this dollar build-up. In order to increase the effective yearly cost of borrowing in the United States for foreigners by 1%, the Interest Equalization Tax was enacted in 1963 (Ferguson, 2006). This action was harsh enough to stop European borrowers from using the Yankee bond market, and issuance was switched to the emerging bond market, which rapidly expanded. Outward direct investment was subject to voluntary limitations under the Voluntary Restraint Program until matching balance of payments profits were increased in 1965. US banks were discouraged from lending to foreign borrowers, including foreign subsidiaries of US firms, for periods longer than one year. Mandatory limits on outbound direct investment released the rules in 1968. As a consequence, the Eurobond market became the sole source of long-term financing for many US multinational corporations' international operations (Ho & Li, 2014).

A strong Deutsche Mark segment of the Euro-bond market had also been established by the decade's conclusion. The exchange rate forces the liberalisation during that time period and had a significant role in the expansion of the euro-dollar bond market. The German authorities could afford to adopt a somewhat permissive approach to the establishment of a Deutsche Mark foreign bond market since they were faced with consistent upward pressure on the Deutsche Mark during the 1960s, which they normally tried to oppose. Particularly because such capital outflows reduced the upward pressure on the currency, German investors were allowed to purchase overseas Deutsche Mark bonds. Similar rationale suggested that foreigners should avoid purchasing local German bonds. Due to the introduction of a withholding tax on domestic German bonds in 1964, non-German investors were strongly encouraged to purchase overseas bonds rather than those denominated in the local Deutsche Mark. Foreign Deutsche Mark bonds had been issued as early as 1958; as non-German securities firms became more engaged in the underwriting and marketing of these bonds, the proportion of non-German investors in this market increased. The overseas Deutsche Mark bond market had, in effect, transformed into a Eurobond market as primary and secondary market procedures began to mimic those used in the USD Eurobond market (Huang & Zhu, 2011).

Eurobond primary and secondary markets today make up a major sector. Eurobonds worth more than $220 billion were introduced in 1989, and secondary market trading volume surpassed $2 trillion. It is plausible to assume that securities firms earn many billions of dollars annually as a result of their involvement in these markets, with the number $22 billion perhaps being near to the mark. Although the majority of it is made by branches headquartered in London, the hub of the Eurobond market, given the diverse nationality makeup of securities companies active in the market, this revenue must be evenly dispersed throughout the developed countries (Fabella & Madhur, 2003) the development of domestic bond markets is increasingly seen as one of the key requirements to strengthen the financial sectors of East Asian countries and to reduce their vulnerabilities to future financial crises. There is a great diversity in terms of the level of bond market development across East Asian countries. Judged by several indicators of bond market development, Hong Kong, China and Singapore are ahead of other countries, followed by a second tier consisting of Korea; Malaysia; and Taiwan, China and a third tier consisting of People's Republic of China, Philippines, and Thailand. Indonesia's bond market is perhaps the most nascent among East Asian bond markets. Initiatives to develop bond markets in East Asia should focus on: (i) Maintaining a low inflation, steady interest rate, and stabilised macroeconomic environment; (ii) Creating an efficient marketplace for government bonds that would act as a benchmark for the corporate bond market; (iii) Improving corporate governance; (iv) Broadening investor base; (v) Strengthening the bond market's regulatory structure.

TABLE 10.1 Worldwide Credit Ratings (2022) (Country-wise by Different Agencies)

Country	*S&P*	*Moody's*	*Fitch*	*DBRS*
Argentina	CCC+	Ca	CCC–	CCC
Australia	AAA	AAA	AAA	AAA
Austria	AA+	Aa	AA+	AAA
Bahrain	B+	B	B+	—
Bangladesh	BB–	Ba	BB–	—
Belgium	AA	Aa	AA–	AA
Botswana	BBB+	A	—	—
Brazil	BB–	Ba	BB-	BB (low)
Bulgaria	BBB	Baa	BBB	—

(*Contd.*)

Country	*S&P*	*Moody's*	*Fitch*	*DBRS*
Canada	AAA	Aaa	AA+	AAA
Chile	A	A	A–	N/A
China	A+	A	A+	A (high)
Colombia	BB+	Baa	BB+	BBB (low)
Croatia	BBB+	Baa	BBB+	—
Cyprus	BBB	Ba	BBB–	BBB
Czech Republic	AA–	Aa	AA–	—
Denmark	AAA	Aaa	AAA	AAA
Egypt	B	B	B+	—
Finland	AA+	Aa	AA+	AA (high)
France	AA	Aa	AA	AA (high)
Germany	AAA	Aaa	AAA	AAA
Greece	BB+	Ba	BB+	BB (high)
Hong Kong	AA+	Aa	AA–	—
Hungary	BBB–	Baa	BBB	—
Iceland	A	A	A	—
India	BBB–	Baa	BBB–	BBB (low)
Indonesia	BBB	Baa	BBB	—
Ireland	AA-	A	AA–	AA (low)
New Zealand	AA+	Aaa	AA+	—
Pakistan	CCC+	Caa	CCC+	—
Philippines	BBB+	Baa	BBB	—
Singapore	AAA	Aaa	AAA	AAA
South Africa	BB–	Ba	BB–	—
Sri Lanka	SD	Ca	RD	—
Switzerland	AAA	Aaa	AAA	AAA
Thailand	BBB+	Baa	BBB+	—
United Kingdom	AA	Aa	AA–	AA
United States	AA+	Aaa	AAA	AAA
Zambia	SD	Ca	RD	—

Source: worldgovernmentbonds.com

Note: **Investment Grade:** AAA to BBB **Speculative Grade:** BB–B to CCC to D

S&P—Standard and Poor DBRS—Dominion Bond Rating Service

Investment into international bond depends on the credit rating of countries from where it is being issued which is presented in Table 10.1 where AAA to BBB is the Investment grade whereas speculative grade is given to BB to D. Country-wise credit rating is being shown in Table 10.1.

10.4 WORLD'S BOND MARKET: A STATISTICAL PERSPECTIVE

The estimated size of the worldwide bond market is close to $47 trillion. The US bond market is the biggest in the world in terms of size. More than $25 trillion in debt is now outstanding on the US bond market. Since the year 2000, the international bond market has doubled in size. Over the last several years, the amount of outstanding developing bond market has substantially increased. In 2000, outstanding bonds for developing nations as a whole represented 36% of GDP, up from only 24% in 1994. The percentage of short-term debt in domestic debt in Latin America has significantly decreased throughout this time. According to figures from the International Capital Market Association, there were around $10 trillion worth of bonds outstanding by the end of 2006. The bonds issued by the many multinational corporations are the reasons which helped in the growth of the international bond market so quickly. In Figure 10.1 it can be clearly seen that USD tops the international bond market in terms of largest deal with 562.3 billion USD followed by Euro (321.3) and Paul Sterling (GBP) 43.8 billion USD respectively.

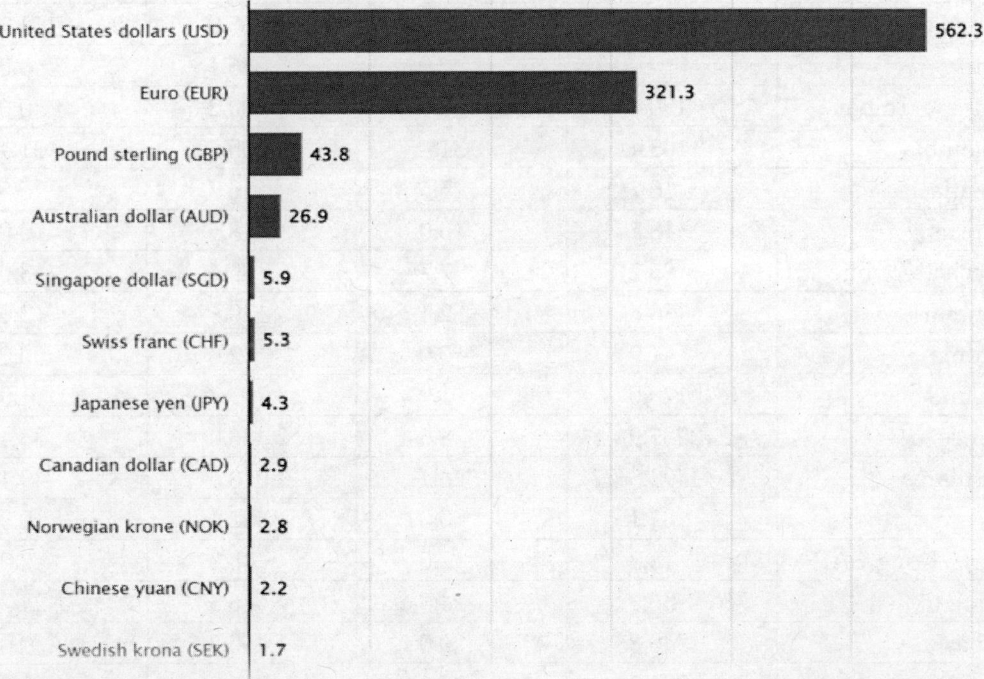

Source: Statista

FIGURE 10.1 Largest Deals in International Debt Markets in 2nd Quarter of 2022, Currency-wise: (in billion USD)

Table 10.2 present the outstanding government securities worldwide which shows the expansion of international bond market among the investor as the detailed explanation for domestic as well foreign currency is being given for the government. While Table 10.3 shows the worldwide distribution of central government debt securities market by instrument and maturity.

TABLE 10.2 Long-terms Government Securities Outstanding Worldwide at the end of 2020 (in billion US dollar)

Country	*Central Government*		*General Government*	
	Domestic Currencies	*Foreign Currencies*	*Domestic Currencies*	*Foreign Currencies*
All Countries	43,680.9	988.3	57,145.1	1,1189.1
Argentina	46.8	113.1	58.8	113.1
Australia	588.0	1.0	864.7	1.5
Austria	313.4	2.1	319.9	3.4
Belgium	461.4	3.6	508.6	3.6
Brazil	1,214.4	44.2	1,282.4	46.5
Bulgaria	3.1	11.7	3.1	11.7
Canada	663.7	9.3	1,265.9	144.7
China	—	0.0	7,056.1	0.0
Chinese Taipei	196.6	0.0	200.2	0.0
Colombia	103.4	31.4	105.5	31.4
Croatia	10.7	25.5	10.7	25.5
Cyprus	18.5	0.0	18.5	0.0
Czech Republic	85.2	7.7	85.6	8.0
Denmark	130.6	2.1	130.6	2.0
Estonia	1.9	0.0	2.0	0.0
Finland	129.0	1.9	131.2	1.9
France	2285.9	8.6	2,486.0	33.4
Germany	1493.5	26.1	2,018.3	49.4
Greece	82.1	0.0	82.1	0.0
Hong Kong SAR	18.3	2.0	18.3	2.0
Hungary	86.3	24.3	86.3	24.3
India	940.8	0.0	1,450.2	0.0
Indonesia	271.5	85.1	275.5	85.1
Ireland	170.2	0.0	170.2	0.0

(Contd.)

Country	Central Government		General Government	
	Domestic Currencies	Foreign Currencies	Domestic Currencies	Foreign Currencies
Israel	190.2	43.7	190.2	43.7
Italy	2446.7	18.1	2,464.4	18.4
Japan	8377.5	0.0	9,079.6	7.7
Korea	772.5	9.4	794.8	9.4
Latvia	12.5	0.4	12.5	0.4
Lithuania	21.0	2.8	21.0	2.8
Luxembourg	14.4	0.0	14.4	0.0
Malaysia	209.5	5.7	209.9	6.5
Malta	6.9	0.0	6.9	0.0
Mexico	349.5	80.7	352.9	80.7
Netherlands	368.8	0.7	374.4	0.7
Norway	57.5	0.0	73.1	0.0
Peru	34.0	15.8	34.0	15.8
Philippines	121.3	34.9	121.3	34.9
Poland	205.9	53.9	214.1	53.9
Portugal	200.2	4.8	205.0	4.8
Romania	52.3	52.0	52.8	52.0
Russia	183.3	37.9	202.9	37.9
Saudi Arabia	131.1	774	131.1	774
Singapore	103.1	0.0	103.1	0.0
Slovakia	53.3	2.3	53.3	2.3
Slovenia	39.9	1.7	39.9	1.7
South Africa	202.9	20.9	204.1	20.9
Spain	1,282.1	0.8	1,334.1	1.1
Sweden	95.6	21.3	115.9	24.6
Switzerland	75.5	0.0	122.7	0.0
Thailand	157.1	0.0	186.5	0.0
Turkey	106.7	103.2	106.7	103.8
United Kingdom	2,490.8	0.0	2,571.9	0.0
United States	16,003.3	0.0	19,121.1	0.0

Source: BIS 2021

TABLE 10.3 Summary of Central Government Debt Securities Market by Instrument and Maturity at the end of 2020 (in billion US dollar)

Country	*Domestic currency, Floating rate*	*Domestic currency, Straight fix rate*	*Domestic currency, Inflation indexed*	*Foreign currency*
Argentina	1.98196	10.63102	34.18968	43.66296274
Australia	0	558.0464	29.02551	0
Belgium	3.163462	458.2401	0	3.645466482
Brazil	415.4061	461.5367	335.5055	4.081669412
Canada	0	601.8702	40.29109	0
Chile	—	—	—	—
Chinese Taipei	0	196.7415	0	0
Colombia	0	68.9279	32.45652	—
Czechia	9.405108	75.84133	0	1.59541238
Germany	15.65165	1545.66	75.88995	26.09058447
Hong Kong SAR	0	13.61983	4.630362	0
Hungary	7.705415	72.5985	5.986281	1.840869191
India	45.42352	935.4891	0.157739	0
Indonesia	28.6571	247.092	0	0.404159834
Israel	13.59401	103.1216	73.47607	0
Korea	0	764.6988	7.811263	0
Malaysia	0	209.4824	0	0
Mexico	178.9742	78.42485	92.09295	0
Peru	0	33.19745	0.802899	0
Philippines	1.203751	117.5173	—	0.498104019
Poland	51.53621	146.1314	1.318681	0
Russia	63.17837	112.437	7.7109	0
Saudi Arabia	24.53333	106.576	0	0
Singapore	—	—	—	—
South Africa	0	151.1763	51.71509	—
Spain	27.2416	1183.046	71.90802	0
Thailand	0	157.1089	0	0
Turkey	19.17477	54.56058	33.78384	24.34893293
United Kingdom	0	1879.216	611.6187	0
United States	498.5	13931.2	1579.3	0

Source: BIS 2021

10.5 CLASSIFICATION OF BONDS

Eurobonds, Foreign Bonds, and Global Bonds are the terms used to describe the international bonds that non-domestic companies issue in a domestic market given in Figure 10.2. Regardless of the type—foreign bond, Eurobond, global bond, foreign-pay bond, investors in these bonds will receive a full return on their initial investment plus interest as guaranteed by the government or business that issued the bond. Although these bonds appear to be the same, they are different investment possibilities.

10.5.1 Foreign Bond

A foreign institution or firm may issue a bond in a nation other than its home country. This is known as a foreign bond. A foreign bond is typically priced throughout the currency of the country where it is anticipated to be sold. For instance, a Japanese business that needs American investors to fund its operations would choose to float a US dollar bond in the country. These bonds are known by the name of the nation in which they were issued. Yankee bonds, for instance, are made in the United States by a non-American corporation but are issued in dollars. The so-called "Samurai bonds" are issued by a non-Japanese firm in Japan and are priced in yen. A non-British firm in Britain issues bulldog bonds in pounds sterling. The "Matilda bonds" are Australian dollar-denominated bonds that were offered in the Australian market by a foreign, non-Australian corporation in an effort to obtain money from local Australian investors.

10.5.2 Eurobond

A bond issued outside of a particular jurisdiction is referred to as a "Eurobond". It does not specifically mention European-only bonds. A corporation issuing bonds using a currency other than its own issuing a "Eurobond." For instance, suppose an Indian business issued USD-denominated Eurobonds—US dollar currency bonds—in Japan. Similar to this, bonds issued by an Indian corporation and denominated in Japanese yen are known as Euro yen bonds when they are issued in the US. Similar to this, "Euro sterling" bonds are issued in other countries but have a sterling denominator.

10.5.3 Global Bond

Bonds considered to be global are those that are simultaneously offered and traded in several markets throughout the world. In most cases, these bonds are issued by governments or multinational corporations with the intention of selling them to a significant number of investors located in other countries. The bond is denominated in the currency of one particular market.

10.5.4 Foreign-Pay-Bond

Bonds that are issued by a local corporation in their home country but are denominated in a different currency that the domestic currency are referred to as foreign-pay bonds. An example of a foreign-pay bond would be one that was denominated in US dollars and issued by an Indian company called Infosys.

FIGURE 10.2 Classification of International Bonds.

10.6 ADVANTAGES AND DISADVANTAGES OF INVESTING IN INTERNATIONAL BONDS

10.6.1 Advantages

Diversification

One of the most significant benefits of buying foreign bonds is the diversification they provide. Since the yields on an international bond are often unaffected by negative developments in the home economy, diversification into such instruments may help decrease investors' exposure to catastrophic losses. Therefore, if your home country experiences severe flooding, your investment in a foreign nation is protected from the consequences of this occurrence.

Better Returns

The interest rates offered by overseas bond markets are higher than those offered by local bond markets. Foreign investors should be aware that the additional risk comes with the higher rewards offered by the issuers to make up for the higher risk. Hence, diversifying into the international bond market might boost portfolio performance.

Exposure to the Large Market

The international bond market is a great way for people to diversify their portfolios by investing in other economies. Thus, you may buy British bonds on the international bond market if you believe the British economy will flourish in the future. You may take advantage of the thriving economy of another country in this way.

Hedging

Investing in a foreign bond also acts as an instrument of hedging if the investors are exposed to losses due to a decline in the value of the US dollar. As a means of recouping their losses, they may buy bonds issued by countries whose currencies are showing signs of strength and appreciation.

10.6.2 Disadvantages

Political Risk

Diversification is offered by investments in the international bond market, but there are also hazards involved. One element for high risk is an unexpected political outburst. Losses for investors may result from the other country's unstable economy. Even though similar dangers exist with domestic bonds as well, the investor is well aware of them and is able to keep a close check on them. In the case of international bonds, It may be difficult for the investor to assess both the issuer's financial health as well as the economic and political climate of the foreign country.

Interest Rate Risk

Bond investors face interest rate risk when market conditions threaten to diminish the value of their holdings as a result of fluctuations in interest rates. The value of bond would normally decrease if interest rates increase and increase the value of bond if interest rates decrease. In general, bonds with longer maturities are more susceptible to market interest rate fluctuations than bonds with shorter maturities.

Default Risk

Risk associated with non-payment of a bond issuer regarding the payment of interest as promised and/or will not have enough money to pay down the principal when the bond expires is known as credit risk or default risk. Lower rated bonds are more susceptible to this danger.

Currency Risk

The danger that the value of your investment denominated in a foreign currency may decrease due to fluctuations in exchange rates is known as currency risk. For example, an investor investing in a German bond denominated in Euros and keep it until maturity, for instance, you will be repaid your initial investment and any income accrued on it in Euros. Even though the value of the actual German bond does not change, your return on investment might be lower if the Euro drops dramatically compared to the US dollar over that period.

Exchange Rate Instability

Bonds from several international issuers are available to investors in currencies other than their own. Hence, the investor is vulnerable to swings in the exchange rate between the two currencies. Upon bond maturity, for instance, the issuer will make payment in the bond's native currency. There is a possibility that the same amount of money might be turned into a smaller quantity based on the investor's local exchange rate.

Liquidity

Foreign bond also suffers with the problem of liquidity. Domestic bonds make it simple for investors to cash out their investment since it will be simple to find a buyer for a domestic bond. However, since so few individuals invest in overseas bonds, so selling the bond becomes a tedious task for the investor. This results in poor relative liquidity for bonds across international bond markets.

SUMMARY

1. International bonds are bonds issued by a nation or business that is not the investor's home country. They are traded on global bond markets and are often issued in the issuer's own currency. They pay interest at regular intervals and return the capital to the holder when the bond matures. The global bond market is rapidly growing as businesses search for the most affordable form of borrowing money. The foreign bond market has drawn private sector lending out of domestic markets, making up a significant portion of the overall amount of bonds existing on the international bond market.
2. The primary motive for creating a bond market was to fund fiscal deficits, but the need to control capital inflows has also led to the development of debt markets. The most important rationale is to create market interest rates that represent the opportunity cost of money at each maturity, which will improve financial markets more comprehensive. Borrowers throughout the private sector also require access to long-term credit, either directly from capital markets or via banks' intermediary services, and projects for permanent investments that are projected to pay off only in the long run must be financed by corporations.
3. Due to the introduction of a withholding tax on domestic German bonds in 1964, non-German investors were strongly encouraged to purchase overseas bonds rather than those denominated in the local Deutsche Mark. Foreign Deutsche Mark bonds had been issued as early as 1958; as non-German securities firms became more engaged in the underwriting and marketing of these bonds, the proportion of non-German investors in this market increased.
4. Several of the reasons that had fueled the development of the Eurobond market in its early years ceased to be significant once the Bretton Woods system collapsed in 1972 and the switch to floating exchange rates. Due to growing financial liberalization, particularly in Japan and the United Kingdom, falling long-term interest rates, and a developing swap market, the issuance of Eurobonds increased eightfold between 1981 and 1986. But issuance volumes in the Eurobond market have been fluctuating at $50 billion each quarter since 1986, with no discernible rising trend.
5. Foreign bonds are typically priced throughout the currency of the country where they are sold, and are known by the name of the nation in which they were issued.
6. A bond issued outside of a particular jurisdiction is referred to as a "Eurobond".
7. Global bonds are issued by governments or multinational corporations to sell to investors in other countries, denominated in one currency.
8. Foreign-pay bonds are bonds denominated in a different currency than the domestic currency.

KEY WORDS

- Farmer Richman Model
- International Bond Market
- Foreign Bond
- Eurobond
- Foreign Pay Bond
- Interest Rate Risk

QUESTIONS

1. Define the evolution of international bond in different phase.
2. What is the need for the development of international bond market?
3. What are the different types of international bond? Explain with example.
4. Explain the advantages and disadvantages while investing in international bond market.
5. What are the different kinds of risk involved in international bond? Also explain the risk mitigation mechanism for international bond.

REFERENCES AND SUGGESTED READINGS

1. Abakah, E.J.A., Addo, E., Gil-Alana, L.A., & Tiwari, A.K. (2021). Re-examination of international bond market dependence: Evidence from a pair copula approach, *International Review of Financial Analysis*, 74, 101678. https://doi.org/10.1016/j.irfa.2021.101678
2. Adelegan, O.J., & Radzewicz-Bak, B. (2016). *What Determines Bond Market Development in sub-Saharan Africa?*
3. Albagli, E., Ceballos, L., Claro, S., & Romero, D. (2019). Channels of US monetary policy spillovers to international bond markets, *Journal of Financial Economics*, *134*(2), 447–473. https://doi.org/10.1016/j.jfineco.2019.04.007
4. Barr, D.G., & Priestley, R. (2004). Expected returns, risk and the integration of international bond markets, *Journal of International Money and Finance*, 23(1), 71–97. https://doi.org/10.1016/j.jimonfin.2003.10.005
5. Bhattacharyay, B.N. (2012). Bond Market Development in Asia: An Empirical Analysis of Major Determinants, In *SSRN Electronic Journal* (Issue 300). https://doi.org/10.2139/ssrn.1898047
6. Bredin, D., Hyde, S., & Reilly, G.O. (2010). Monetary policy surprises and international bond markets, *Journal of International Money and Finance*, 29(6), 988–1002. https://doi.org/10.1016/j.jimonfin.2010.02.005
7. Burger, J.D., & Warnock, F.E. (2003). Diversification, Original Sin, and International Bond Portfolios, In *International Finance Discussion Papers* (Issue d).
8. Burger, J.D., & Warnock, F.E. (2006). Local currency bond markets, *IMF Staff Papers*, *53*(2006), 133–146.

9. Burger, J.D., Warnock, F.E., & Warnock, V.C. (2018). Bond Market Development in Developing Asia, *SSRN Electronic Journal*, 448, https://doi.org/10.2139/ssrn.2707539
10. Clare, A.D., & Lekkos, I. (2005). An Analysis of the Relationship Between International Bond Markets, *SSRN Electronic Journal*. https://doi.org/10.2139/ssrn.258021
11. Dungey, M., Fry, R., González-Hermosillo, B., & Martin, V. (2006). Contagion in international bond markets during the Russian and the LTCM crises, *Journal of Financial Stability*, 2(1), 1–27. https://doi.org/10.1016/j.jfs.2005.01.001
12. Fabella, R., & Madhur, S. (2003). Bond market development in East Asia: Issues and challenges, *ERD Working Paper Series*, 35, 1–24.
13. Ferguson, N. (2006). Political risk and the international bond market between the 1848 revolution and the outbreak of the First World War, *Economic History Review*, 59(1), 70–112. https://doi.org/10.1111/j.1468-0289.2005.00335.x
14. Fidora, M., Fratzscher, M., & Thimann, C. (2007). Home bias in global bond and equity markets: The role of real exchange rate volatility, *Journal of International Money and Finance*, 26(4), 631–655. https://doi.org/10.1016/j.jimonfin.2007.03.002
15. Hale, G.B., Jones, P.C., & Spiegel, M.M. (2020). Home currency issuance in international bond markets, *Journal of International Economics*, 122, 103256. https://doi.org/10.1016/j.jinteco.2019.103256
16. Hardie, I. (2006). The power of the markets? The international bond markets and the 2002 elections in Brazil, *Review of International Political Economy*, *13*(1), 53–77. https://doi.org/10.1080/09692290500396651
17. Hartmann, P., Manganelli, S., & Monnet, C. (2006). Capital markets and financial integration in Europe, *Competition and Profitability in European Financial Services: Strategic, Systemic and Policy Issues*, 553, 281–306. https://doi.org/10.4324/9780203086698
18. Ho, B.C., & Li, D.A.N. (2014). A mirror of history: China's bond market, 1921–1942, *The Economic History Review*, 67(2), 409–434.
19. Homer, S. (1975). The Historical Evolution of Today's Bond Market, *Explorations in Economic Research*, 2(3), 378–389.
20. Huang, H., & Zhu, N. (2011). The Chinese Bond Market: Historical Lessons, Present Challenges and Future Perspectives, *SSRN Electronic Journal, April* 2007. https://doi.org/10.2139/ssrn.991760
21. Ilmanen, A. (1995). Time-Varying Expected Returns in International Bond Markets, *The Journal of Finance*, 50(2), 481–506.
22. Leigland, J. (2020). Accelerating Municipal Bond Market Development in Emerging Economies: An Assessment of Strategies and Progress, *Wiley Online Library*, 21(1), 1–9. http://journal.um-surabaya.ac.id/index.php/JKM/article/view/2203
23. Pearson, R. (2015). The development of international insurance. In *The Development of International Insurance* (pp. 1–280). https://doi.org/10.4324/9781315655925
24. Piljak, V. (2013). Bond markets co-movement dynamics and macroeconomic factors: Evidence from emerging and frontier markets, *Emerging Markets Review*, 17, 29–43. https://doi.org/10.1016/j.ememar.2013.08.001

25. Plummer, M.G., & Click, R.W. (2005). Bond market development and integration in ASEAN, *International Journal of Finance and Economics*, 10(2), 133–142. https://doi.org/10.1002/ijfe.268

26. Pradhan, R.P., Arvin, M.B., Norman, N.R., & Bahmani, S. (2020). The dynamics of bond market development, stock market development and economic growth: Evidence from the G-20 countries, *Journal of Economics, Finance and Administrative Science*, 25(49), 119–147. https://doi.org/10.1108/JEFAS-09-2018-0087

27. Smaoui, H., Grandes, M., & Akindele, A. (2017). The Determinants of Bond Market Development: Further Evidence from Emerging and Developed Countries, *Emerging Markets Review*, 32, 148–167. https://doi.org/10.1016/j.ememar.2017.06.003.

CHAPTER 11

International Equity Market

LEARNING OUTCOMES

After reading this chapter, the reader will be able to:

- Describe Important Aspects of International Equity Market
- Name Major Stock Exchanges in India
- Discuss Major Stock Exchanges in the USA and Europe
- Discuss Instruments of International Equity Market

11.1 INTERNATIONAL EQUITY MARKET: AN OVERVIEW

The stock exchanges across several nations where investors have the opportunity to invest in a company's shares. Individual investors, institutional investors, and businesses purchase equity shares or holdings in public corporations. The goal is to acquire a portion of the company's equity capital in order to profit from and develop along with the company's development and become a partner in the business (French & Poterba, 1991; Longin & Solnik, 2001). There are tools available for this reason via which a US-based investor may invest money in the London Stock Exchange. Furthermore, this chance has accelerated globalisation and broadened the range of money transfers between nations. Even globally, the secondary market serves as a link between investors and investee enterprises in need of capital. Investors may invest internationally in two different ways: first, via dealer markets, and second, through agency markets. Additionally, it is sometimes referred to as the OTC market when an investor transacts with a dealer via dealer marketplaces (Darbar & Deb, 1997; Küçükçolak, et al., 2019). Additionally, the dealer is in charge of executing investor transactions on the OTC market. However, the general public cannot see these transactions. In contrast, brokers in the agency market are in charge of carrying out the investor's transactions. The global growth is expected to slowdown to 3.8% in 2023 from 4.4% in 2022 as per the IMF report published in October, 2022. As different growing economies expand at different rates, investing across the international market enhances the likelihood of bigger earnings than just investing in the local market. In a market economy that is still emerging, both the growth rate and the risks are high. In addition, developed countries send a significant amount of money to these developing markets (Chouksey, 2019; Dumas, et al., 2017).

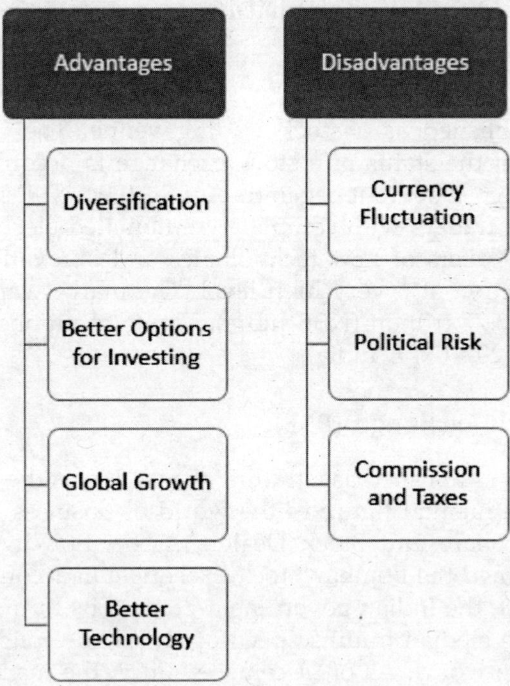

FIGURE 11.1 Advantages and Disadvantages of Investing in International Equity Market

TABLE 11.1 World's Top 10 Stock Exchanges in Terms of Market Capitalisation by 2022 (in trillion US dollars)

Rank	*Stock Exchange*	*Country*	*Market Capitalisation*
1	New York Stock Exchange (NYSE)	US	26.64
2	NASDAQ	US	23.46
3	Sanghai Stock Exchange (SSE)	China	7.63
4	Euronext	Europe	7.33
5	Tokyo Stock Exchange (TSE)	Japan	6.795
6	Hong Kong Stock Exchange (HKSE)	Hong Kong	6.13
7	Shenzhen Stock Exchange	China	5.74
8	London Stock Exchange (LSE)	UK	4.05
9	Bombay Stock Exchange (BSE)	India	3.96
10	National Stock Exchange	India	3.77

Source: Statista

11.2 MAJOR STOCK EXCHANGES IN INDIA

11.2.1 National Stock Exchange (NSE)

In 1992, NSE was established as a stock trading venue. The Securities and Exchange Board of India granted it the status of a stock exchange in accordance with the Securities Contracts (Regulation) Act, 1956, so it began trading in 1994. NSE became the first exchange in country that assists it traders with completely automated electronic trading. Since NSE was one of the early adopters of new technologies and innovative ideas, the company's systems are able to function at a very high level. The market capitalization of NSE as of December, 2022 is US$ 3.77 trillion (NSE India). The total number of companies listed in NSE is 1,696 as of July, 2021(NSE India).

11.2.2 Bombay Stock Exchange (BSE)

On July 9, 1875, BSE was established as a trading venue. It was the very first stock exchange across all of Asia. An influential figure in the world of business, Premchand Roy Chand, established the Native Share and Stock Dealers Association in 1875. This organisation would eventually be named the Bombay Stock Exchange. In accordance with the Securities Contracts Regulation Act, the Indian government granted its formal approval in the month of August 1957. Also, its median trading speed of six microseconds each deal makes it the quickest exchange in the world. As of Decemeber, 2022, the market capitalization of BSE is US$ 3.96 trillion (BSE India). The total number of companies listed in BSE is 5,749 as of July, 2021 (BSE India).

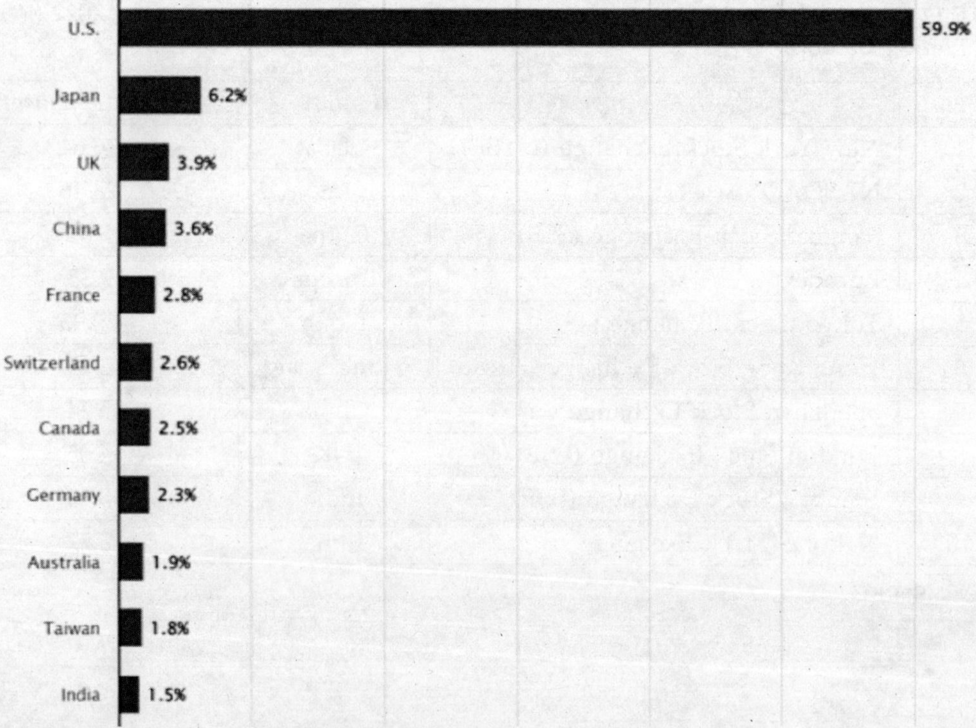

Figure 11.2 Equity Market Share by Country

11.3 MAJOR STOCK EXCHANGES IN THE UNITED STATES OF AMERICA (US)

11.3.1 New York Stock Exchange (NYSE)

New York Stock Exchange (NYSE) was founded on May 17 1792, by twenty-four brokers who signed the Buttonwood Agreement, which set a floor commission rate charged to clients and bound the signers to give preference to the other signers in securities sales. It is the world's most extensive Stock exchange by market capitalization of its listed companies at US$ 27,766.01 billion as of December, 2022 and 2,873 companies are listed on New York Stock Exchange as of July, 2021(NYSE 2021).

11.3.2 NASDAQ

The NASDAQ is the exchange which is known for the trading of technology stocks. The National Association of Securities Dealers (NASD), currently known as the Financial Industry Regulatory Authority (FINRA), established it in 1971. As per the report published by Focus world exchanges on July, 2021, the market capitalization of NASDAQ is US$16,237.59 billion and 2,987 companies are listed on NASDAQ as of December, 2022. This index, which is well known for being strongly weighted towards technology, includes a number of subsectors within the technology industry, such as software, biotech, semiconductors, and more. This exchange includes certain securities from different sectors, although being noted for its substantial amount of technology equities.

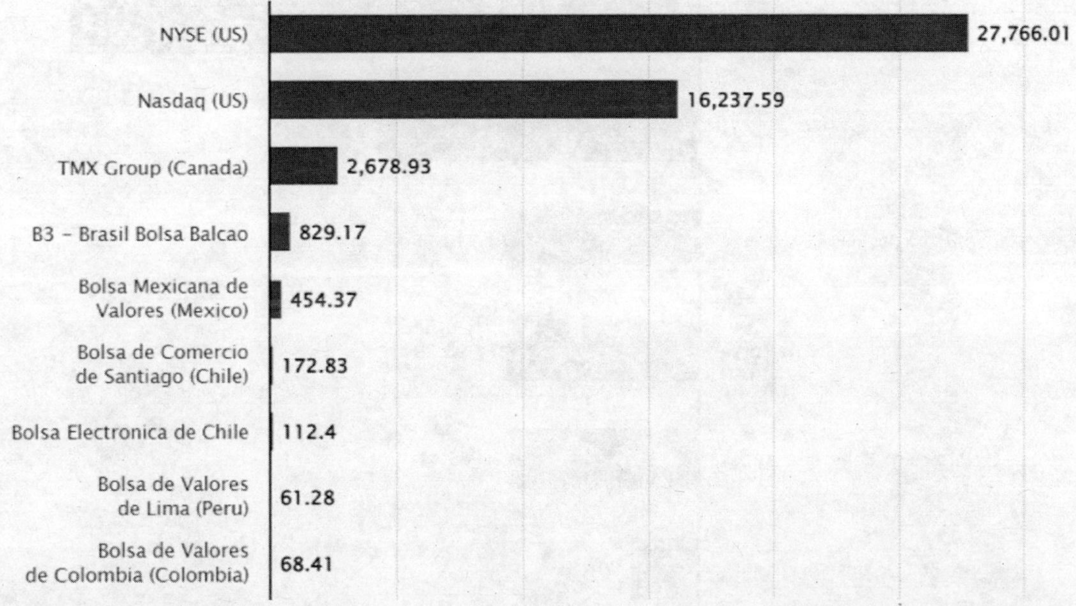

Source: Statista

FIGURE 11.3 Stock Exchanges in US in Terms of Market Capitalisation by 2022 (In billion US dollars)

11.4 MAJOR STOCK EXCHANGES IN EUROPE

11.4.1 Euronext

The Euronext stock exchange has offices in Brussels, London, Amsterdam, Paris, and Lisbon, among other European cities. It has over 1,200 issuers as of 2022, making it the biggest exchange in Europe with a $5,517 billion market valuation. The merger of the Paris Bourse, the Amsterdam and Brussels Stock Exchanges, and Euronext took place in 2000. It joined forces with NYSE Group in 2007 to become NYSE Euronext, and it successfully completed its IPO as a separate business in 2014. It provides market solution, settlement services, and listing market data.

11.4.2 London Stock Exchange

The London city is the headquarters to the London Stock Exchange. With a market value of $2823.4 billion, it is among the biggest stock exchanges in the world and the second largest in Europe. The London Stock Exchange dates back almost 300 years making it an oldest stock exchange in the world. It was established in 1801 and is a member of the London Stock Exchange Group, which was established in 2007 as a result of the merger of the LSE and the Milan Stock Exchange. Companies of all sizes have the chance to list on the LSE's multiple listing marketplaces. London permits international businesses to list their items as well.

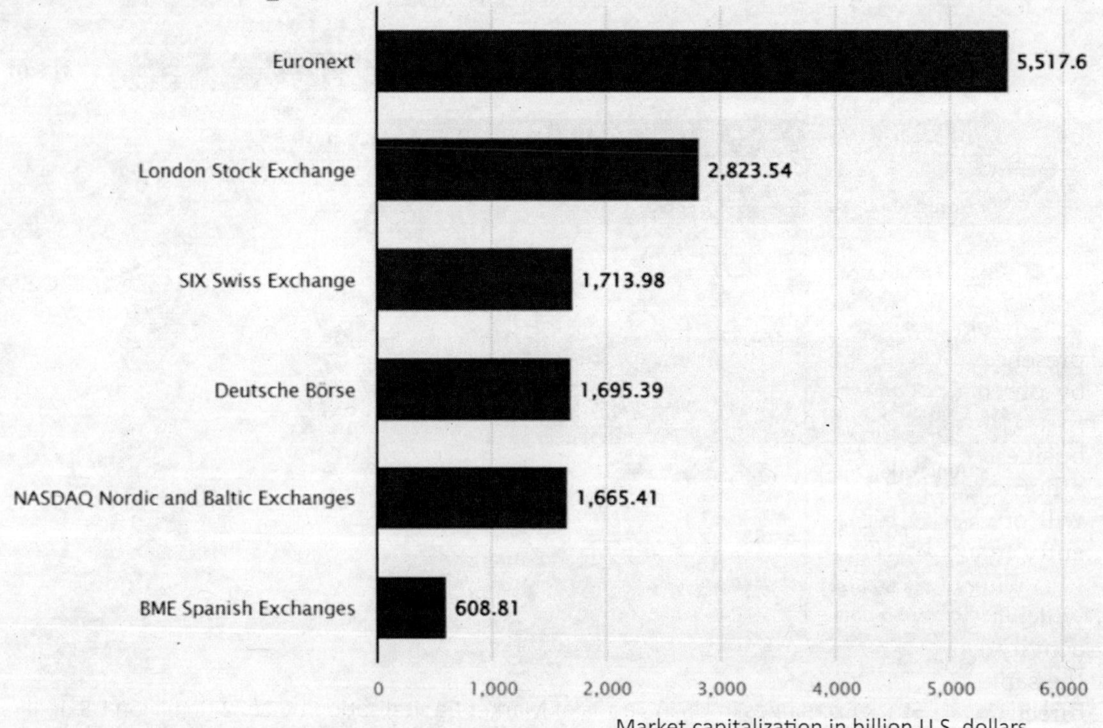

Source: Statista

FIGURE 11.4 Stock Exchanges in Europe in Terms of Market Capitalisation by 2022 (In billion US dollars).

11.5 INSTRUMENTS OF INTERNATIONAL EQUITY MARKET

11.5.1 Direct Investing

Direct investment is also referred to as FDI (foreign direct investment). FDI refers to investing the money into a foreign company with the intention of acquiring a majority ownership. Without having to purchase ordinary shares, FDI provide ownership position in return of the money invested (Huth, 1994; Malik, 2021). The primary distinction between direct investment and portfolio investment is that the acquisition of equity shares or preferred stock of a foreign firm, and the element of control desired are the latter two. Intangible assets, such as intellectual property, are often the only ones for which non-financial contributions to control are considered significant (Wongswan, 2006). Foreign direct investment (FDI) often involves more than just a simple cash transfer of ownership; it may also include supplementary aspects like organisational and managerial skills or technology. Individuals may make foreign direct investments, but businesses looking to establish a foothold in another nation are more likely to do so.

FIGURE 11.5 Types of Instruments in International Equity Market.

In vertical type of direct investment, the investor increases a company's worldwide presence. To illustrate, think of a major American manufacturer that expands worldwide by purchasing a parts distributor or opening new dealerships.

Horizontal direct investments are perhaps the most common kind of FDI. Any business that already has a foothold inside one country expands into another through a horizontal direct investment. For example, a fast food franchise with American origins will open locations in China. For both vertical and horizontal FDI, the term "green-field entry into a foreign market" is applicable.

The term "conglomerate direct investment" is used to describe the practice by which an already-established company in one country expands into an unrelated business activity in another country. Being a new business, opening up shop in a foreign country at the same time presents unique challenges for this kind of direct investment. Conglomerate direct investment might take the form of a company's construction of a theme park in a foreign country.

FIGURE 11.6 Classification of FDI.

11.5.2 American Depository Receipts

American Deposit Receipts are issued with increasing involvement from the global equity markets (ADRs). ADRs provide investors a broad range of global investment options and let foreign banks access far-flung global marketplaces. A few figures support the claim: In comparison with the approximately 5000 firms listed on US exchanges, there are over 37,000 companies listed globally; the US generates over 71% of the global GDP; yet one fourth of the world's biggest corporations are American (Bessembinder, et al., 2021). ADRs are negotiable certificates or "receipts" issued in the US that indicate holding of shares of a non-US-based corporation (Watanabe, et al., 2013). ADRs are used to trade the shares of several non-US corporations on US stock markets. Due to the fact that ADRs are regarded as US securities that are recognised as domestic under US law and that benefit from the protection and openness provided by US securities laws. Using ADRs, US investors to purchase shares of overseas corporations without engaging in international business. Prices for ADRs are expressed in US dollars, and they may also be traded similarly to US company shares. ADR includes two types: sponsored and unsponsored. A bank starts a sponsored ADR there at the request of an issuer from a foreign firm. One or more shares of the overseas stock may be represented by each ADR, which is granted by a United States depositary bank (Babu, 2019). Owners of ADRs have the option to purchase the foreign shares they stand in for, but most US investors find it more convenient to just possess the ADR. While the majority of underlying equities are bearer securities, ADRs (apart from Rule 144A issuance) are listed securities that provide ownership rights protection. A US bank issues a negotiable certificate on behalf of a certain number of shares of an overseas

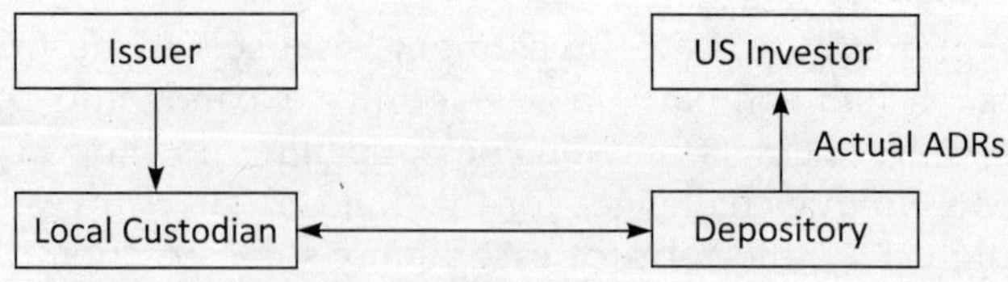

FIGURE 11.7 ADR Scheme.

stock which is trading on a US exchange (Kearney & Lucey, 2004). A US financial firm is the foreign owner of the underlying security for ADRs, which are denominated in US dollars. Administration and tariff expenses that would be imposed on each transaction are decreased due to ADRs.

Depository Agreement

An agreement made between the local custodians and the depositary bank is known as a depositary agreement. A bank is designated by an issuer as the depositary for the Depositary Receipt (DR) scheme it sponsors. In addition to acting as a registrar, transfer agent, and payment agency for the DR programme, the depositary issues and cancels ADRs. Investors may contact the issuer directly or via a broker or the depositary's direct investment scheme. Among the major participants in ADRs are JP Morgan Chase, Citibank, Deutsche Bank, and Bank of New York Mellon. Through a broker (conventional or internet), an investor may acquire ADRs (Lobão, 2019). ADRs are traded on the NASDAQ, NYSE, or AMEX.

An ADR's structure is determined by the goals set. ADR issuers may aim to increase their investor base or raise money. ADRs are divided into three tiers, each with its own criteria.

Level 1 ADRs are the most fundamental type of ADRs when foreign corporations either don't meet the requirements or don't want their ADR to be published on an exchange. An organisation may easily and affordably determine the level of interest in its assets in North America by using Level 1 ADRs, which are available in the over-the-counter market. The SEC also has the laxest regulations for Level 1 ADRs.

Level 2 kind of ADR is traded on an exchange. The SEC has a few extra standards for Level 2 ADRs; however, they also get greater visible trading volume.

The most prestigious **Level 3** ADR is when an issuer launches an ADR public offering on a US exchange. In the US financial markets, these ADRs are able to raise money and increase their visibility significantly.

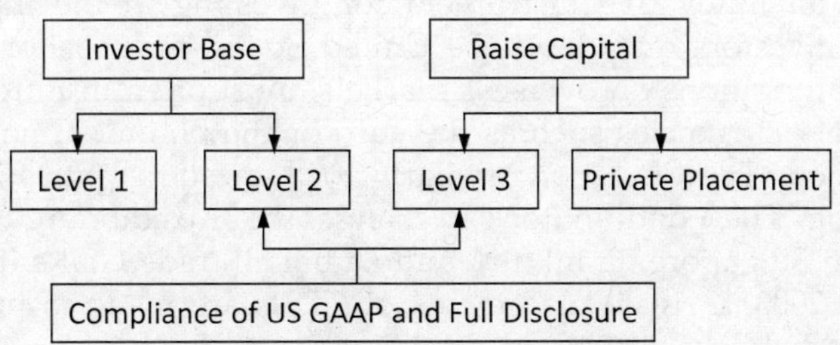

FIGURE 11.8 ADR Structure.

Benefits and Weakness of ADRs

Benefits

- ADRs provides an eased-up opportunity of investing in foreign company's stocks.
- ADRs are being traded in US dollar which provides the better trading value.

- The money involved in administration cost can also be reduced while investing in ADRs and tax burden can also be avoided in each transaction.
- Foreign firm prefers ADRs due to its exposure in US stock market and tap the investors from the market. Also, the firms get better exposure to the world's best companies and get better valuation than the domestic equity markets.
- ADRs are traded in accordance to the US regulations.
- Trading in ADRs is convenient and often considered as more tax efficient instrument while investing.
- ADRs provide the opportunity for diversifying the portfolio using the US dollar as well.

Challenges

As ADRs are the non-US market securities, they are prone to specific risks which are related with the ADRs.

- **Country Risk:** The risk associated with the home country regarding their political imbalance, economic fluctuations and social conditions will have impact on the stock prices listed on US market as well.
- **Inflation Risk:** Inflation risk which is an extension of exchange rate risk also impacts the prices of ADRs as the general price level increases and purchasing power of the individuals falls.
- **Currency Risk:** As ADRs are non-US based securities, they suffer from the currency risk as well. Although the ADRs are being traded in US dollar and the dividends also paid US dollar as well.
- Companies needs to follow the accounting standards as per the US stock market which sometime also creates a conflict to the non-US firms.

11.5.3 Global Depository Receipts

GDRs emerged as an innovative instrument for investing in the international financial markets. To reach investors outside of the United States, a depository bank would issue shares of foreign corporations on overseas markets, most often in Europe. Some GDRs are denominated in other currencies such as the euro or the pound, although the dollar is by far the most common. They function similarly to domestic equities in terms of trading, clearing, and settling. The London Stock Exchange, the Luxembourg Stock Exchange, and the stock markets in Singapore, Frankfurt, and Dubai all trade GDRs (Brennan, et al., 2005; Connolly & Wang, 2003). Private placements of GDRs are made to institutional investors before they become publicly traded.

11.5.4 International Equity Fund

International equity fund which is also referred as global mutual funds are one of the best way for investing into international market as the investors don't need to make much hassle for the same. In this, investors opt out for those mutual funds which specially focuses on the international equities. Mutual funds with an international concentration are available in a range of strategies, from extreme to cautious. They could be nation- or region-specific.

They may follow an international stock index passively via an index fund or aggressively through an actively managed fund. But watch out for expenses: Compared to their local equivalents, globally oriented mutual funds can incur greater charges and fees.

SUMMARY

1. The stock exchanges across several nations where investors have the opportunity to invest in a company's shares. Individual investors, institutional investors, and businesses purchase equity shares or holdings in public corporations.
2. Investors can invest in international equity market by different ways: first, via dealer markets, and second, through agency markets. Additionally, it is sometimes referred to as the OTC market when an investor transacts with a dealer via dealer marketplaces.
3. Major Stock Exchanges across the world:

   India: Bombay Stock Exchange (BSE)
   National Stock Exchange (NSE)

   US: New York Stock Exchange (NYSE)
   National Association of Securities Dealers Automated Quotations (NASDAQ)

   Europe: Euronext
   London Stock Exchange
4. Foreign direct investment is the most frequent name for direct investment. Investments made into foreign companies with the goal of gaining a controlling stake are referred to as FDI. Without the need to buy common stock, direct investments provide financial financing in return for an ownership position.
5. In vertical type of direct investment, the investor expands an existing company's international operations. As an example, consider an American automaker that develops dealerships or buys a parts supply company overseas.
6. The most typical kind of direct investment is likely to be a horizontal direct investment. In horizontal direct investments, an organisation that currently has operations in one nation sets up shop in another. It's possible that a fast-food chain with American roots may launch restaurants in China. The phrase "green-field entrance into a foreign market" also applies to horizontal direct investment.
7. An established corporation in one nation adds an unrelated commercial activity in another country refers to the conglomerate direct investment. This kind of direct investment is especially difficult since it calls for starting a new company and setting it up abroad at the same time. An example of conglomerate direct investment can be a corporation building a theme park in another nation.
8. American Deposit Receipts (ADRs) are issued with increasing involvement from the global equity markets. ADRs provide investors a broad range of global investment options and let foreign banks access far-flung global marketplaces.

9. GDRs emerged as an innovative instrument for investing in the international financial markets. To reach investors outside of the United States, a depository bank would issue shares of foreign corporations on overseas markets, most often in Europe.
10. International equity fund which is also referred as global mutual funds are one of the best ways for investing into international market as the investors don't need to make much hassle for the same.

KEY WORDS

- International Equity Market
- Direct Investing
- American Depository Receipts
- Global Depository Receipts
- International Equity Fund

QUESTIONS

1. What are the main reasons for investing in the international equity market? Explain the advantages and disadvantages of international investing.
2. Explain in brief about the following stock exchanges:
   (a) National Stock Exchange
   (b) Bombay Stock Exchange
   (c) Euronext
   (d) London Stock Exchange
   (e) New York Stock Exchange
   (f) NASDAQ
3. What are the various instruments for investing in the international equity market?
4. Explain ADRs as an investing instrument by focusing on ADR scheme and its structure.
5. Differentiate between ADRs and GDRs with suitable examples.

REFERENCES AND SUGGESTED READINGS

1. Babu, A.S. (2019). Investors' Attention and American Depository Receipts Pricing: Evidence from Indian Stocks, *Asian Journal of Empirical Research*, 9(12), 381–386. https://doi.org/10.18488/journal.1007/2019.9.12/1007.12.381.386
2. Bessembinder, H. (Hank), Chen, T.F., Choi, G., & Wei, K.C. (John). (2021). American Depository Receipts: The Long-Term US Investor Experience, *SSRN Electronic Journal*, 0–24. https://doi.org/10.2139/ssrn.3762706

3. Brennan, M.J., Henry Cao, H., Strong, N., & Xu, X. (2005). The dynamics of international equity market expectations, *Journal of Financial Economics*, 77(2), 257–288. https://doi.org/10.1016/j.jfineco.2004.06.008
4. Chouksey, A. (2019). Indian capital market in context of tapping international market through depository receipts, *Journal of Prabhandan and Taqniki*, 2(2).
5. Connolly, R.A., & Wang, F.A. (2003). International equity market comovements: Economic fundamentals or contagion, *Pacific Basin Finance Journal*, 11(1), 23–43. https://doi.org/10.1016/S0927-538X(02)00060-4
6. Darbar, S.M., & Deb, P. (1997). Co-movements in international equity markets, *Journal of Financial Research*, 20(3), 305–322. https://doi.org/10.1111/j.1475-6803.1997.tb00251.x
7. Dumas, B., Lewis, K.K., & Osambela, E. (2017). Differences of opinion and international equity markets, *Review of Financial Studies*, *30*(3), 750–800. https://doi.org/10.1093/rfs/hhw083
8. French, K.R. & Poterba, J.M. (1991). Investor diversification and international equity markets, In *The American Economic Review* (Vol. 81, Issue 2, pp. 222–226). http://www.nber.org/papers/w3609
9. Huth, W.L. (1994). International Equity Market Integration, *Managerial Finance*, 20(4), 3–7. https://doi.org/10.1108/eb018467
10. Kearney, C., & Lucey, B.M. (2004). International equity market integration: Theory, evidence and implications. *International Review of Financial Analysis*, 13(5 SPEC. ISS.), 571–583. https://doi.org/10.1016/j.irfa.2004.02.013
11. Küçükçolak, A., Büyükakın, F., & Küçükçolak, N. (2019). Cointegration of Equity and Gold Markets : Evidence from, *International Journal of Economics and Financial Issues*, 9(2), 32–40.
12. Lobão, J. (2019). Seasonal anomalies in the market for American depository receipts, *Journal of Economics, Finance and Administrative Science*, 24(48), 241–265. https://doi.org/10.1108/JEFAS-09-2018-0088
13. Longin, F., & Solnik, B. (2001). Extreme correlation of international equity markets, *Journal of Finance*, 56(2), 649–676. https://doi.org/10.1111/0022-1082.00340
14. Malik, D. (2021). Foreign Direct Investment in India: Trends and Determinants Foreign Direct Investment in India: Trends and Determinants, *Our Heritage*.
15. Watanabe, A., Xu, Y., Yao, T., & Yu, T. (2013). The asset growth effect: Insights from international equity markets, *Journal of Financial Economics*, 108(2), 529–563. https://doi.org/10.1016/j.jfineco.2012.12.002
16. Wongswan, J. (2006). Transmission of information across international equity markets, *Review of Financial Studies*, 19(4), 1157–1189. https://doi.org/10.1093/rfs/hhj033.

CHAPTER 12

International Capital Structure and Cost of Capital

LEARNING OUTCOMES

After reading this chapter, the reader will be able to:

- Provide an Overview of International Capital Structure
- Describe Market Structure
- Discuss Advantages and Disadvantages of Cross-listing
- Explain the Law of One Price
- Interpret Portfolio Theory and Arbitrage Pricing Theory
- Explain and Differentiate between Domestic and International Capital Asset Pricing Model

12.1 INTERNATIONAL CAPITAL STRUCTURE: AN OVERVIEW

The capital structure of a company and the proportion of the various types of funding that are included in it are considered to impact the cost of capital for that company, but this is not the only factor to take into account when evaluating the cost of capital in the international market, or the cost of capital for multinational corporations. Multinational companies are those that operate in more than one country. However, in this chapter, for the cost of capital in an international context, those firms are being considered which are listed in more than one country are considered.

The structure of the international financial market is a key concern when pricing assets in an international setting, as per the previous studies, there are two principal components of the global financial market. First, determine whether the market is segmented so that no effect can be seen from one market to another. Next, assess whether a country's financial industry is integrated so that there appears to be no variation in the cost of capital across markets. Since the cost of capital in an integrated market is the same in all nations, it doesn't matter whether a company raises money from inside its own country or from outside it. Interestingly, the other aspect is that the market is less than fully integrated, or we can say that the market is partially segmented. Once they do, the companies might be able to issue securities in both local and international markets, increasing the potential for wealth creation for their shareholders. Table 12.1 shows the previous research on integration testing and its results.

TABLE 12.1 Summary of Past Results for Market Integration

Author	*Valuation Model*	*Methodology*	*Data*	*Result*
Solnik	IAPM	Fama-Mcbeth	Europe	Cannot reject integration
Stehle	IAPM	Modified Fama-Macbeth	US	Could not discriminate between integration and segmentation
Errunza and Losq	Mild segmentation IAPM	Modified Stehle	European market	Not consistent with mild segmentation
Wheatley	Consumption-based IAPM	MLF-Gibbons Stambaugh	Developed markets	Cannot reject integration
Jorion and Schwartz	IAPM	Maximum likelihood estimates	US-Canada	Rejected integration
Berges-Lobera	IAPT	Traditional factor analysis	US-UK Canada Spain	Rejected integration (except Canada-US)
Cho, et al.	IAPT	Inter-battery factor analysis	Developed markets	Rejected integration
Alexander, et al.		Event study of dual listing	Canada, Japan, Australia, South Africa, Denmark, UK	Rejected integration (except Canada-US)

Source: (Errunza, et al., 1992)

12.2 MARKET STRUCTURE

12.2.1 Theoretical Background

For a better understanding, we have divided the world financial market into three parts based on the level of integration:

Integration of Market

The integration of the world financial market will result in international portfolio diversification by investors. That means while calculating the market portfolio in the capital asset pricing model, the market portfolio (MP) in the asset pricing formula will be of "world", which includes all the assets worldwide. In this, the risk-measured beta should represent the world's systematic risk. Specifically, in the Integrated world financial market, the future cash flows will be the same across the nations.

Assets are priced in the complete integration of the market as:

$$R_i = R_f + \frac{R_m - R_f}{Var\,(R_m)}\,\text{Cov}(R_i, R_m) \tag{1}$$

where, R_i = Return of asset; R_f = Risk free rate; R_m = Return of market

While pricing the Internationally tradable assets, world beta will be considered and priced accordingly.

Segmentation of Market

After integration, the other principal component of market structure is segmentation. Now, supposedly consider the world financial market segmented where investors are restricted from investing in domestic portfolios and not allowed to diversify their portfolios internationally. In this case, while calculating the portfolio, the market portfolio (MP) considered for pricing will be the domestic market. The risk measured beta should be domestic, representing the systematic domestic risk. Here, the additional future cash flows prices differently across the countries as the investors perceive different risk aversion of systematic risk across the nations.

In an entirely segmented market, the domestic assets are priced as follows:

$$R_i = R_f + A^D D\,Cov\,(R_i, R_D) \tag{2}$$

The assets from multinational foreign firms listed on the exchange will be priced as follows:

$$R_g = R_f + A^F F\,Cov(R_g, R_f) \tag{3}$$

where R_i and R_g are the current equilibrium level of domestic and foreign assets, R_f will be the risk-free rate assumed for both domestic and foreign countries. A^D and A^F denote the risk aversion measure of domestic and foreign securities. $Cov(R_i, R_D)$ and $Cov(R_g, R_F)$ denote the covariance between future returns on securities and the domestic and foreign country market portfolio.

Partial Integration

Asset Pricing is complicated in the partially integrated market where some assets are cross-listed and others are not; the pricing of non-tradable assets will be priced as follows:

$$R_i = R_f + A^W W\,Cov(R_i, R_w) + A^D D[Cov(R_i, R_D) - Cov(R_i, R_D)] \tag{4}$$

$Cov(R_i, R_D)$ will be the indirect covariance between future returns of non-tradable assets and domestic market portfolios induced by the tradable assets. Figure 12.1 shows the effect and pricing pattern of securities in different market structure.

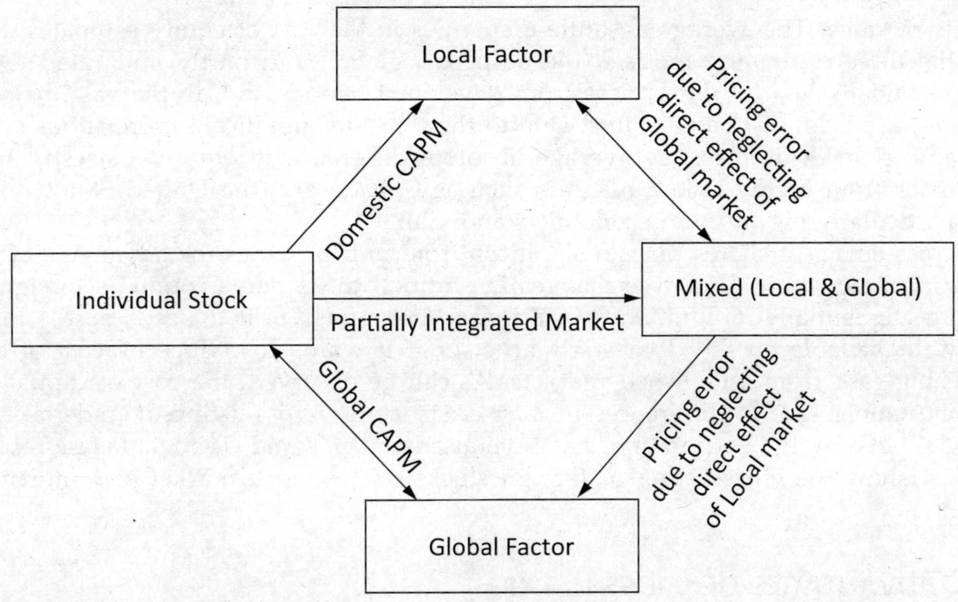

Source: (El Hedi Arouri, et al., 2013)

FIGURE 12.1 Effect of Domestic and International Market on Cross-listed Stock.

El Hedi Arouri, et al., (2013), in their paper, shows the cost of capital across the countries and compute it using domestic CAPM, global CAPM, and partially integrated CAPM. The sample countries include Brazil, Canada, France, Malaysia, Mexico, and the US. The details are given in Table 12.2, where the countries, number of firms, and the average degree of segmentation by domestic, global, and partially integrated CAPM are shown.

TABLE 12.2 Cost of Capital difference Across the Countries in different Market Structures

Country	*No. of firms*	*Domestic CAPM*	*Global CAPM*	*Partially Integrated CAPM*
Brazil	106	0.423	175.678	181.091
Canada	212	0.069	22.247	15.338
France	131	0.192	54.355	49.453
Malaysia	78	0.486	123.433	85.435
Mexico	89	0.670	97.396	198.771
US	517	0.042	11.218	10.314

Source: Ross, S.A. (2005). Capital structure and the cost of capital. *Journal of Applied Finance*, 15(1), pp. 664–671.

Brazil (176 points) has the greatest absolute average value, whereas Mexico has the highest absolute average value (199 points). The businesses from Brazil and Malaysia have absolute mean values larger than 100 points, while the firms from Brazil and Mexico exhibit the same. The average absolute disparities in the cost of equity estimates derived from the three competing models (the domestic, global, and partly integrated CAPMs) are substantially less for enterprises from developed nations and, in the vast majority of instances, are below 50 basis points. Due to the typically significant correlations between local and global variables, the average absolute difference in equity cost estimates for enterprises from highly linked markets such as Canada and the United States does not seem particularly big from an economic standpoint.

Cross-listing of shares plays a significant role as it provides the advantage of listing shares in one or more foreign exchanges in addition to its home country's foreign stock exchange. Essentially, a company would cross-list its assets if it needs access to more money unavailable on the domestic market or if it wants to reduce its cost of capital by seeking cash from established markets. As can be observed, the cost of capital varies between nations due to differences in market structure. Cross-listing, if undertaken as a strategic move by the corporation, has several advantages and disadvantages. Table 12.3 and 12.4 show the cross-listing of foreign stocks on US stock market and Indian stock market.

12.3 ADVANTAGES OF CROSS-LISTING

12.3.1 Access to Capital

Cross-listing provides companies with opportunities to raise funds from larger markets. Hence giving them access to more exchanges.

12.3.2 Expanded Investor Base

By cross-listing their shares in foreign markets, companies can expand their investor base as the cross-listing increases the visibility of the company's name outside the domestic setting.

12.3.3 The Secondary Market for the Company's Stock

Cross-listing creates a secondary market for the companies to raise new capital from foreign markets.

12.3.4 Enhances Liquidity of the Stock

Cross-listing enhances the stock's liquidity by providing an additional market for the company's share.

12.3.5 Improved Corporate Governance and Transparency

Before cross-listing stock to foreign markets, companies must fulfil the listing and disclosure criteria given by the exchanges. So, it improves the governance procedure of the companies and also brings transparency to their financials as they complete the dual requirement of domestic as international foreign exchanges.

12.4 DISADVANTAGES OF CROSS-LISTING

12.4.1 Increased Cost

The process of cross-listing requires fulfilling the guidelines given by the exchanges. So, it increases the cost as well.

Securing insider information is tough once the securities are listed in foreign exchanges as they require specific information while cross-listing, and sometimes users derive it for personal benefits.

12.4.2 Volatility Spillover

Once a company's stock gets listed on the foreign exchange, it also brings volatility spillover effect from those markets to the domestic market.

TABLE 12.3 Foreign Companies Listed on the US Stock Market (Selected)

Country	*Firms*
Taiwan	Taiwan Semiconductor Manufacturing, Chunghwa Telecom Co Ltd., United Microelectronics Corp, Advanced Semiconductor Engineering Inc, Silicon Motion Technology Corporation, Himax Technologies, ChipMOS technologies
China	Alibaba Group Holding, JD.com Inc, NetEase Inc, Pinduoduo Inc, Baidu Inc, NIO Inc, XPeng Inc, Li Auto Inc, BeiGene, DiDi Global Inc, KE Holdings Inc, ZTO Express, Trip.com Group Limited
Japan	Toyota Motor Corp, Sony Group Corporation, Mitsubishi UFJ Financial Group Inc, Honda Motor Co Ltd, Sumitomo Mitsui Financial Group Inc, Takeda Pharmaceutical Company Limited, Mizuho Financial Group Inc, Canon Inc, Orix, Nomura Holdings Inc, MEDIROM Healthcare Technologies Inc
The Netherlands	ASML Holding NV, ING Groep NV, Koninklijke Philips NV, Argenx SE, Aegon NV, VEON Ltd, MYT Ltd., Pharming Group N.V., Trivago NV
Switzerland	Novartis AG, ABB Ltd, UBS Group AG, Credit Suisse Group AG, Molecular Partners AG, WISeKey International Holding AG, Addex Therapeutics
United Kingdom	Royal Dutch Shell, Royal Dutch Shell, AstraZeneca PLC, HSBC Holdings PLC, Unilever PLC, Rio Tinto PLC, Diageo PLC, GlaxoSmithKline PLC, BP PLC, British American Tobacco PLC, BHP Group PLC
Denmark	Novo Nordisk A/S, Genmab A/S, Ascendis Pharma, Zealand Pharma A/S, Evaxion Biotech A/S, Orphazyme A/S, Forward Pharma
Germany	SAP SE, BioNTech SE, Fresenius Medical Care AG, Evotec SE, MorphoSys AG, Jumia Technologies AG, Mynaric AG, VIA optronics AG, Biofrontera AG, Spark Networks Inc, voxeljet

(*Contd.*)

Country	Firms
India	HDFC Bank Ltd, Infosys Ltd, ICICI Bank Ltd, Wipro Ltd, Tata Motors Ltd, Dr. Reddys Laboratories, WNS Holdings, SIFY Technologies Limited
Australia	BHP Billiton Ltd, Westpac Banking Corp, WPP PLC, James Hardie Industries, Mesoblast, Opthea Limited, Immutep Limited, Kazia Therapeutics, Advanced Human Imaging Ltd, Alterity Therapeutics Limited, Genetic Technologies, Immuron Limited, Bionomics Limited

Source: adrbnymellon.com

TABLE 12.4 Foreign Companies Listed on the Indian Stock exchange (Selected)

Country	Firms
Switzerland	ABB Ltd., Bata, Nestle
United States	Proctor & Gamble, Abbott Laboratories, Colgate Palmolive, Gillette, Honeywell, Oracle Corporation, Whirlpool Corporation, Pfizer
Germany	Bosch
United Kingdom	Hindustan Unilever, Castrol, AstraZeneca Pharma, GlaxoSmithKline, Thomas Cook
Japan	Maruti Suzuki, Panasonic
France	Saint-Gobain

Source: Datastream

Financial market integration results from various postulates from the past, such as Cournot's law of one price, Markowitz portfolio theory, and the international asset pricing model, which is a development over the traditional capital asset pricing and Arbitrage pricing theory in an international setting.

12.5 LAW OF ONE PRICE (COURNOT 1927)

Cournot gives the law of one price in 1927, which states that the price of identical assets or commodity will have the same price across the globe regardless of their location when the particular factors are taken into consideration which includes:

1. No transaction cost
2. No transportation cost
3. No legal restrictions
4. Same currency exchange rates
5. No price manipulation by buyers and sellers

This law provides essential fundamental support to the concept of integration, allowing companies to raise capital among integrated stock markets.

12.6 THE PORTFOLIO THEORY (MARKOWITZ 1952)

An investment portfolio refers to the diversification of financial assets and grouping them into various assets such as stocks, currencies, bonds, commodities, and funds that the investor purchases to generate his income and meet the financial objectives. Markowitz gives the investors the trade-off between the stocks which are high in risk and give a high return. The other side is issuing debt and treasury bills with low risk and return. In his book "The Theory of Investment Value", John Burr Williams advocated that a stock's value should be equal to the present value of its future dividend stream. However, because dividends are unpredictable, William advises valuing a stock based on the estimated value of its discounted future dividend stream. Roy also suggested making judgments based on the portfolio's overall mean and standard deviation. He proposed, in particular, selecting the portfolio that maximises portfolio $(E - d)/\sigma$, where d is a fixed (for the analysis) terrible return and is the standard deviation of return (Markowitz, 1999). However, if an investor is solely concerned with the expected values of securities, they must also be concerned with the portfolio's expected value. To maximise a portfolio's expected value, one must invest in the securities with the highest expected return (Markowitz, 1991). Investors must make the optimum portfolio with the most gains and the least risk (Marling & Emanuelsson (2012). While deciding on investing, an investor must have to make three decisions:

1. Amount a person wants to invest in the asset market
2. The assets in which a person wants to invest
3. The amount allotted to each type of assets

The Markowitz model was the first significant quantitative examination of such advantages (Witt & Dobbins, 1979). Integrated financial markets also allow the firm to raise the fund from the market, reducing their capital cost and maximizing their profits.

12.7 ARBITRAGE PRICING THEORY (ROSS, 1976)

Stephen Ross developed the Arbitrage Pricing Theory (APT) in 1976 as an alternative to the CAPM model, which assumes that the market sometimes misprices the securities. The APT, according to Brennan, is "a minimalist model of security market equilibrium" that "logically precedes our other utility-based models and should be verified before considering the predictions of greater utility specifications (Shanken, 2019)". A multifactor asset pricing model states an asset's return can be predicted by expected return and many macroeconomic factors that capture the systematic risk (Bansal & Vishwanathan, 2016). The Arbitrage pricing theory plays a vital role in a fully integrated market where securities are internationally tradable. APT by Ross provides a testable alternative to the traditional CAPM, as it is proposed that the CAPM model is static and follows the assumption of fixed beta (Roll & Ross, 1967). Because it completely matches what appears to be the CAPM's intuition, the APT is a highly suitable substitute. Allowing the beta to vary with time can be justified by the business cycle (Mahdy F. Elhusseiny, et al., 2019). So, using all the information to form expectations is reasonable, which gives rise to Conditional CAPM. So, while evaluating assets considering the market information fits the data much better than the traditional CAPM, it fails while explaining the asset pricing in the short run (Choe, et al., 2016).

Assets are priced in Arbitrage pricing theory:

$$E(R)_i = E(R)_z + (E(I) - E(R)_z) \times \beta_n$$

where,

$E(R)_i$ = Expected return on the asset
R_z = Risk-free rate of return
β_n = Sensitivity of the asset price to macroeconomic factor
E_i = Risk premium associated with factor *i*.

12.8 DOMESTIC VERSUS INTERNATIONAL CAPITAL ASSET PRICING MODEL (CAPM)

12.8.1 CAPM (Capital Asset Pricing Model, Sharpe 1964)

CAPM focuses on the relationship between systematic risk and the expected return on financial assets, widely used to price risky securities and calculate the firms' capital cost (Bollerslev, et al., 2016). One of the finance's most fundamental theoretical underpinnings is the Capital Asset Pricing Model (Hundal, et al., 2019). General equilibrium models of capital asset pricing have recently received much attention. Sharpe (1964) and Treynor (1961) devised the mean-variance formulation, which was expanded and explained by Lintner (1965), Mossin (1966), Fama (1968a; 1968b), and Long (1968a; 1968b) (1972). Treynor (1965), Sharpe (1966), and Jensen (1967) are also notable. Suppose the financial market is fully segmented where none of the assets is internationally tradable, i.e., the pricing of non-tradable assets. In such instances, they will be priced based on the domestic country's systemic risk. Nevertheless, if the market is completely integrated and all assets are internationally tradable, local and foreign currency assets will be valued according to systematic global risk (Karp & Van Vuuren, 2017) by predicting the variation in excess portfolio returns on the Johannesburg Stock Exchange. Portfolios of stocks were constructed based on an adapted Fama-French (1993). Here, the cross-listing of assets plays a crucial role in defining the pricing of assets. The CAPM is based on the idea that not all risks affect the firm; risk can also be diversified (Perold, 2004). The model's principal output describes the relationship between predicted risk premiums on individual assets and their "systematic risk." $E(R_j) = E(RM)_j$ (Black, et al., 2003). The CAPM's appeal is that it makes accurate and intuitive predictions about quantifying risk and the relationship between return and risk (Fama & French, 2004). Due to its relevance in making financial decisions such as investing, obtaining capital, and analyzing portfolio performance, the link between risk and return has long been the primary topic in finance (Kuehn, et al., 2021).

12.8.2 International Asset Pricing Model

Asset pricing in a global context has been researched by a numerous researchers including (Bai & Green, 2020; Buckberg, 1995a; De Santis & Gerard, 1997; Harshita, et al., 2015; Harvey, 1991; Musawa, Kapena, & Shikaputo, 2020; Musawa, Kapena, Shikaputo, et al., 2020; Wang, et al., 2013) in which they stressed the value of CAPM's international version for assessing asset pricing models. The question of whether the global market is segmented or integrated was also a major topic of discussion (El Hedi Arouri, et al., 2013; Errunza, Vihang R., Miller, 2016; Errunza, et al., 1992; Patro, 2001; Pirinsky & Wang, 2011; René M.

Stulz, 1995; Thomadakis & Usmen, 1991). When evaluating asset price in a global context, cross-listing is yet another essential issue to consider. The question arises over whether the non-tradable assets should also be or whether they should be priced according to domestic pricing portfolios, both of which must be taken into account when discussing the cross-listed share, which is tradable on international markets (Alpanda & Kabaca, 2020; Fama & French, 1992; Hail & Leuz, 2009; Li, 2019). Many asset pricing models have only been evaluated within the confines of the local market, particularly in closed economies where domestic assets are valued and domestic asset diversification is all that exists. Fama and Mcbeth (1973) and Stephen Ross(1980) show the single economy test of CAPM and APT. Mispriced securities, seasonal fluctuations, company size and dividend yields are just some of the anomalies that pop up in country-by-country research (Korajczyk & Viallet, 1989). Investment return and risk, including currency risk, may be evaluated with the use of the International Capital Asset Pricing Model (RenéM M. Stulz, 1981). Rates of return on local and international assets calculated using several alternative models. Both the local and international forms of the models are contrasted when valuing assets in different countries (Lee, et al., 2016). With International CAPM, investors are rewarded for exposure to overseas currency markets in addition to the time value of money compensation and market risk premium (Buckberg, 1995b). Consideration is given to the impact of fluctuations in the value of a foreign currency on an investor's holdings. Despite being central to these ideas, our comprehension of financial market integration has improved because of them. If the price is determined by risk, then businesses that participate in these marketplaces may be used to learn about the interconnectedness of the industry.

ICAPM provides investors with a way of calculating expected returns in local currency:

$$E(R)_i = RFR + \beta(R_m - R_f) + \beta(FCRP)$$

where,

RFR = Domestic Risk-free rate

β = World systematic risk

$R_m - R_f$ = Premium for global market risk measured in domestic currency

FCRP = Foreign currency risk premium

12.8.3 Specific Versions of Asset Pricing Models

The Conditional CAPM

The CAPM is a one-period equilibrium model from a theoretical standpoint, and as such, it is not meant to account for temporal dependence. However, it is generally recognised that the distribution of asset returns exhibits volatility clustering, which presents itself as a temporal dependency in variances from a practical standpoint (Brailsford & Faff, 1997). The CAPM does not account for typical stock returns across the board. For example, small stocks have outperformed large stocks throughout time, firms with high book-to-market (B/M) ratios outperform businesses with low B/M ratios, and equities with high prior-year returns continue to beat equities with low prior-year returns, according to the CAPM (Lewellen & Nagel, 2006). A significant difficulty in financial economics is valuing unpredictable future cash flows (Adrian & Franzoni, 2009). It is usually believed that the larger an agent's estimated return for investing in stocks, the higher the risk (Hansson & Hördahl, 1998).

The conventional wisdom holds that the static CAPM fails to capture the cross-section of average stock returns adequately. The CAPM is assumed to hold conditional, meaning that betas and the market risk premium change over time. The traditional CAPM proposes that the model is static and follows fixed beta's assumption. The business cycle can justify allowing the beta to vary with time (Jagannathan & Wang, 1996). The resulting equilibrium is an information-dependent conditional CAPM (Kumar, et al., 2008).

The conditional CAPM can be represented as:

$$E(R_{pt}) = \Upsilon_0 + \Upsilon_1 B_p$$

where, $\Upsilon_0 = R_{ft}$ and $\Upsilon_1 = E(R_{mt}\ 01 - R_{ft})$

under a positive expected excess market return (Ismail & Shakrani, 2003). So, using all the information to form expectations is reasonable, which gives rise to Conditional CAPM. So, while doing the valuation, the assets considering the market information fit the data much better than the traditional CAPM. Still, while explaining the asset pricing in the short run, it fails.

TABLE 12.5 Summary of Various Pricing Models

Model/Theory	*Variables*	*Note*
Standard CAPM	Beta, Risk-free Rate of Return, Risk, Market Return.	This model is based on ten hypotheses emphasizing the symmetric market and the existence of information in the market.
Downward CAPM	Semi-variance criterion and beta in an undesirable situation which is based on semi-variance.	This model can be used when the distribution of return is lower or upper than the symmetric level.
Adjusted CAPM	Liquidity risk in estimating investors' beta.	Liquidity risk of securities and liquidity risk of return is considered in this model.
Conditional CAPM	Beta is explained based on the division of market variance by share and market return covariance.	This model expresses those investors don't share the exact expectations because of the changes in market situation.
Concurrent CAPM	Beta is explained based on the growth in inventors' consumption and growing consumption in the market.	The extensive amount of consumption Beta shows the increased return on risky assets.
Reward-BETA	Return is divided into two parts: expected and unexpected return of shares	For estimating return beta, the mean of monthly beta of the share in the last period is divided by the mean of the beta of the market in the current period and this return beta is used for forecasting the return of the share in the next period.

Source: (Raei, et al., 2011)

SUMMARY

1. Segmentation of the world market where no effect from one market to other is visible, while integration appears where no restrictions appear in the portfolio diversification by the investors.
2. Assets are priced in the complete integration of the market as:

$$R_i = R_f + \frac{R_m - R_f}{Var(R_m)} Cov(R_i, R_m)$$

where, R_i = Return of asset; R_f = Risk free rate; R_m = Return of market
3. In an entirely segmented market, the domestic assets are priced as:

$$R_i = R_f + A^D D \, Cov(R_i, R_D)$$

4. The assets from multinational foreign firms listed on the exchange will be priced as:

$$R_g = R_f + A^F F \, Cov(R_g, R_f)$$

5. Asset pricing is complicated in the partially integrated market where some assets are cross-listed and others are not; the pricing of non-tradable assets will be priced as:

$$R_i = R_f + A^W W \, Cov(R_i, R_w) + A^D D \left[Cov(R_i, R_D) - Cov(R_i, R_D)\right]$$

$Cov(R_i, R_D)$, will be the indirect covariance between future returns of non-tradable assets and domestic market portfolios induced by the tradable assets.
6. Cross-listing of shares plays a significant role as it provides the advantage of listing shares in one or more foreign exchanges in addition to its home country's foreign stock exchange.
7. The law of one price provides essential fundamental support to the concept of integration, allowing companies to raise capital among integrated stock markets.
8. The Markowitz portfolio theory was the first significant quantitative examination where integrated financial markets also allow the firm to raise the fund from the market, which reduces their cost of capital and maximises their profits.
9. Stephen Ross developed the Arbitrage Pricing Theory in 1976 as an alternative to the CAPM model, which assumes that the market sometimes misprices the securities.
10. CAPM majorly focuses on the relationship between systematic risk and the expected return on the financial assets, widely used to price risky securities and calculate the firms' capital cost. In contrast, the International CAPM model is a financial model that helps investors evaluate the return they seek for a certain level of risk, including foreign risk associated with various currencies.

KEY WORDS

- Integration
- Segmentation
- Cross-listing
- Capital Asset Pricing Model
- International Capital Asset Pricing Model
- Portfolio Theory
- Arbitrage Pricing Theory

QUESTIONS

1. Explain the cost of capital in an international setting.
2. Define integration and segmentation as a phenomenon of financial market structure.
3. "Pricing of asset differs across the different market structure." Give reasons.
4. What are the various postulates and theories supporting international portfolio diversification? Explain considering the statement "Cost of capital differs across the countries."
5. Explain the different versions of asset pricing models in brief.

REFERENCES AND SUGGESTED READINGS

1. Adrian, T., & Franzoni, F. (2009). Learning about beta: Time-varying factor loadings, expected returns, and the conditional CAPM, *Journal of Empirical Finance*, 16(4), 537–556. https://doi.org/10.1016/j.jempfin.2009.02.003
2. Alpanda, S., & Kabaca, S. (2020). International Spillovers of Large-Scale Asset Purchases, *Journal of the European Economic Association*, 18(1), 342–391. https://doi.org/10.1093/jeea/jvy053
3. Bai, Y., & Green, C.J. (2020). Country and industry factors in tests of Capital Asset Pricing Models for partially integrated emerging markets, *Economic Modelling*, 92(April 2019), 180–194. https://doi.org/10.1016/j.econmod.2019.12.019
4. Bansal, R., & Vishwanathan, S. (2016). A New Approach to International Arbitrage Pricing, *The Journal of Finance*, 48(4), 1231–1262.
5. Black, F., Jensen, M.C., & Scholes, M. (2003). The Capital Asset Pricing Model: Some Empirical Tests, In *Studies in the Theory of Capital Markets*. https://doi.org/10.2139/ssrn.908569
6. Bollerslev, T., Engle, R.F., & Wooldridge, J.M. (2016). *A Capital Asset Pricing Model with Time-Varying Covariances Author (s): Tim Bollerslev, Robert F. Engle and Jeffrey M . Wooldridge Published by : The University of Chicago Press Stable URL: http://www.jstor.org/stable/1830713 Accessed : 27–06–2016 19*. 96(1), 116–131.

7. Brailsford, T.J., & Faff, R.W. (1997). Testing the conditional CAPM and the effect of intervaling: A note, *Pacific Basin Finance Journal*, 5(5), 527–537. https://doi.org/10.1016/S0927-538X(97)00018-8
8. Buckberg, E. (1995a). Emerging stock markets and international asset pricing, *World Bank Economic Review*, 9(1), 51–74. https://doi.org/10.1093/wber/9.1.51
9. Buckberg, E. (1995b). Emerging Stock Markets and International Asset Pricing. *The World Bank Economic Review*, *9*(1), 51–74.
10. Choe, D.C., Eun, C.S., & Senbet, L.W. (2016). American Finance Association International Arbitrage Pricing Theory: An Empirical Investigation Author (s): D. Chinhyung Cho, Cheol S. Eun and Lemma W. Senbet Source: *The Journal of Finance,* Vol. 41, No. 2 (Jun., 1986), pp. 313–329 Publish. 41(2), 313–329.
11. De Santis, G., & Gerard, B. (1997). International asset pricing and portfolio diversification with time-varying risk, *Journal of Finance*, 52(5), 1881–1912. https://doi.org/10.1111/j.1540-6261.1997.tb02745.x
12. El Hedi Arouri, M., Rault, C., Sova, A., Sova, R., & Teulon, F. (2013). Market structure and the cost of capital, *Economic Modelling*, 31(1), 664–671. https://doi.org/10.1016/j.econmod.2013.01.004
13. Errunza, Vihang R., Miller, D. P. (2016). *Market Segmentation and the Cost of Capital in International Equity Markets Author (s): Vihang R . Errunza and Darius P. Miller Published by: Cambridge University Press on behalf of the University of Washington School of Business Administration Stable*, 35(4), 577–600.
14. Errunza, V., Losq, E., & Padmanabhan, P. (1992). Tests of integration, mild segmentation and segmentation hypotheses, *Journal of Banking and Finance*, 16(5), 949–972. https://doi.org/10.1016/0378-4266(92)90034-W
15. Fama, E.F., & French, K.R. (2004). The Capital Asset Pricing Model: Theory and evidence, *Journal of Economic Perspectives*, 18(3), 25–46. https://doi.org/10.1257/0895330042162430
16. Fama, E.F., & French, K.R. (1992). The Cross-Section of Expected Stock Returns, *The Journal of Finance*, 47(2), 427–465. https://doi.org/10.1111/j.1540-6261.1992.tb04398.x
17. Geweke, J., & Zhou, G. (1996). Measuring the pricing error of the Arbitrage Pricing Theory, *Review of Financial Studies*, 9(2), 557–587.
18. Hail, L., & Leuz, C. (2009). Cost of capital effects and changes in growth expectations around U.S. cross-listings, *Journal of Financial Economics*, 93(3), 428–454. https://doi.org/10.1016/j.jfineco.2008.09.006
19. Hansson, B., & Hördahl, P. (1998). Testing the conditional CAPM using multivariate GARCH-M, *Applied Financial Economics*, 8(4), 377–388. https://doi.org/10.1080/096031098332916
20. Harshita, Singh, S., & Yadav, S.S. (2015). Indian Stock Market and the Asset Pricing Models, *Procedia Economics and Finance*, 30(15), 294–304. https://doi.org/10.1016/s2212-5671(15)01297-6
21. Harvey, C.R. (1991). The World Price of Covariance Risk, *The Journal of Finance*, 46(1), 111–157. https://doi.org/10.1111/j.1540-6261.1991.tb03747.x

22. Hundal, S., Eskola, A., & Tuan, D. (2019). Risk–return relationship in the Finnish stock market in the light of Capital Asset Pricing Model (CAPM), *Journal of Transnational Management*, 24(4), 305–322. https://doi.org/10.1080/15475778.2019.1641394
23. Ismail, A.G.b., & Shakrani, M.S.b. (2003). The Conditional Capm and Cross-Sectional Evidence of Return and Beta for *IIUM Journal of Economics and Management*, 1(1), 1–31.
24. Jagannathan, R., & Wang, Z. (1996). The Conditional CAPM and the Cross-Section of Expected Returns A, *The Journal of Finance*, 51(1), 3–53.
25. Karp, A., & Van Vuuren, G. (2017). The Capital Asset Pricing Model And Fama-French Three Factor Model in an Emerging Market Environment, *International Business & Economics Research Journal (IBER)*, 16(4), 231–256. https://doi.org/10.19030/iber.v16i4.10040
26. Korajczyk, R.A., & Viallet, C.J. (1989). An empirical Investigation of International Asset Pricing, *The Review of Financial Studies*, 2(4), 553–585.
27. Kuehn, A.L., Simutin, M., & Wang, J.J. (2021). *American Finance Association A Labor Capital Asset Pricing Model Source: The Journal of Finance*, Vol. 72, No. 5 (October 2017), pp. 2131–2178 Published by: Wiley for the American Finance Association Stable URL : https://www.jstor.org/stable/26653, 72(5), 2131–2178. https://doi.org/10.1111/jofi.12504
28. Kumar, P., Sorescu, S. M., Boehme, R.D., & Danielsen, B.R. (2008). Estimation risk, information, and the conditional CAPM: Theory and evidence, *Review of Financial Studies*, 21(3), 1037–1075. https://doi.org/10.1093/rfs/hhn016
29. Lee, C., Ng, D., & Swaminathan, B. (2016). Testing International Asset Pricing Models Using Implied Costs of Capital, *The Journal of Financial and Quantitative Analysis*, 44(2), 307–335.
30. Lewellen, J., & Nagel, S. (2006). The conditional CAPM does not explain asset-pricing anomalies, *Journal of Financial Economics*, 82(2), 289–314. https://doi.org/10.1016/j.jfineco.2005.05.012
31. Li, H. (2019). Direct overseas listing versus cross-listing: A multivalued treatment effects analysis of Chinese listed firms, *International Review of Financial Analysis*, 66(October), 101391. https://doi.org/10.1016/j.irfa.2019.101391
32. Mahdy F. Elhusseiny, Nyakundi M. Michieka, & Benjamin Bae. (2019). An Empirical Examination of the Arbitrage Pricing Theory: Evidences from the U.S. Stock Market, *Journal of Modern Accounting and Auditing*, 15(2), 69–79. https://doi.org/10.17265/1548-6583/2019.02.002
33. Markowitz, H.M. (1991). Foundations of Portfolio Theory, *The Journal of Finance*, 46(2), 469–477.
34. Markowitz, H.M. (1999). The Early History of Portfolio Theory: 1600–1960, *Financial Analysts Journal*, 55(4), 5–16. https://doi.org/10.2469/faj.v55.n4.2281
35. Marling and, & Emanuelsson. (2012). The Markowitz Portfolio Theory, *Survey Online Http://Www. Math. Chalmers. Se*, 1–6. http://www.math.chalmers.se/Stat/Grundutb/CTH/mve220/1213/gr1_HannesMarling_SaraEmanuelsson_MPT.pdf

36. Musawa, N., Kapena, S., & Shikaputo, C. (2020). A better stock pricing model: A systematic literature review, *Journal of Economic and Financial Sciences*, 13(1), 1–6. https://doi.org/10.4102/jef.v13i1.472
37. Musawa, N., Kapena, S., Shikaputo, C., Harshita, Singh, S., Yadav, S.S., Bai, Y., Green, C.J., Wang, M.C., Fang, M., Ye, J.K., HARVEY, C.R., De Santis, G., & Gerard, B. (2020). International Stock Market and the Asset Pricing Models, *Journal of Finance*, 92(1), 294–304. https://doi.org/10.1111/j.1540-6261.1997.tb02745.x
38. Patro, D.K. (2001). Market segmentation and international asset prices: Evidence from the listing of world equity benchmark shares, *Journal of Financial Research*, 24(1), 83–98. https://doi.org/10.1111/j.1475-6803.2001.tb00819.x
39. Pirinsky, C.A., & Wang, Q. (2011). Market segmentation and the cost of capital in a domestic market: Evidence from municipal bonds, *Financial Management*, 40(2), 455–481. https://doi.org/10.1111/j.1755-053X.2011.01149.x
40. Raei, R., Ahmadinia, H., & Hasbaei, A. (2011). A Study on Developing of Asset Pricing Models, *International Business Research*, 4(4). https://doi.org/10.5539/ibr.v4n4p139
41. Reinganum, M.R. (1981). American Finance Association The Arbitrage Pricing Theory : Some Empirical Results Author (s): Marc R. Reinganum Source: *The Journal of Finance*, Vol. 36, No. 2, Papers and Proceedings of the Thirty Ninth Annual Meeting American Finance Association, *The Journal of Finance*, 36(2), 3–12. http://www.jstor.org/stable/2327013
42. Roll, R., & Ross, S.A. (1967). An Empirical Investigation of the Arbitrage Pricing Theory, *Angewandte Chemie International Edition*, 6(11), 951–952, 35(5), 5–24.
43. Shanken, J. (2019). The Arbitrage Pricing Theory: Is it Testable? *The Journal of Finance*, 37(5), 1–114.
44. Solnik, B. (1983). International Arbitrage Pricing Theory, *The Journal of Finance*, 38(2), 449–457.
45. Stener-victorin, E., Moran, L.J., Robertson, S.A., Stepto, N.K., & Norman, R.J. (2019). An Empirical Examination of the Arbitrage Pricing Theory: Evidence from Jordan. *Infinity Press*, 12(2), 1–10.
46. Stulz, René M. (1995). The cost of capital in internationally integrated markets: The case of Nestlé, *European Financial Management*, 1(1), 11–22. https://doi.org/10.1111/j.1468-036X.1995.tb00003.x
47. Stulz, René M.M. (1981). A model of international asset pricing, *Journal of Financial Economics*, 9(4), 383–406. https://doi.org/10.1016/0304-405X(81)90005-2
48. Thomadakis, S., & Usmen, N. (1991). Foreign Project Financing in Segmented Capital Markets: Equity versus Debt., *Financial Management*, 20(4), 42. https://doi.org/10.2307/3665711
49. Wang, M.C., Fang, M., & Ye, J.K. (2013). Financial integration of large-and small-cap stocks in emerging markets, *Emerging Markets Finance and Trade*, 49(SUPPL. 4), 17–31. https://doi.org/10.2753/REE1540-496X4905S402
50. Witt, S.F., & Dobbins, R. (1979). The Markowitz Contribution to Portfolio Theory, *Managerial Finance*, 5(1), 3–17. https://doi.org/10.1108/eb013433

Glossary

American Deposit Receipts are issued with increasing involvement from the global equity markets (ADRs). ADRs provide investors a broad range of global investment options and let foreign banks access far-flung global marketplaces.

Appreciate It is the increase in the currency exchange rate of domestic currency when the rates are quoted in direct terms, i.e., foreign currency per unit of domestic currency.

Arbitrage Pricing Theory is a multifactor asset pricing model states an asset's return can be predicted by expected return and many macroeconomic factors that capture the systematic risk.

Arbitrage The purchasing and selling of currencies/commodities/assets simultaneously in different markets to make profits by taking advantage of price differences.

Ask Price The price at which brokers/dealers buy a currency in forex market.

Balance of Payments It is a systematic accounting record of all economic transactions during a given period of time between the residents of the country and the rest of the world.

Balance Sheet Hedge A technique to diminish translation exposure of a corporation by removing the mismatched assets and liabilities denominated in the same currency.

Bid Price The price at which dealers/brokers offer to purchase currency in the forex market.

Bilateral Netting A system to reduce transaction exposure, in which the counterparties adjust net receivables and payables between them and only the net amount is transferred.

Bretton Woods System An exchange rate system that was followed from 1944–1971, to stabilize various currencies and facilitate international trade. Under the system, the US dollar was fully convertible in gold and vice-versa at the rate of $35 per ounce.

Call Option An option to purchase underlying asset in future at a rate fixed today.

Capital Account Transactions affecting the country's foreign assets and liabilities are included under this BOP account.

CAPM focuses on the relationship between systematic risk and the expected return on financial assets, widely used to price risky securities and calculate the firms' capital cost.

Casual Observation Theory is the overseas development of industrial companies with headquarters in a given country reflects the foreign expansion of banks with that country's headquarters in numerous foreign markets.

Comparative Advantage Proposed by Ricardo in 1817, Theory of Comparative Cost Advantage focuses on the relative productivity differences between the products.

Conditional CAPM allows beta to vary with time unlike the static CAPM.

Conglomerate Direct Investment is used to describe the practice by which an already-established company in one country expands into an unrelated business activity in another country.

Covered Interest Arbitrage When the IRP doesn't hold, an arbitrager has the opportunity earn sure profits without undertaking any risk.

Cross Exchange Rate An exchange rate between two currencies that is derived out of their respective rates with a third currency (base currency).

Current Account Transactions involving imports and exports as well as unilateral transfers are segregated under this BOP head.

Currency Risk The risk associated with the value of your investment denominated in a foreign currency may decrease due to fluctuations in exchange rates is known as currency risk.

Currency Swap A swap contract where counterparties exchange the interest rate on their debt raised in their respective currencies.

Default Risk Risk associated with non-payment of a bond issuer regarding the payment of interest as promised and/or will not have enough money to pay down the principal when the bond expires is known as credit risk or default risk.

Depreciate It is the decrease in the currency exchange rate of domestic currency when the rates are quoted in direct terms, i.e., foreign currency per unit of domestic currency.

Direct Investing refers to investing the money into a foreign company with the intention of acquiring a majority ownership.

Economic Exposure The long-term effect of foreign exchange volatility on cash flows of a firm.

Efficient Market Hypothesis This hypothesis assumes that the information is freely available to available and hence, the price of an asset incorporates all the relevant information.

Eurobond A bond issued outside of a particular jurisdiction is referred to as a "Eurobond". It does not specifically mention European-only bonds.

Eurocredits are eurocurrency loans made by eurobanks to companies, national countries, subprime banks, or multilateral agencies for terms ranging from short-term to medium-term.

Eurocurrency Market The marketplace where Eurodollars are traded is called the Eurocurrency Market.

Eurodollars The dollars that were placed in the bank were called as Eurodollars.

European Monetary System Established in 1979 by countries of Europe, it was an adjustable exchange rate regime aimed at stabilizing the currencies and control inflation.

European Monetary Union It is the union of European countries that decided to irrevocably adopt euro as their common currency.

European Union A union of 20 european countries, where there is no restriction on flow of goods, capital and people.

Exposure Coefficient It represents economic exposure of a firm. It is obtained by regressing the value of assets in home currency on currency exchange rates.

Exposure Netting This strategy involves hedging only the net exposure arrived after adjusting forex receivables and payables.

Financial Hedging Hedging through financial contracts like forwards, options and swaps is termed as financial hedging.

Foreign Bond A foreign institution or firm may issue a bond in a nation other than its home country. This is known as a foreign bond.

Foreign Direct Investment (FDI) An ownership stake in a foreign company or project is known as a foreign direct investment (FDI) and is made by a foreign investor, business, or government.

Foreign Exchange (FX) Markets The market where currencies are bought and sold.

Foreign Exchange Risk The variability in firm's cash flows or operating profits due to variations in currency exchange rates.

Foreign Subsidiary A subsidiary of multinational corporation that is located at a country other than home country.

Foreign-Pay-Bond Bonds that are issued by a local corporation in their home country but are denominated in a different currency that the domestic currency are referred to as foreign-pay-bonds.

Forward Market The market where currencies are traded today but settled at a future date at a specified price.

Forward Market Hedge Hedging forex risk via forward market operations.

Forward Premium/Discount When forward rate of a currency is higher (lower) than the spot rate, it is termed as forward premium (discount).

Futures Standardized exchange traded financial contracts, that are settled at a future date.

General Agreement on Tariffs and Trade (GATT) Predecessor of WTO, it was a multilateral agreement between member countries to promote international trade.

Global Bond Bonds considered to be global are those that are simultaneously offered and traded in several markets throughout the world.

Global Depository Receipts An innovative instrument for investing in the international financial markets. To reach investors outside of the United States, a depository bank would issue shares of foreign corporations on overseas markets, most often in Europe.

Gold Standard Under the gold exchange standard, the currency of one country could be converted into the currency of other country on the basis of their conversion rate with the gold.

Gold-Exchange Standard Under this system, currency of one country (US dollar) was fully convertible to gold at a fixed rate and all the other countries had to use that currency as their reserve.

Gravitational Pull Effect occurs when banks go overseas to service their domestic clients who have relocated abroad.

Hedger A forex market participant, whose objective is to minimize or eliminate foreign exchange risk.

Hedging through Invoice Currency A hedging technique, under which the exporter or importer invoices the deal in home currency to avoid forex risk.

Horizontal Direct Investments are the most common kind of direct investment (DI). Any business that already has a foothold inside one country expands into another through a horizontal direct investment.

Integration of the world financial market will result in international portfolio diversification by investors.

Interest Rate Parity (IRP) A condition under which the forward rate of a currency with respect to the other currency is determined by the interest rate differential between the two countries.

International Asset Pricing Model Assets are priced according to the world systematic risk.

International Bank Transfers The firms can send and receive money easily because of the smooth currency conversion mechanism. Due to global banking, the corporation are able to pay bills abroad.

International Equity Fund referred as global mutual funds are one of the best way for investing into international market as the investors don't need to make much hassle for the same.

International Monetary Fund (IMF) Created at Bretton Woods conference in July 1944, the goal of IMF is to promote macroeconomic and financial stability of the member countries.

International Monetary System It is the system that determines the exchange rates between various currencies across the globe as well as that facilitates trade and investment effectively.

Law of One Price states that the price of identical assets or commodity will have the same price across the globe regardless of their location.

Lead/Lag Strategy A hedging strategy under which the hedger pays in advance for a deal if he expects the invoiced currency to appreciate with reference to the domestic currency or delays the payment if he expects the currency to depreciate with reference to the domestic currency.

Level 1 ADRs are the most fundamental type of ADRs when foreign corporations either don't meet the requirements or don't want their ADR to be published on an exchange.

Level 2 ADR is traded on an exchange. The SEC has a few extra standards for Level 2 ADRs; however, they also get greater visible trading volume.

Level 3 ADR is when an issuer launches an ADR public offering on a US exchange.

London Interbank Offered Rate The banks lend money to one another in the London money market, and that rate is known as the LIBOR.

Merchant Bank Bank that performs both the traditional as well as investment banking functions.

Money Market Hedge A hedging technique that involves borrowing or lending in money markets either domestic or foreign.

Multinational Corporation (MNC) Multinational Corporation (MNC), is any corporation that is registered and operates in more than one country at a time or an enterprise which is having strategic presence in two or more than two distinct regions of the world.

Operational Hedging This hedging technique involves long-term measures like diversifying the market as well as the sourcing destinations.

Option A derivative contract that gives the right but not an obligation to sell or purchase an underlying security at a fixed price in future.

Option Market Hedge Hedging forex risk using call and put option to limit the losses of transaction exposure.

Over the Counter Market When there is no centralized market place and the transactions take place over telephones, computers, etc., it is termed as over the counter market.

Partial Integration Market where some assets are cross-listed and others are not.

Petrodollars The OPEC firms started depositing their portion of oil revenues in banks. These types of deposits are known as petrodollars.

Political Risk Losses for investors resulting from the country's unstable political situation.

Purchasing Power Parity The purchasing Power Parity theory links the buying power of the currencies, i.e., the basket of products or services that could be bought with one unit of the currencies to their respective exchange rates.

Put Option The right but not an obligation to sell a currency at a fixed rate.

Quality Spread Differential The difference between fixed and floating interest rate spread differential of the debt of two parties in a swap transaction.

Random Walk Hypothesis The hypothesis suggests that prices of assets do not follow any set rules, they vary randomly and hence, are unpredictable.

Segmentation of Market is where investors are restricted from investing in domestic portfolios and not allowed to diversify their portfolios internationally.

Speculator One who take positions in market to benefit from the expected rise/fall in the prices of financial assets/currencies/commodities.

Spot Exchange Rate The current currency exchange rate at which transaction is executed is termed as spot exchange rate.

Spot Market The market where spot transactions take place.

The Portfolio Theory refers to the diversification of financial assets and grouping them into various assets such as stocks, currencies, bonds, commodities, and funds that the investor purchases to generate his income and meet the financial objectives.

Transaction Exposure The exposure arising out of contracts involving foreign currency.

Translation Exposure The difference in value of firm's assets and liabilities denominated in foreign currency due to the conversion of their values in domestic/functional currency.

Triangular Arbitrage The trading between three currencies to take advantage of differences in direct and cross exchange rates between currencies.

Uncovered Interest Rate Parity The theory suggests that the interest rate differential between the two countries is equal to the expected change in exchange rates between the two nations.

Vertical Direct Investment increases a company's worldwide presence by investing in similar kind of distribution network abroad.

World Bank Created with the IMF, the objective of World Bank is to promote long-term economic development and poverty alleviation.

World Trade Organization (WTO) Successor of Generalized Agreements on Tariffs and Trade (GATT), the WTO oversees the international trade rules.

Index